Douglas Arthur was born in Liverpool on the 22nd June 1920.

Educated at one of Liverpool's largest Elementary Schools he left there, as head boy, at the age of fourteen. He had represented his school in athletics, boxing and baseball, and was awarded the Bronze Medallion Life Saving Certificate.

Employed in the Building Industry he continued his education at night schools, and was awarded a scholarship in Business Studies before being called up as a Territorial in 1939. He tells of his service 'up the blue' in his memoir, DESERT WATCH.

A prisoner of war for four years, after returning home he became a Director and Company Secretary of a highly successful Plumbing Contractors' business.

Married for 53 years he has three children and six grandchildren.

WITH BEST WISHES,

Doug Cuttins

12ᵗʰ FEBRUARY, 2004

40 MEN – 8 HORSES

Douglas Arthur

---

40 MEN – 8 HORSES

Vanguard Press

VANGUARD PAPERBACK

© Copyright 2003
Douglas Arthur

The right of Douglas Arthur to be identified as author of
this work has been asserted by him in accordance with the
Copyright, Designs and Patents Act 1988

All Rights Reserved

No reproduction, copy or transmission of this publication
may be made without written permission.
No paragraph of this publication may be reproduced,
copied or transmitted save with the written permission of the
publisher, or in accordance with the provisions
of the Copyright Act 1956 (as amended).

Any person who does any unauthorised act in relation to
this publication may be liable to criminal
prosecution and civil claims for damage.

A CIP catalogue record for this title is
available from the British Library
ISBN 1 843860 70 8

*Vanguard Press is an imprint of
Pegasus Elliot MacKenzie Publishers Ltd.*
www.pegasuspublishers.com

First Published in 2003

**Vanguard Press
Sheraton House Castle Park
Cambridge England**

Printed & Bound in Great Britain

Dedication

For my many friends and Comrades of the 106th Lancashire Hussars (Yeomanry) Regiment, Royal Horse Artillery, TA, with whom I was proud and privileged to serve, during those fateful and momentous months from September, 1939 until June, 1941.

Also for the thousands of Allied Servicemen who lost their lives, or became casualties, or who forfeited four years of their youth in German prisoner-of-war camps, following the futile and forgotten Greece and Crete Campaigns in 1941.

Acknowledgement

I am indebted to many friends who have assisted me with this story. Many thanks.

Very special thanks, also, to Maureen for her loving patience and encouragement, and to David, John and Christopher for putting me right with the demon computer.

Contents

Chapter 1

The Cauldron of Greece

I spotted the khaki haversack in the ditch alongside the road just as one of the guards, a tall, lean, blond Alpine Paratrooper, a machine-gun cradled in his arms, shouted incomprehensively to an Aussie infantryman in the slowly moving column in front of me. Taking a chance, when the German ran towards the rebellious Colonial and then thumped him in the middle of the back with the butt of his tommy-gun, I jumped down into the shallow ditch. Picking up the haversack without pausing, I was back in the line of my ragged, fellow prisoners-of-war before he had finished his intimidation of the Aussie.

Examining my prize as I trudged along, I could just about decipher the faded initials *"JM"* printed in smudged, purple indelible pencil on the back of the scruffy, tatty, discarded haversack.

It was obvious that *"JM"*, like me, and everyone else on those fatal, final days of the disorderly retreat to the evacuation beach at Sphakia, had been ordered to destroy or throw away everything he possessed, except the clothes he stood up in.

And all I stood up in, or, rather, staggered along in, on the morning of that never-to-be-forgotten First of June, 1941, was a khaki shirt and battledress trousers.

The pockets of these tattered and dirty remnants of a uniform, once worn with so much pride, carried what was left of my few mundane possessions. A grubby handkerchief; a few carefully kept, treasured photographs; the last two letters I had received from Home, and my Army Pay-Book. (Or what was left of it, for the non-essential pages were missing, long been used for a more essential personal purpose). With each faltering step I made, the silver pocket watch which I had liberated from a surrendering Italian Officer at the Battle of Beda Fomm back in the desert, rattled about in its Cherry Blossom Boot Polish tin, at the bottom of the deep pocket of my battledress trousers.

Underpants, stained with the repeated, terrifying screams of diving Stukas making their personal attacks directly on me, and worn out boots, lacerated by the jagged rocks of the White Mountains of Crete, and socks with holes in the heels the size of half-crowns, just about completed my worldly assets on that bleak morning.

As I ambled along in my slowly moving line of dejected, dispirited prisoners-of-war, I opened *J.M.*'s discarded haversack to discover a badly chipped white enamelled mug, an army spoon blotched with green verdigris, an army-issue safety razor in its flat, metal case, together with three razor blades, one of which was heavily spotted with rust. There was a brightly polished stainless steel mirror in the lid of the case. Further searching in the bottom of the grubby pack revealed an old, dirty-looking shaving brush. The worn-down stub of bristles was stiff and yellow with stale soap. Alongside it were the tacky remains of a stick of "Erasmus" shaving soap, the covering silver foil torn and stained with the dribble from the soap.

And, finally, a *"hussif"*.

The housewife had obviously never been used by *"JM"*, nor even been opened by him judging from its appearance, for inside the pocket of the little canvas bag the darning needles were clean and bright, the hank of grey wool and the card of khaki cotton untouched.

I still have the old razor set and the *"hussif"* to this day.

Although I didn't appreciate it at that particular moment, I had taken my first faltering steps, dragging myself out of the depths of despair. At the dawn of that day, I had been told by one of our Junior Officers, summarily and without ceremony, to destroy my rifle. He said the Allies had capitulated and Crete was now controlled by the Germans. With that order came the awful realisation that I was now a Prisoner of War.

***

Some eight weeks earlier, I was languishing on my back on the warm, wooden deck of a battered, old cargo ship ploughing its way, laboriously, to Greece. I was enjoying the glorious, fresh Mediterranean air and drowsily basking in the warm, spring sunshine. Only half awake, I was startled by sudden, alarming shouts of "Take cover, take cover. Action stations, action stations. Italian bombers. Ities, overhead. Take cover."

Immediately wide awake, I looked up and saw, high in the sky, the cause of the uproar. A formation of six aeroplanes. To my inexperienced eye they were heavy lumbering bombers, flying so high they were little more than silver dots in the crystal-clear blue sky.

In the glare of the afternoon sun I barely had time to focus my eyes on the slowly moving aeroplanes. Then I heard the unmistakable swish of falling bombs and then the rumble of the explosions as the missiles hit the water in a long, straight line about fifty yards away, parallel with the ship. I could taste the salt in the spray drifting over from the fountains of water thrown into the air. In response to the raucous "action stations" alarm on the tannoy, my heart was beating away furiously. I ran along the deck to my allotted life-boat station, hurriedly donning the skimpy life-belt which had been issued when we boarded.

But the bombers, without altering speed, height or direction, were soon lost from my view.

There was an excited babble of relief as the silver dots vanished out of sight, my fellow gunners protesting, loudly, that our Breda light ack-ack guns were lashed away down in the hold. Not that they would have been of much use, anyway. The little gun's range was limited and would not have reached a quarter of the distance of the enemy planes, whose bombs had so narrowly missed us.

Until the abortive attack by the Italian bombers brought me back to reality, I had been in a sort of seventh heaven, enjoying the peaceful cruise across the Mediterranean and relishing the fresh, sea air and the balmier, friendlier sunshine. It was so different from the dry, aggressive, oven-like heat of the desert. For the first time since leaving Alexandria I had noticed a distinct difference in the smell of the sea breeze. Gone were the pungent, spicy sort of waste-pipe smells of Cairo and Alexandria. Instead, I could detect a fresher, almost aromatic scent, which in a vague way reminded me of the back garden at

15

home after the grass had been mown.

As we left the Meditteranean, I saw the reason for the change in the ozone when we reached the first of the many beautiful Greek Islands, scattered about the blue-green water of the Aegean Sea. Most of these lovely islands had cultivated plots or fields around dazzling white houses of the little fishing villages on the water's edge. The hills behind the tiny cottages were covered with bushy trees, some of them still splashed with the remnants of winter snow. It was a delightful panorama to my eyes, after the months I had spent in the flat monotony of the featureless Libyan desert.

We arrived at Piraeus without further visits from our high flying enemies, and disembarked immediately. On the quayside we waited for our vehicles and guns to be slung out from the hold of the old merchantship.

Piraeus, the Port of Athens, was another Liverpool, Bootle, or Haifa. Shipping of all kinds, bustled about the harbour with tremendous activity, their foamy wakes glistening in the late afternoon sun. Tiny Greek caique fishing boats were unloading their day's catch. Crowded ferries crossing the harbour reminded me of the Iris and Daffodil steaming across the Mersey between New Brighton and Liverpool. Battered old tramp steamers looked a bit the worse for wear and, most importantly to me, smart looking, grey painted cruisers and destroyers of the British Navy.

Dockside cranes were unloading the flotsam and jetsam and paraphernalia of war from the ships tied up at the quays. 15cwt trucks, portees and three tonner lorries in freshly painted camouflage, were being slung in nets on to the quayside. Crates, barrels, oil drums, guns, ammunition, tea chests were being packed into dockside warehouses which were not unlike those on the Dock Road, Liverpool – or hurriedly loaded directly on to the waiting R.A.S.C. convoys.

When our turn came, we boarded the portees and set off without any delay, along the dock road heading for Athens. By-passing Athens (regretfully, I by-passed Athens for the whole of my short stay in Greece and only ever saw the Parthenon in the distance on the sky-line), we arrived at Glyfada, a beachside training camp which was to be our home for two weeks.

16

Glyfada is now a modern holiday resort, in the summer months full of British and German tourists. But in those days it was just another hastily erected tented camp, without the luxuries and amenities of the NAAFI and open-air cinema. Also without our Indian friends, the Camp Followers, who had been with us during our stay in Palestine and at Mena Camp. There were no roomy, white marquees with comfortable wooden plank beds raised off the ground. Instead each gun was given a canvas ridge tent which just about managed to accommodate the gun crew and their meagre possessions.

At Glyfada the Regiment was, once again, re-formed and re-equipped. Nos. 1 and 2 anti-tank batteries, which had done so well for themselves in the desert, were turned into anti-aircraft batteries. They were equipped with the same Italian Breda ack-ack guns used by Nos. 3 and 4 batteries in their protection of the desert convoys in Libya. So, a week after landing in Greece and still retaining its proud title, the 106th Lancashire Hussars (Yeomanry), Regiment, Royal Horse Artillery, became a Light Anti-Aircraft Unit. The four batteries were now equipped with Italian guns, part of a cargo of munitions captured by the Navy en-route to Benghazi, Libya.

The gun crews were also re-organised, the anti-tank gunners of Nos. 1 and 2 batteries being reinforced by the more experienced Breda ack-ack gunners from 3 and 4 batteries who had already been in action with the Bredas in the desert. Regretfully, I was parted from my long standing desert companions, but luckily found myself on the same gun as two good friends from Barlborough days, Lance Ferguson and Sergeant George Lunt – the schoolteacher from St. Teresas. George Lunt was the No. 1 and Lance the gun layer. The remainder of the gun crew was made up by two re-inforcements who had joined the unit in Alexandria, and "Yorkie", the elderly Yorkshire reservist who came to us just before we left England. I saw Arthur Taylor, my chum since we joined the Terriers, only once during my short stay at Glyfada. He was driving a stores truck in one of the other batteries.

A new arrival, also, was Lt. "Dickie" Guest who became my Section Officer. A short, stocky man who had played rugby for Waterloo and England, he immediately became very popular

17

with the lads of the Section. Peter McShea, one of the five McShea brothers all serving together in the 106th, was my Section Sergeant. Dave McClean was the No. 1 on the other gun in the section. Another old friend from Barlborough days.

The portees were kitted out much the same as they had been in the desert campaign, but with the addition of the 10ft by 6ft canvas ridge tent. We had been re-issued with khaki battledress, ankle puttees and the standard Army issue waterproof, a rectangular rubber sheet about five foot long by three feet wide. This peculiar, cumbersome piece of military apparel had buttons sewn on in odd places to enable it, supposedly, to double as a mackintosh. When the spring rains came and I was forced to don this masterpiece, I found it always let the rain in down my neck. Yet it failed to protect the lower part of my back and my legs. After my first soaking I found it too wet to use for its correct purpose, as a groundsheet under the blanket. Out of practice after the months in the rain-free desert, I cursed, firstly the unaccustomed rain and then the rubber sheets.

True to pattern, we were kept in total ignorance of the situation on the Northern borders of Greece. But we knew that although the Greeks had successfully stopped the Italians in their tracks, Germany had declared war on Greece. There was a renewed urgency about the Regiment's re-organisation.

Our "training" on the Breda at Glyfada was brief. We were shown the basic rudiments of how to clean, load, aim, and fire the gun, and to clear the many stoppages to which it was prone. My job, was much the same as it had been with the Bofors anti-tank gun. To drive the portee with the gun mounted on it, altering the position of the truck when instructed by the No.1. If the gun was in a dug-in position, I became a general dogsbody and ammunition handler.

On the final day of our two weeks introduction to the Breda, and the daily practice handling this new and unaccustomed weapon, we actually fired the gun, everybody aiming and firing live shells at a drogue target-sleeve, some five hundred feet in the air. The drogue was towed by an ancient Lysander monoplane, like a pre-war aerial advertisement for "Sunlight Soap" or "Ovaltine" being flown across the crowded Aintree racecourse on Grand National day. Trundling along at a steady 110 miles an hour from left to right across our range of vision, in no way did it resemble the frightening, screaming Stuka dive bombers we were to encounter later, diving vertically out of the skies directly on to the gun. Being the driver, I was the last to take a turn, but my practice burst was interrupted by the anguished cries of our Commanding Officer, Colonel Hely.

"For God's sake, Sergeant Major, stop that man firing that bloody gun before he shoots the Lysander down."

Years later, when I spoke of this at one of our Old Comrades meetings, Tim Hely, being the gentleman he was, said he couldn't remember the incident.

Our two weeks scanty training culminated with a brief lecture by the Battery Sergeant Major informing us that we would be on the move again, shortly, and warning us that Greece had the highest instance of venereal disease in Europe. "So don't have anything to do with the female population, and, anyway, any man catching anything will be put on a charge. You know what that means. Don't you, you'll be for it?"

So, in the second week of March, 1941, Batteries Nos. One and Two left Glyfada, heading due North to an unknown destination.

The much vaunted "few days leave or rest", promised before we set off back down the desert from Beda Fomm to Alexandria, never materialised.

Chapter 2

The Woody Woodpecker Song

I thoroughly enjoyed driving through the spectacular mountains and countryside of central Greece. Bright spring flowers and colourful blossoms I had never seen before, overflowed from hedges and gardens at every bend.

The roads, though, were rough and badly in need of repair. I had to take particular care rounding the steep, unprotected hairpin bends on the mountain passes, some of which were scarcely more than tracks anyway.

We drove through seemingly poverty-stricken little villages clinging precariously to the rocky mountainsides, the villagers turning out enthusiastically in force to cheer, vociferously, Mr Churchill's saviours of Greece, on their way to repel the Germans. Fruit, vegetables and flowers, and even bottles of wine, were thrown into the trucks by the excited populace as we passed by. Always accompanied by their exuberant rendering of the "The Woodpecker Song". This popular, anti-Mussolini propaganda ditty was on the lips of nearly all Greeks, in the early days of the unsuccessful Italian invasion of Greece. The lads in the trucks, infected by the excitement of the ecstatic villagers, and ever ready for a song, joined in with gusto with the English, obscene, version.

Our destination turned out to be Larissa, a little town in the North of Greece at the end of a railway line. When we finally arrived, there was no welcoming, flower-strewn, choral reception. Larissa looked as if it had been on the receiving end of a heavy bombing raid. We learned that the devastation was caused, not by bombing, but by a recent severe earthquake, which had left many of the houses and buildings demolished or badly damaged. Debris cluttered the sidewalks and roads, making progress difficult through the town. Many of the shops and tavernas, still apparently undamaged, were closed and shuttered. The occupants had disappeared into the mountain villages to join relatives and friends, after Germany declared war.

Larissa was a railhead. Rations, petrol and ammunition dumps had been established there for transport by road to our front line troops awaiting the anticipated German invasion. There was also a makeshift landing strip on the outskirts of the town, where the Royal Air Force had based six Hurricane fighters and a couple of ancient Gladiators.

***

The 106th's job was to defend the town against low level bombing and strafing; in particular the airstrip, railway station and a bridge over the only road to the North from the town.

On our arrival, my gun was positioned by the Section Officer, in the centre of the flat roof of a newly-built Police Station and Municipal Office. It was situated on a hill in the centre of the town. The position was high enough to give the gun a clear, unimpeded 360 degree firing circle. That's what the Section Officer said.

Not yet occupied, the imposing looking office block, a modern, architectural showpiece compared with the rest of the buildings in Larissa, seemed to be solid and well constructed. There had been some heavy rain that day so we looked forward to a dry indoor billet instead of the muddy groundsheet of our damp little Scout tent. We turned an ignorant, blind eye to the obvious signs of damage to the building caused by the earthquake; external tiles missing from walls and lying in fragments on the ground, zig-zag cracks in the floors and the integral, concrete stairs to the roof coming adrift from the wall.

The only earthquake we had ever heard of, was in the film about San Francisco, so we never gave it a second thought. Cheerfully singing the "Woody Woodpecker Song", we set about taking the Breda off the portee, stripping it down and carrying the parts, piece by piece, up the three flights of rickety stairs, each flight shaking ominously as we clumped up and down. We had just about finished re-assembling the gun and had carried the rest of the contents of the portee up to the flat roof, including the heavy boxes of ammunition and the filled sandbags to protect the gun, when a Royal Engineer Major walked onto the roof.

He saw the three stripes on George Lunt's arm and said to him,

"What Regiment are you, Sergeant, and who told you to put this gun up here?"

"We're the 106th, R.H.A. sir," said George, "Lt. Guest, our Section Officer, positioned the gun, sir."

"Well you can't stay here," the Major said, emphatically, "It's far too dangerous. There's been a severe earthquake and this building will probably fall down if there's another one. Even the firing of your gun might be enough to collapse it. So get hold of your Section Officer, as soon as you can and tell him I said the gun has to be moved to another position."

I heaved a sigh of relief when I heard the Officer's words.

In my mind's eye, I had already seen German Messerschmitts circling around our suicidal perch and swooping down on us, without warning, like the shite-hawks at Mena Camp in Egypt. Known to every serving soldier in the Middle East, these black, noisy scavengers winged around the cook-house at Mena Camp looking for easy meat from some unsuspecting gunner's plate of curry, as he carried it from the cook-house to the mess-tent.

Sergeant George Lunt didn't hesitate to carry out the Engineer Officer's order. Tired as we were, we didn't need very much persuasion to strip the gun again and carry it, and the accompanying equipment, back down to the portee. On my final trip down the concrete stairs, carrying the last of the boxes of ammunition, I distinctly felt a momentary, stomach-churning, swaying movement. Expecting the building to fall on top of me, I leaped down the last six steps, clutching the box of ammo tightly to my chest. Half a dozen large glazed tiles fell off the wall with a frightening clatter around my feet. I scampered out through the door before you could say "Woody Woodpecker".

Our new position was to protect the bridge over the road, on the outskirts of the town. We were sited in a field, on one side of the road. The other gun in my section was dug in on the far side of the road. Although still apprehensive about the Messerschmitts, I felt much safer after we had finished digging a gun-pit to the required depth. It was only a shallow depression, two or three feet deep, to accommodate the gun and its crew. We filled sandbags with the spoil from the hole, and built a low wall around the pit as an added protection.

We made ourselves as comfortable as we could in the mire and mud of the field, half the crew on guard in the gun pit, and the other half "resting" on the pathetic rubber groundsheets in the little Scout tent.

Original drawn by unknown POW in Stalag 383, handed to OCA by Geoff Swinnerton, son of the late Bdr Jack Swinnerton. Refurbished by Eric Davies June 1997

The tent, with the portee parked alongside, was pitched near a farmhouse on a corner of the field away from the gun position. It transpired that the farmer had lived in New York for three years in the early thirties and spoke excellent English. We became quite friendly with him and his family. Until the bombing started a few days later we were able to buy forgotten luxuries like fresh milk, eggs, fruit and vegetables.

We also became friendly with the locals, some of the young

girls in fact wanting more than friendship. They saw the chance to earn themselves some money, or tins of coveted Fray Bentos corned beef. One girl became very attached to Jock McDonald, the only Scot on the gun. It was hysterical, one afternoon when Sergeant Lunt was attending a conference at Battery Headquarters. The lads vacated the Scout tent so that Jock could carry on a somewhat brief courtship with some privacy. Very little privacy, as it turned out, for whilst the canvas hid from view the couple inside, it didn't deaden the sound of their frantic activity. Nor the sound of the chorus of encouragement and advice Jock was receiving from some of his comrades on the outside.

"'urry up, Jock, get on with it for Christ's sake, the Jerries are nearly 'ere. They're only up the fuckin' road and they'll have yer balls for garters if yer not careful." All this was accompanied by frenzied hammering with a metal tent peg on the canvas of the scout tent.

Jock emerged from the tent fastening the brass buttons of his battledress trousers.

"Yer lousy bastards," he shouted, "you knew bloody well I was comin'. Couldn't you tell 'em to wait a bit?"

But, the B.S.M.'s lecture, back in Athens, on the perils of venereal disease in Greece, graphically recalled by Sergeant George Lunt, frightened off the rest of the crew. George confessed, afterwards that he was scared that the Scout Tent might turn into a mobile brothel.

Pedlars called, selling knick-knacks, souvenirs and lemonade drinks, and we had photographs taken by an itinerant photographer. Suspicious of him at first, when someone suggested he could be a fifth columnist taking photos of the guns for the Germans, the farmer, Andreous the Yank, said he was OK and he'd known him for years. As a souvenir, the photographer took a trick photograph of George Lunt handing himself a cigarette. (Although George didn't smoke.)

So my first few days in Larissa were very quiet, without any hint at all of what was to come in the very near future. I was even able to write a letter Home, which, strangely enough, got back to England safely. It was the last of my letters from the Middle East to survive the years in the old shoe box of Rene's.

No. 890650. Dvr. ARTHUR. D.
No. 1 BATTERY,
106ᵗʰ (L.Y.) Regt. R.H.A.,
M.E.F.
Tuesday, 25th Mar., '41.

Dear Mum,

Received last week your welcome letter dated 23rd March enclosed with Alf's. At the same time I got the one from Dad and Rene and also one each from Frank and Hilda. I'll reply to all of them as I get the opportunity.

You enclosed an envelope which had been returned from Haifa and you said you got a bit of a shock when you saw it. There was no need, really, because I told you in some of my earlier letters from the desert, that most of the mail was going all over the place after me.

I was very glad to hear from Dad, that he was feeling OK again and hope he is still in the pink and eating like a horse. He must have had a fairly tough time in hospital, according to his letter, for he seems to have fed on rubber tubes for a week or so. Anyway, I'm glad it's all over and as Alf says, you want to rest and take things absolutely easy again.

You don't seem to have had much of a Christmas, but perhaps the next one may be a lot better for all of us. I had a fairly dull Christmas, I may of told you. We were outside Fort Cuppuzzo at the time and the weather was pretty bad, and to make matters worse the water was salty and we couldn't make a proper drink. However, we made the best of it and had a good sleep and a bit of a sing song.

I was very glad to hear from you and both Dad and Alf, that all at Home are pleased with the successes of the lads in the desert. At the time, I remember we were all wondering very much what the people in Blighty were thinking. We were all looking forward to the letters and papers of that date. We didn't take a very great part in it until the battle at Bengazi, where our Regiment made a bit of name for itself. I mentioned it in my last letter, but, of course, I can't tell you the whole story properly until I get Home. It was during that campaign that I got one or two souvenirs a wristlet watch and big pocket watch given me by an Italian Officer. I also had a lovely piano accordion in a wooden case, but it began to get battered about so I got rid of it. I also got a lovely camera which had a roll of films in it, so we took some up there in the blue. I enclose one of myself and the lads I was with all the time, on our truck ("The Liverpool Boys"). The other, is two of the lads cooking chips. On the left is Tom Kenwright who knows Hilda very well, (show it to her if you see her) and the other chap is Jack Beck. He lives in Dovecote. Do you think we look dirty or just sunburnt? Actually we were both.

By the way Tom MacCrimmon was with me at the time and he was OK and getting lots of letters. I suppose his people will hear from him before very long.

Well, Mum, we are out of the "burning waterless desert" and instead we are now in a very beautiful country, exactly the opposite. Summer is just beginning and the snow has started to melt from the mountain tops. At the moment we are in a wonderful spot, the best we've ever been in. On the other side of the road from us is a farm house and we get fresh milk every evening. It costs very little. Every morning an old chap from the town brings out to us, on his way to work, a couple of dozen eggs and one or two loaves of new brown bread. The eggs cost about 1.1/2d each.

The town isn't up to much as it had a pretty bad earthquake a few months ago and it caused a lot of damage. A lot of people cleared out and I don't blame them. The most important thing, though, the cimema is still open and I went last night. It was an ancient picture and I'd seen it before. An Army picture called, O.H.M.S. An interesting feature about it was the troop-ship they use in the story. It was the same ship that took us to Palestine.

I was very interested to hear about Harold being offered a commission, he's getting on fine, isn't he? Here's me an old soldier of eighteen months and still a common Driver. I wish you could get him and Ken to write, Mum, I'd love to hear from them. If they can't use their military address they could use yours.

Well, Mum, this is all for now and I'll write again very shortly as I've plenty of time on my hands. Remember me to all

and I'll write next to Dad and Rene.
Cheerio,
Doug.
P.S. I forgot to tell you I'm fit as a fiddle and still
one of the very few not on the doctor's sick list.
(Touch wood) Don't address letters M.E.F.Y.
just put M.E.F.

Like all servicemen uprooted from Home, letters were a life line with the every day things I had blithely taken for granted before my call up. And what had become even more important to me, they were a link with the undemonstrative love of my Mother and the family life I had left behind. So it was little wonder that I was seeking letters from my siblings. By this time, of course, they had all been called up and had joined the letter-writing fraternity themselves.

My four brothers also served in the Army during the War, despite my Father's oft repeated promise after his service in the Engineers in the 1914 war, that none of his sons would wear khaki. Alfred Edward, the eldest, a sergeant in the Pay Corps. Harold Milward, the second eldest, was commissioned in the Ordnance Corps in 1944 and finished his service as a Major. Kenneth George, son No. 3, five year older than me, first saw service with the Nottinghamshire Hussars, a Yeomanry Territorial Unit similar to the 106th Lancashire Hussars before being transferred to the Ordnance Corps. And my younger brother, Walter, a fitter with R.E.M.E, served in the Western Desert and Italy.

* * *

In the lull before the storm, (or should I say before the Storm-Troopers), Lance Ferguson and I took advantage of our sparse off-duty periods by exploring what was left of Larissa and its surroundings, after the devastation of the earthquake.

There wasn't very much to see. Most of the shops were closed but we found a little taverna open and I was introduced to the foul tasting Greek Ouzo and the delicious, but expensive, Mavro Daphne.

The one and only cinema in the town was also still open, noisily patronised at every performance by the British and Colonial troops in the area. Most of them, like us, straight from the Libyan Desert and starved of any entertainment of any kind for months. Lance and I eagerly joined the queue, one evening, to see two out-of-date black and white films which were showing during the few days we were there. One was the "O.H.M.S." film I told Mother about in my letter. The other featured Errol Flynn in another film about the 1914 world war. He played the part of a dashing fighter pilot in the Royal Flying Corps, piloting a tiny biplane apparently made of galvanized wire and cardboard, setting fire to dozens of enemy aircraft on remote landing fields and bombing munitions factories and strafing troops in the trenches on the way back to his base. All on the same first flight after he had left his flying school!

Seasoned desert veterans, we were watching this Hollywood fairy tale, some with tongue in cheek and some shouting for the manager to put a Mickey Mouse cartoon on, when I had my second frightening experience of an earthquake. At least, my immediate thoughts were that we were about to experience an earthquake at first hand.

Lance and I were in the front row of the little balcony at the rear of the Cinema, when without any warning the seats seemed to lurch to one side with a sickening, trembling movement, and then "floated" back to their original position. My hands froze on the brass rail in front of me, with my first terrified reaction that the balcony was going to fall, me with it, on the heads of the rowdy Australian patrons in the rear stalls, beneath us.

The film stopped immediately. (For the third time. There had already been two stoppages to change the reels). The auditorium lights flickered on, the manager came out to the front of the screen. Barely making himself heard over the mixture of cat-calls, boos and cheers of the Australians in the audience, he explained, in a heavily American accented, broken English, that there had been another minor tremor. There was nothing to worry about, and he was going to carry on showing the film.

"THERE'S NOTHING TO WORRY ABOUT," the man said, "IT'S ONLY A BIT OF A TREMOR."

In the last few days we had seen at first hand the ravages of the earthquake which had almost destroyed Larissa. Furthermore we had just watched on the trembling cinema screen, the enormous damage Errol Flynn had caused with his little aeroplane on The Western Front.

So Lance and I left Errol enjoying a spot of well earned leave, with Mademoiselle from Armentiers in a haystack at the back of the Officers' Mess, to the accompaniment of the derisive, bawdy comments of the Aussies, as we hurriedly vacated the cinema. We spent the rest of the evening, and what was left of our pocket money, on Mavro Daphny in the deserted Taverna. I thanked my lucky stars that I didn't have to go back to the gun on top of the Police Station.

***

During our wanderings around the little town, Lance and I had blundered on some mysterious, canvas covered mounds neatly spaced at intervals across the grass in a field near the railway station. It was a Service Corps food supply dump. When the R.A.S.C. guard on the other side of the field had his back turned, our closer investigation revealed that the canvas covers were hiding all kinds of appetising food and delicacies like tinned pilchards and salmon, tinned plums and pears, and precious Nestle's condensed milk. Goodies that we hadn't seen for months. To add to our excitement we discovered, also, that one of the little mounds, conveniently placed on the edge of the field, concealed stone demijohns of rum lined up in orderly, military rows under the canvas sheet.

Expectations had been high, when we arrived in Greece, that our food would be better than the spartan fare we had put up with in the desert, but there had been very little improvement. Basically our food ration was much the same as it had been in North Africa, except that there was a bit more of it without the sand. There was, of course, the ever present corned beef and rock hard biscuits. Bread was issued occasionally and sometimes there were potatoes with a few fresh vegetables. The real luxury to us desert veterans was being able to buy eggs and milk from our American friend on the nearby farm. However, this became a somewhat dangerous shopping expedition, when the Andreous

Family decided to spend most of the daylight hours with his brother in the hills.

He told us that, when he was away, we could help ourselves to the eggs in the hen-house, provided we left the money for them on the window sill in the tumbledown coop. What he didn't tell us was that he had left his two vicious German Shepherds chained up in the farmyard, on a long slip chain to look after his property whilst he was away. I took my turn to collect the eggs from the hen-house, taking my life in my hands as I slid past the frightening, demented guard dogs, rushing up and down the length of chain across the muddy farmyard. They were frothing at the mouth in their efforts to get at me, and howling with frustration when the chain brought them to an abrupt halt, before they could take the seat out of my pants. Even after dodging the dogs we conscientiously and honestly, always left the money for the eggs.

The Andreous family, with Yorkie, Lance, Bill, Jock and me.

Lance Ferguson and I decided, after we had stumbled on the R.A.S.C. cache in the field, that it would be far less risky, and far less expensive, to help ourselves to some of the goodies from the ration dump than to face the terrible wrath of the half-wild dogs in the farmyard. When Yorkie, our laconic, hard-bitten ex-regular reinforcement, heard about the jars of rum, he immediately volunteered to help.

Just before sun-up next morning, accompanied by Lance and Yorkie, I drove the portee along the edge of the field, and conveniently "broke down" by the canvas mound concealing the rum. Whilst I had the bonnet raised to search for the fault, my two companions were able to make a quick foray into the supply dump, hurriedly transferring into the open back of the vehicle jars of rum, large tins of peaches and pears and the once much despised pilchards-in-tomato-sauce from the first days of our call-up in Barlborough, now turned into a mouth-watering delicacy.

Somebody also threw on board a mysterious, unmarked cardboard box, which turned out to be full of flat little envelopes containing condoms. I and most of the gun-crew had never before even seen these deflated balloons but, realising they were french letters (as they were called in those days), concluded they must have been for "Officers, for the use of". Somebody suggested we should hand them over to our Section Officer!

Unfortunately our early morning activities came to a sudden end. We had to make a hasty retreat when we saw two of the R.A.S.C. lads, rifles in hand, dashing out of their guard hut. I had no guilty conscience about making the raid and in fact regretted that we hadn't been able to help ourselves to more of the carelessly guarded provisions. Later, I was also disappointed that I did not have the opportunity to make better use of the flat envelopes in the box of mysteries.

It transpired that our first raid on the luxuries of Larissa was also the last, for, very shortly afterwards, and before we had the opportunity to try our luck again, the Germans overran the town and the ration dump.

The Germans looted the lot.

Tinned fruit, tinned fish and best Jamacian rum, condoms and all, plus a cache of countless cigarettes which we hadn't stumbled across on our own expedition. As an added bonus, the Germans also captured a petrol dump in the next field containing thousands and thousands of gallons of petrol.

Chapter 3

Delayed Action

As we sampled the contraband rum that evening, our escapade became funnier and funnier, as the rum got tastier and tastier. As first I, and then Lance, related to our fellow gunners how Yorkie had burrowed under the canvas sheeting with his backside in the air, like a whippet down a rabbit hole, to get at what he thought were larger flagons of the rum. Our colourful description of his hurried reappearance, clutching a jar of rum in each hand and one under each armpit, after our warning cries when we had been spotted, became more hilarious with each swig of rum. So did the Scouse mimicking of his Yorkshire "coom on lads, let's fook off, quick," when he saw the Service Corp guards running across the field towards us.

The next day, with some unknown sixth sense, we treated ourselves to a gargantuan breakfast. Illicit tinned fruit was followed by porridge made with biscuits and lashings of Nestle's condensed milk, rounded off with corned beef and eggs fried in olive oil.

We had just finished this long remembered, delicious repast, when someone spotted a single plane, very high in the sky flying slowly, round and round in wide circles over the town and our position. Far too high for us to even see the markings, and certainly far too high for us to engage with our light anti-aircraft guns. We guessed it was a German reconnaissance 'plane, particularly when it turned away and headed North, as three of our six Hurricanes took off from the airstrip and started climbing towards it.

It was not very long before we realised that we had guessed correctly.

Shortly before mid-day, I had my first fleeting glimpse of black German crosses decorating the wings of a dozen or more

Messerschmitt fighters, as they flew over us at a frightening speed in the direction of the airfield. Taken completely by surprise by the suddenness of the attack, the speed, and the noise, and the tree-top height of the attacking planes, we somewhat belatedly opened fire with our little Breda ack-ack gun for the first time in earnest. Without much success, I'm bound to say. Horrified and helpless we saw two of the three Hurricanes based at the airstrip shot down as they were taking off. The third became airborne and we cheered when we saw it bring down one of the enemy fighters. Out of our range, we were unable to support the heavy fire put up by our fellow gunners from No 2 Battery, based on the perimeter of the muddy grass landing strip, and could only watch, helplessly. We learned, later, that twenty four Messerschmitts took part in the attack on the airfield and our Breda guns had been successful in bringing down one of them.

But that first attack by the German fighters on the airfield was only a forerunner to the bombing of Larissa. It heralded another lightning blitzkrieg by the Germans with the overrunning of Greece, and the overwhelming of the puny Allied force of desert veterans. It was the start of a daily, nerve-wracking, non-stop bombing and strafing, by the completely unopposed German Air Force, which lasted from first light in the morning until dusk. The ceaseless harassment by the Stukas and Dorniers and Messerchmitts of the Luftwaffe carried on throughout our demoralising and hasty retreat back to the south of Greece.

That first morning, the Messerschmitts departed as quickly as they had appeared, leaving behind a strange, shocked silence. Locked in our positions in the gun pit, we all realised the enormity of what had happened at the airfield.

Almost immediately, with no time to collect my thoughts and still dazed and shaken by the sudden attack by the fighters, I heard the steady, throbbing noise of the engines of hundreds of heavy bombers getting louder and louder as they approached us from the North – or what I believed to be hundreds of bombers – because I had never before seen so many aeroplanes in the sky at the same time, friend or foe. We opened fire with our little gun at this awe-inspiring armada flying over us in tight formation, almost wing to wing, with the other gun in the section joining in. A useless gesture of defiance, really, for the planes were far too high and completely out of range. Nevertheless, the very act of firing at the lumbering, black aeroplanes, seemed to bolster our courage. So did the loud, foul mouthed curses we yelled at the unheeding German pilots.

Our gun fell silent, as we sensed that Sergeant George Lunt was trying to make himself heard over the thunder of the aeroplanes.

"Hold your fire, Lance, hold your fire," he was bawling, "we're nowhere near in range."

Then I swiftly became aware of another vaguely familiar, threatening, frightening noise. A kind of swishing, screaming or whistling sound, against the background of the throbbing bombers.

It was the unmistakable sound of falling bombs.

A noise which became quite commonplace over the next few dreadful weeks. So did the distinctive banshee wailing and shrieking of Stuka dive-bombers.

Petrified with fear, we all, instinctively, flung ourselves down on the floor of the shallow gun-pit. All thoughts of firing the gun were forgotten. Like the others, I sought the doubtful protection of the sand-bagged wall, by huddling up against it with my knees drawn up to my body. Desperately I tried to make myself as small as possible, with hands and arms around my face and head, handicapped by the muddy boots of one of my comrades pressing hard against my steel helmet. Suddenly conscious of the boxes of live ammunition stacked around the floor of the gun pit, I half turned my head and caught a fleeting glance through my spread fingers, of the deadly black cylinders dropping down on us.

Not in a direct vertical fall, but at an angle, projected forward by the speed of the flying aeroplanes. In a ghastly optical illusion, the rotating bombs seemed to be falling slowly, like a film in slow motion, heading directly for our gun-pit.

Then the whole of the muddy field, with me in the middle of it, erupted in a series of gigantic ear-splitting explosions.

One after another, like the rolling, rumbling, thunderclaps of an electrical thunderstorm I had once experienced on the top of Snowdon in North Wales.

Lumps of soil and mud, clods of grass, stones, pebbles and bits of jagged metal, were tossed violently into the air, then to rain down on the gun and the occupants of the gun-pit, with a noise like hailstones hammering on a corrugated roof. Fleetingly I saw one of the farmer's goats, which a few minutes previously had been peaceably grazing on the sparse grass of the paddock, tossed into the air like a piece of brown paper, winging its uncontrollable way in a storm.

After what seemed a lifetime, the thunder ceased, and the rattling of falling debris died away. I could smell the pungent, acrid stink of cordite drifting across the field in wisps of black smoke. Steeling myself for the next lot to fall, I lay motionless in the bottom of the gun-pit, in the unnatural silence that followed the deafening explosions. Thankfully, I then became aware of the fading sound of the engines of the departing bombers.

Trembling, I clambered to my feet to find Sergeant Lunt already peering over the top of the sandbags, checking on the mayhem the bombers had caused. I saw that the muddy field was dotted with bomb craters and the corpses of three goats. Miraculously, neither our gun nor the pit were damaged. Although ashen faced and temporarily speechless, none of the crew appeared to be injured.

George and I were joined by Lance Ferguson and Bombardier Jenkinson, the No. 2 on the gun, a newcomer to the Unit. Bill was a Londoner, with a strong Cockney accent, one of the reinforcements who had joined us in Glyfada straight out from England. He had seen action on heavy ack-ack guns in London during the blitz, and knew far more about high level enemy bombing than we did. Since joining us he never ceased to remind us of the fact.

We climbed out of the pit, and could see that the gun on the other side of the road had been hit. It was slewed over on its side, the barrel lying askew on the parapet of the sandbagged wall. Our mates had received a direct hit. The gun rendered completely useless, Tom Kenwright badly wounded and Ernie Mack, the layer, had received what he thought were superficial shrapnel wounds to his legs. Before we had time to find out the full extent of the damage, our second-in-charge, Bombardier

Jenkinson let out a yell.

"Christ," he shouted, "the bastards have dropped fuckin' delayed action bombs. We can't stay here."

There was panic in his voice as he shouted again.

"Those 'oles are bloody delayed action bombs, They could go off any fuckin' time. In five minutes or five bleedin' hours. The're goin' to blow up any minute, I'm tellin' you, and we can't stay 'ere."

He was pointing, wild-eyed, at three circular holes in the ground. Neat, clean, round holes which looked as if they had been formed in the muddy soil by a McAlpine pile-driver, drilling bore holes for a block of high rise tenements. Two of the holes were no more than five or six feet from the sandbagged wall of the gun pit. The third was closer still, and had formed a half circle in the outer part of the sand bagged wall itself before entering the ground. This deadly looking cavity, I saw to my horror, was about three feet away from where I had been grovelling with fright, in the bottom of the gun pit a few very short moments earlier. It was miraculous that the falling red-hot metal had missed my head by only a fraction. Something like a dart landing on a dartboard on the wrong side of the treble twenty. But this wasn't a dart, it was a bomb. For all I knew, a thousand pounder, and obviously aimed with precision at our circular dart-board of a gun-pit! It was also nothing short of miraculous that none of the three bombs had detonated when they hit the ground, blowing us all to Kingdom Come, as well as the gun.

The rest of the crew scrambled out of the pit.

Overwhelmed by the magnitude of the attack, dazed, and open mouthed, we gathered around one of the deadly holes, stupidly looking down the cavity to see if we could spot the bomb hidden in its depths.

Bombardier Jenkinson went hysterical.

"This is delayed action shite," he shouted again, his Cockney accent more pronounced than ever. "The fuckin' things'll blow up any second. I've seen dozens of these goin' up in the raids on London. Blowin' rows of 'ouses sky 'igh. And I tell yer what, you can please your bloody selves, but I'm not stayin' 'ere any longer."

And he didn't.

He was off like a greyhound in the first race at Stanley Track on a Saturday night, to fling himself headlong into the muddy ditch on the other side of the field.

His panic spread to the rest of us, and, without further discussion, and deferring to his oft repeated experiences in the bombing of London, en masse, we took to our heels after him. Including the steady, unflappable, conscientious Sergeant George Lunt who I thought would never run away from anything, or anybody. We left everything. The gun and ammunition in the pit, the scout tent containing all our personal belongings, sleeping gear, rations, water, and what was left of the purloined rum and tinned fruit. Under the scanty cover of olive trees, we also abandoned the portee containing the precious emergency rations, petrol, boxes of ammunition and sundry personal souvenirs of Palestine, Egypt and Greece.

We reached the "safety" of the ditch at the far side of the field, and stood in six inches of muddy water to wait with bated breath for the delayed-action bombs, and the gun to blow up. As if confirming the Bombardier's dire warning, the silence was then broken by the distant crump, crump of explosions.

"There y'are," cried Bill, triumphantly, "that was delayed actions goin' orf. Dropped just after we copped it over there, a few minutes ago. I 'ope some poor bugger 'asn't bought it, standin' around lookin' at the flamin' things, like what we were."

For what seemed ages to me in the strange, eerie silence which followed the departure of the aeroplanes, we crouched in the ditch getting wetter and wetter, more nervous and more miserable and waited expectantly, for the bombs to explode. What conversation there was, strangely enough, being carried out in whispers as if the Germans were the other side of the hedge, or any loud conversation might detonate the bombs.

But there were no explosions from the field. Delayed or otherwise. After a while, I could see that George Lunt was realising his responsibility as No. 1, and was getting concerned about the unattended gun being left on the other side of the field.

Unable to contain himself any longer, he said, "Come on, lads, we'll have to get the gun out of the pit. We can't leave it there. If the Jerry fighters come over again, we'll have to have a go at them, that's what we're here for. We can't do that if we leave the gun in the pit, and stay here in the ditch."

There was not much response from the "lads", except a muttered, "you'll have to get the fuckin' thing out yourself, then, won't you?" from the Bombardier.

George didn't seem to hear the remark, but turned to me and said, "Well I'm going to have a shot at getting the gun out of that pit, and I'll do it by myself if necessary. But you're the driver, Doug, so you'll have to come over to help me get it on the portee, and drive it away from the bombs. We'll have to be quick about it before they go off."

I climbed out of the ditch, reluctantly, to follow him, sick at heart, my thoughts unable to shake off the image of the falling bombs and the holes around the gunpit. But I found that the act of setting out to do something relieved some of the tension and strain that had overtaken me when the bombs dropped. Anyway, I knew I was the only one there who could drive the truck and I couldn't let him go alone. I felt better when Lance Ferguson, in his sing-song Geordie accent said, "Whey eh, lads, I'll give you a hand then."

The three of us set off, running, across the field, dodging the bomb craters which were already beginning to fill up with muddy water.

The young sailors at the Royal Tournament, in later years, couldn't have touched us with the speed with which we demolished the sandbagged wall of the gun-pit, pulled the gun out, and loaded it onto the portee. We must have broken all records, known and unknown, in our haste to get away from the frightening presence of those delayed action bombs.

We stuffed sandbags from the wall down the bomb holes, in a forlorn hope that they would be some protection if the bombs did erupt, and then quickly made a sort of sloped runway from the floor of the pit, for dragging the gun up and into the field. I ran to the portee, pulled off the camouflage of branches and vegetation, and drove it over to the gun. I was thankful to see that Yorkie had sheepishly followed our example and had arrived to give us a hand. He also rescued his rum, or what was left of it. As he said later, "I couldn't leave the bleedin' rum there, could I?"

In treble quick time we had loaded the gun and

38

ammunition, and thrown most of the gear from the tent, piecemeal, into a heap in the back of the portee. We left the tent behind in the olive trees.

I didn't need George Lunt's, "OK Doug, get to the other side of the field as quick as you can." Nor Yorkie's. "Coom on Dougie, fook off before those bleedin' bombs blow up." I was off across the field, weaving in and out of the craters, expecting the bombs to blow up, any second, behind me.

I don't know, to this day, whether those delayed action bombs ever went off, as we left Larissa that same evening. For all I know they may still be buried deep in the soil of a blissfully ignorant farmer's sheep paddock, on the outskirts of the little town. Or perhaps they built a new earthquake-proof Police Station and Municipal Office over them.

But I like to believe, in retrospect, that those bombs were not "delayed action" at all.

I like to believe they were duds.

Simply duds. Defective. No bloody good.

Perhaps the end product of some tired, disillusioned female German munitions worker, on the late afternoon shift, her heart not really into the job, and worried stiff about what to give the kids for their dinner, when she got home. Or did I owe my life to an unknown "Auslander" slave worker? An overworked, Polish Prisoner-of-War, slowly expiring of starvation and brutality, carrying out sabotage at great risk to his already worthless life, in a Krupps munitions factory.

***

In the absence of any instructions from more senior N.C.Os or officers, George Lunt selected another position in the field, which he hoped was a safe distance from the dormant bombs, which we were still expecting to explode. Nervously, with heads looking over our shoulders we had started to dig another gun-pit, when we received a belated visit from Peter McShea, our Section Sergeant.

"Pack in, lads," shouted Peter, almost before he got out of the truck on the edge of the field. "Pack up. We're pissing off. The Jerries are only up the road and we're going back to Athens.

We're off as soon as it gets dark."

Then he added, as an afterthought, "Is everybody OK? Nobody injured? Any casualties? Dave Mclean's gun is out of action and Ernie Mack and Stenson got peppered in the legs with shrapnel and Tom Kenwright's badly wounded and they've taken him away."

He didn't seem to notice that we were not in our original position.

His information was received with mixed feelings. Worry about the wounded on the other gun, and wondering what would happen to them because nobody had ever told us what the drill was if any of us copped it. Relief that we were moving away from Larissa. Trepidation and alarm that "the Jerries are up the road".

By late afternoon, as darkness set in, the Battery began the long and exhausting retreat South, down the shabby narrow roads of Greece. This time without the plaudits of the populace, and their oft repeated choruses of "The Woodpecker Song".

Larissa had taken the full force of the bombing, and we slowly made our way through what was left of the town, picking our way through the bomb craters and the shattered remains of the houses and little shops. Passing the site of our first gun position on the top of the Police Station, I could see in the fading light, that the new building had collapsed like a house of cards. It might have been built by a youngster on the parlour table and blown over by his teasing little sister. The floors and walls of the building had fallen in on themselves, and the blackened, flat, concrete roof – the original site of our gun – was lying like the Ace of Spades on top of the heap of rubble. I silently thanked, once again, the unknown Engineer Major who had condemned the gun position, and had ordered us to find another site.

We also passed the little cinema where Lance and I had had a brief encounter with Mr Flynn and his flying machine, and the scene of our hurried departure from the balcony after the "earthquake". There was nothing much left of the cinema. It was as if the Germans were getting their own back on Errol for the damage he had inflicted on them in the 14/18 war. All that was left of him was part of his paper image advertising the film, flapping forlornly, on the only wall left standing.

We moved out of Larissa when darkness fell.

Chapter 4

Flight from Larissa and Retreat from Greece

Convoys crawling round the mountains,
Tail-lights glimmering in the blackness.
Lorries falling over edges.
Daylight bringing screaming Stukas

A single bomber coming over.
Two ambulances seeking cover.
A clump of trees, a lorry hidden…
This one full of ammunition.

Torn branches, stripped of springtime greenness,
Hung with little bits of bandage,
Limbs, intestines, whiteness, redness,
Like the spruce festooned at Christmas.

The Royal Navy sailing swiftly:
Hero, Hasty, Havock, Hotspur,
Isis, Kingston, Wryneck, Griffin,
Decoy, Diamond, Defender.

Convoys leaving. *Slamat* blazing.
Ulster Prince in flames at Navplion.
Hellas burning at Piraeus,
Packed with wounded and civilians.

Soldiers waiting for the Navy
Patiently at Kalamata.
Cooks and butchers, clerks and bakers,
Driving Germans from the harbour.

Thousands snaking down the beaches.
Four destroyers sending whalers.
Boats and scrambling nets, rope ladders.
Morning: orders to surrender.

Acres of prisoners lacking shelter.
Meagre food, infected water.
Cases of dysentery spreading rapidly.
Soon diphtheria and malaria.

Hot sun beating, starved men marching.
Weakest dropping, guards dispatching.
Bootless feet and wounds to carry.
Beaten Greeks who show compassion.

Locomotives pulling wagons.
Human cargo tightly herded.
Lice, foul air, poor sanitation,
Darkness, heat, deceased companions.

Thirst and hunger, fear and anger.
Nervy guards with ready guns.
Harsh punishment for all defiance.
Greece in 1941.

RETREAT FROM GREECE. Estelle Lancaster April 2001

It *was* dark. Pitch black. No street lights, no moon, no stars. No glowing fag-ends to alert the German Luftwaffe of our presence on the roads. Although we were soon to learn, that Jerry planes seldom flew after dark. Our progress South, in what we all knew now was a hasty, ignominious retreat, was made during the hours of darkness.

Driving from then on, became a nerve-wracking, harrowing nightmare. The side lights and the tiny, red rearlight on all vehicles were blacked out, except for a thin strip in the centre of each lamp. There were, of course, no stop-lights. The slowly moving convoy became a frustrating crawl of tightly packed vehicles. The blind leading the blind along the tortuous, winding roads, some not much more than cart tracks clinging to the side of a mountain. A five hundred foot drop on one side and a steep, almost vertical wall on the other side, disappearing upwards into the blackness of the night, and obliterating any feeble effort of the stars to show us the way.

Only two hundred yards out of Larissa, we lost the first of our trucks.

Section Sergeant Peter McShea in the section 15cwt. Morris immediately ahead of me, driven by one of the new re-inforcements who had joined us at Athens, suddenly vanished completely from my sight. Peter's truck was loaded to capacity, and more, with the spare kit and sundry accoutrement of the section. Petrol, tools, ammunition, rations, spares of all kinds, heaped in the back of the truck, making a pile some three or four feet high and held in place with a canvas cover tied at the corners. I say he vanished suddenly, but we were only crawling along at about five miles an hour. The vague silhouette of the truck I was following, slowly tilted to one side, and then disappeared out of my sight.

I came to a hurried stop on the crumbling lip of a huge crater, into which half of the road had disappeared. Just in time, I avoided following Sgt. McShea and his driver, and disappearing over the edge myself with my gun-crew. As George Lunt and I hurriedly got out somebody produced a torch and shone it down the crater. The section truck was lying upside down in the bottom of the huge bomb-hole, its four wheels still spinning. Then I was amazed to see Peter McShea and the driver scrambling up the side of the crater, seemingly uninjured but covered in mud. Sergeant McShea was verbally abusing the driver, because he had not seen the bomb hole in time to avoid going over the edge.

At that moment a Military Policeman on a motor bike stopped alongside my truck.

Without preamble, and barely giving him time to climb out of the muddy hole in the ground, the M.P. said to the badly shaken Peter, "You'll have to leave the truck, Sergeant, you won't have time to get it out of that shit."

"What about all the kit?" said Sergeant McShea, without very much enthusiam I'm bound to say.

"You'll have to leave the bleedin' stuff, won't you?" said the M.P. "There's 'undreds of vehicles at the back of you, and you're holdin' them all up. The bastard Jerry tanks are only up the road and will be 'ere by first light. So get in one of the other trucks, leave everythin' and fuck off as soon as you can."

Peter, still in shock, didn't need any second bidding and jumped on to my portee, squeezing alongside George Lunt in the front seat. Understandably, he instructed me to "go careful, Young Doug, for Christ's sake, go careful." Under the guidance of the M.P., I drove past the huge crater, in the bottom of which the wheels of his upside down truck were still spinning slowly.

It wasn't very long before I caught up with the now stationary convoy. Sergeant McShea left me to join the Section Officer in the 5cwt at the head of the Battery. He was one of the first Sergeants I had served under back in our T.A. Camp at Trawsfynned, and became another lost ship passing in the night. I did not see him again, after this incident until 1948 when I was on a business call at Liverpool University where he worked in the Fabric Department.

The convoy was stationary for a good half hour and then moved off suddenly, without warning. It came to a grinding halt five minutes later at a hairpin bend, where a three tonner had broken down and was in the process of being pushed over the side of the mountain. This was the start of many such holdups we were to encounter that night, and the two succeeding nights. At the longer, frustrating, irritating halts, a Military Policeman on a motor-cycle, halted alongside each of the stationary trucks of the convoy. He noisily hammered on the bonnet with a metal starting handle, shouting, "don't go to sleep, driver, no fuckin' sleepin'. Keep awake. You too, Sergeant. We'll be movin' on in a minute." Two or three sleeping drivers with exhausted gunners dead to the world in the back of their trucks, could hold up the entire retreating Allied army.

This "stop and go" snail's progress went on all night. A sort of ghost train of slowly moving vehicles grinding up and down the mountain roads. In the middle of that awful night, despite the bumping and jolting over the dreadful roads, despite the pleas to stay awake by the Military Policemen when we came to a halt, the lads on my gun were fast asleep. Including Sergeant George

Lunt, my No. 1 who had said, "OK Doug, I'll keep an eye open on this side for you." For long, lonely spells, I was the only one awake on the portee. To stop myself from nodding off, I had jammed tools from the truck repair kit under the thin leather cushion of the driving seat, to make myself as uncomfortable as possible. My backside, if I relaxed too much, biting into the jaws of a 12" monkey wrench. Or the jaws biting into my backside, I wasn't too sure which.

But even sitting and squirming on the wrench and two-pound lump hammer, there was one hair-raising moment when exhaustion finally overtook my concentration.

My eyes closed, and I dropped off to sleep.

Momentarily, it was one of the few occasions when the convoy was not stopping and starting every two or three minutes. We were making reasonably steady progress at about 15 miles and hour. I dozed off. Coming to life with a sudden, startling, frightening jerk, my hands still firmly gripping the steering wheel, I was just in time to regain control of the portee. I took a sharp, right hand turn to stay on the road, instead of driving straight over the side of a hundred foot drop to the valley below.

I never dozed off again.

Shortly afterwards, I was wide awake, my heart still beating rapidly from the shock of my near miss, when I had to maneouvre past a slowly moving detachment of Greek Pioneers. The mounted equivalent of our Royal Army Service Corps. The Muleteers, on foot, in a long single file, each man silently leading a scraggy little mule, took up most of the road and were barely visible in the darkness. The mules – truly Beasts of Burden – were completely exhausted after their long trek from the slopes of Mount Olympus or some place up North. They struggled along with heads hanging down dejectedly between their legs, loaded with all kinds of military stores and equipment.

As I drove slowly past the queue of beaten animals and their dispirited handlers, a bracket on the side of the portee snagged the lashings holding two steel-rimmed cartwheels on the back of one of the mules.

Not aware, at first, that I had picked up an unwilling passenger, I carried the poor beast along with its legs threshing wildly in mid-air. It was like some bizarre, comical scene from a "Popeye" cartoon. The muleteer running alongside shouting in unintelligible Greek, unable to atract my attention or to wake the sleeping gunners in the back of the truck. I braked suddenly when I eventually heard the screams of fright from the now crazed mule. As I stopped, the rope loosened itself from the bracket. The animal stumbled, fell to its knees and then disappeared, cartwheels and all, over the edge of the road and down the mountainside. Its ghost-like screams faded away as it vanished into the darkness.

Leaving the unfortunate animal to its fate and goaded on by the M.P. who had caught up with me once again on his motor bike, I had no time to stop to commiserate with the hysterical muleteer. His cursing, and the shrieks of the mule still ringing in my ears, I hurried on to catch up with the disappearing convoy. I was more determined than ever not to fall asleep and drive over the edge of one of the awful mountain roads, or snag another animal and pitch it over the side of a cliff.

I was tired and red-eyed for want of sleep, my backside sore and tender through the ministrations of the lump hammer and monkey wrench, and hungry. I had not eaten since before the air-raid on Larissa fifteen or more hours ago. I was desperate for a hot drink, as the terrible nightmare of my headlong flight seemed to go on for hours, and I longed for daylight to come.

When the morning light did eventually put in an appearance over those craggy mountain tops, it brought an even more frightening peril.

Chapter 5

"Ulster Prince" Runs Aground

Daylight found us in the middle of another enforced halt. Unfortunately, this was on a long, straight, narrow road crossing a valley from one range of mountains to another. The road was crammed, as far as the eye could see, with stationary vehicles. Some of the occupants had climbed out and lit suicidal fires under the olive trees, to make the tea they had all been longing for.

We, on our portee, were about to follow suit, when the first of the Messerschmits came roaring over the mountain top. They were following the contours of the road which was packed, nose to tail – like a traffic hold-up on a modern motor-way – with what seemed to me to be half of the Allied transport in Greece.

Twelve of them, one behind the other, just about clearing the tops of the olive trees lining the road. Low enough to catch a glimpse of the pilots, and to plainly see the black crosses on the underside of the wings, as they flashed by.

The planes came screaming down the long straight road. The unexpected, terrifying noise of the flying death machines was punctuated with repeated bursts of their machine-guns. There was a rapid, plop-plopping noise alongside the roadway, marking the sudden appearance of a continuous line of neat little holes, spaced out at regular intervals in the soil and grass a foot or so from the verge. There was a mad scramble among the gunners in the back of the portee to get the gun into action. They were too late. The fighters had vanished over the distant mountain top, one after the other, as quickly as they had arrived. They left behind them three burning trucks, the black smoke billowing into the sky to guide their comrades in the following flight to the target.

Surprisingly, the convoy started to move off again, albeit at

47

a walking pace, and there was a stampede of tea-brewers from the olive trees to re-join their transport. We hadn't gone very far when we halted yet again. This time to watch, opened mouthed, the first of many attacks of Stuka dive-bombers shrieking down in follow-my-leader fashion, on vehicles at the head of the column. Too far out of range for us to open fire, we watched the spectacle glad that we were not on the receiving end.

We quickly learned which attack on the convoy was the most threatening, and which one we could engage with some hope of success. To our elation, our gun was successful in downing one of the fighters.

For the next day, after another morning of non-stop, low-level attacks by the German planes, "Yorkie", our ex-regular Reservist – who had been quaffing some of the rum we had pinched from the ration dump at Larissa – insisted on taking over the aiming and firing of the gun. Well and truly fortified, he sat on the seat behind the open sights of the Breda. When the next flights of raiders came weaving down the road at their accustomed tree-top level, he let them have five or six pans of shells, as fast as they were loaded into the breach by Lance Ferguson. Each pan accompanied by a torrent of foul-mouthed curses, acquired during his seven year stint in the regulars in India. To his surprise and our delight, thick black smoke streamed out from the engine of one of the planes as it roared over our heads and we watched it bank away sharply, losing height and then crashing on the mountainside ahead of us.

A rousing cheer, heralding our success, went up from the hundreds of troops taking refuge in the olive trees flanking the road. The sight of the Messerschmitt rapidly losing height, black smoke streaming from it, made us all feel that our skimpy training had not been entirely in vain. I was to learn later that this was not the only success of the little guns of the 106th. Our portees were by now spaced out at intervals along the snaking column of retreating vehicles. Four Messerschmitt fighters met their fate by the Bredas of the two batteries of the 106th, during the two day retreat from Larissa.

***

The purgatory of the headlong retreat ended for me after we crossed the Corinth Canal, and arrived at the little fishing port of Nauplion on the Bay of Argos in the Aegean Sea. The Navy had already started to evacuate troops, and the 106th guns became part of the rear-guard, providing the only anti-aircraft defence for the embarkation port. Our gun was positioned on the headland above the harbour, overlooking a sandy beach and the blue waters of the Bay of Argos.

That night, after drawing lots for guard duty, we "kipped down" on the wet grass alongside the truck, leaving one man on guard in case the Germans crept up on us. He was to waken his relief after his spell of an hour. Utterly exhausted we all fell into a deep sleep including, at some stage during the night, the man who should have been on guard!

The Germans didn't creep up on us that night, but four of our Greek Allies did. The guilty guard woke up suddenly to find four young Greek soldiers helping themselves to our belongings in the back of the truck. His cries of alarm woke the rest of the crew, and four of us chased after the thieves, who gave us the slip in the next olive grove. It was obvious that like us they were hungry, so they helped themselves to our meagre stock of corned beef, biscuits and a couple of the tins of the fruit which we had pinched in Larissa.

This was the only occasion we experienced this sort of intrusive behaviour by the Greeks during our few hectic weeks in their country.

Next day, shortly after we had once again excavated the clay soil and were ensconsed in our deeper than ever gun-pit, a smart, trim looking, two-funnelled ship made its way, cautiously, into the harbour. One or two of the boys immediately recognised it as the "Ulster Prince".

Before the outbreak of the war the "Ulster Prince" was an Irish Sea Passenger Ferry regularly sailing between Liverpool and Belfast. It was very familiar to some of the 106th lads, one-time dockers in the port of Liverpool.

Lieutenant (E) Gerald Hughes in his story "*The Ulster Prince Goes to War*", relates how the Passenger Ferry was commissioned into the Royal Navy early in September, 1939 and converted into a troop transport carrier. After the fall of France she was in constant action evacuating troops from the Continent. She rescued troops from St. Nazaire and was heavily involved in both the landings and evacuation at Narvik, Norway. She made a hair-raising, dangerous trip to Lisbon, Portugal where she successfully rescued some 500 British civilian escapees from Central and Southern France.

The "Ulster Prince", and her Liverpool crew, was already a veteran, when, refitted as an assault ship, she was transferred to the Mediterranean. There she was continually in action, making perilous night-time dashes along the coast of Africa, with essential supplies to the besieged fortress of Tobruk, and running the gauntlet from Tobruk to Alexandria with Allied casualties and hundreds of Italian prisoners of war, alternating with ferrying supplies and troops over to Crete and Greece.

The writing was already on the wall that the fruitless campaign in Greece was lost. The "Ulster Prince" became part of a large Naval Task-force held in readiness at Suda Bay, Crete, to evacuate troops from Nauplion and Kalamata and other ports in Southern Greece.

On the 24th April, after the capitulation of the Greek Government, and the subsequent belated decision of the Allied Middle East Command to rescue our troops, the "Ulster Prince", escorted by two destroyers, was sent on ahead of the main relief force. Under constant heavy air attack after they had left Crete, they arrived in Nauplia Sound around mid-day.

From our position on the headland overlooking the little harbour, we watched the "Ulster Prince" inch her way across the water of the harbour. She came to a standstill a few hundred feet from the jetty. It was obvious to us that she had run aground, when we clearly saw the churning of the sand disturbed by the propellers, as the Captain made repeated abortive attempts to free the ship from the sand-bank. We watched, dismayed, as the stern slowly swung around and blocked the entrance to the harbour, for her two accompanying destroyers.

"It's stuck on the sand," said Lance Ferguson, "That's bloody torn it. We'll not get out tonight."

When we saw the "Ulster Prince" enter the bay our first thoughts and hopes had been that we would get away from

Greece that night. Wishful thinking. Instead, when the last of the German planes had vanished out of sight in the gloom of the early evening we watched the crew disembark, four of them joining us to share the last of our rations.

All Liverpudlians, they told us that the crew had been put ashore except for a skeleton crew of volunteers led by Lieutenant (E) Gerald Hughes, to keep the main engines going and attempt to free the ship from the sandbank. We were not able to offer them a five course dinner that night. Speaking with the voices of experience, after months of short, sometimes non-existent rations, on our advice they ate with relish the "blind" scouse we had managed to scrape together. We used our last tin of corned-beef, a tin of tomatoes and a few wrinkled potatoes, and thickened the mixture with broken hard-tack biscuits we found on the bottom of the portee. Washed down with the watered dregs of rum from two of the stone jars that had been overlooked by the victorious Yorkie, it was a meal fit for a king.

The crew of the "Ulster Prince", eventually, luckily or unluckily, depending which way you saw it, was successfully repatriated. Months later they reached home safely. Some of them went on to serve with great distinction in Atlantic and Russian convoys, one or two even finishing the war with "The Forgotten Fleet" in the Far East campaigns.

The stranded ship in the bay attracted more attention than ever from the enemy aircraft. As their planes put in an appearance at first light our gun also came under direct attack. Terrifying, but not always accurate, their repeated attempts to bomb the stricken ship were balked by the hail of fire from the Breda guns of the 106th, positioned on the headland. Usually, the Stukas made their attacks in formations of six or seven planes. But it was a lone plane that caused the first real damage to the ship and set her on fire. I distinctly saw the bombs drop from the belly of the plane and land amidships. The fires started almost immediately. The Stuka, however, never recovered from its dive. Without regaining height, it flew directly towards us, quite low. The frightening wailing of its klaxon shrieking in our ears, it took the full force, head on, of the continuous rapid fire of our gun. Passing right over the gun pit it crashed in a ball of flame some two hundred yards away. It was unfortunate that we hit him with our salvo of shells after he dropped the bombs on the "Ulster Prince", and not before.

Later, we took turns to inspect the crashed aeroplane. Completely destroyed, it was unrecognisable as a flying machine, and the burnt and charred wreckage was spread over a wide area of the hillside. There was no trace of the pilot except for a single, black leather, knee-length flying boot, with the gruesome remains of a foot and part of the calf of a leg still inside it. It was a small boot, strangely and horribly intact. Except for some charring around the edge of the sole. It was highly polished but so small, that some of the lads were quite convinced that the pilot had been a woman.

Late that afternoon we got the welcome news we had been longing for since arriving at Nauplion. We were told we were being taken off after nightfall. We had to destroy the Breda and its portee and all kit, with the exception of the driver's and Sergeant's rifles and ammunition. We would only be allowed to board our rescue vessel with a rifle, a steel helmet and the small webbing side pack containing a limited amount of personal gear.

It was quite easy to render the Breda gun useless. We threw the breechblock into the sea, destroyed all the small moving parts, hammered off the aiming sights and twisted the barrel out of shape.

But it was surprising how difficult it was to destroy the truck, short of setting it on fire, which we were warned not to do. I drained off the water, oil and petrol, switched the engine on and left it running with the choke fully extended. There could only have been a small amount of petrol left in the tank, but the engine seemed to run for ages before it eventually seized up with smoke billowing out from the cylinder head. I took out the sparking plugs and stripped away all the electrical leads, the battery, the carburettor, the pump, and buried them with the Breda ammunition. The solid rubber tyres on the truck were slashed into ribbons, and the radiator fins beaten until they split. We were all resolved that the Germans would not get much use out of our gear.

After darkness fell we made our way down to the quayside to join a subdued, orderly queue of soldiers being quietly urged by two sailors into what appeared to me to be an oversized rowing boat with a sail, tied to the quay.

"Come on lads, we haven't got all night," urged one of the sailors. "We've got to get on our way long before daybreak and the Jerry planes come over again. Pack yourselves in as tight as you can, there's a lot more still to come. Rifles and side packs only. Anything else, throw over the side."

My rifle was slung over one shoulder. A side pack containing all my worldly possessions – five rounds of 303 ammunition, a pair of dirty, sweaty socks, shaving gear, a grubby towel, a couple of letters from Home and a pocket watch in a Cherry Blossom boot polish tin – was slung over the other shoulder.

Exhausted, unkempt and unwashed, I was apprehensive and had mixed feelings about the embarkation. I was thankful to be leaving behind the shambles of the demoralising and shameful retreat. I looked forward, hopefully, to returning to Egypt and the almost forgotten luxuries of a bath, a haircut and shampoo and, who knows, perhaps a spot of leave. But, at the same time, remembering the ever present Luftwaffe, completely unopposed in the air over the skies of Greece, I felt very nervous about embarking on a perilous sea journey, even as a guest of the Royal Navy.

But it was a fait accompli, as they say. I didn't have a choice, anyway. So, ever the optimist, I clambered over the side of the Greek caique, with the little boat rising and falling quite alarmingly on the heavy swell of the water against the quayside. It was a small, peculiarly shaped wooden fishing boat, stinking of stale fish. To a land-lubber like me, it seemed overburdened with ropes and nets and spars and canvas sails furled around long wooden booms. By the dim light of a partly blacked-out lantern perched on top of the mast, the caique, to my worried, inexperienced eye already lying dangerously low in the water, was packed from stem to stern with a motley crowd of silent, apprehensive servicemen. Gunners, sappers, and privates of this, that and the other units of the British Army, they sat patiently waiting for the little boat to ferry us to the embarkation vessels, which the two sailors said were outside the harbour.

When the two matelows had decided they were unable to

pack anymore into the overloaded boat, they cast off and the caique chugged away from the quayside. Five minutes later I could feel the intense heat from the still fiercly burning "Ulster Prince" as we passed within a few yards of her.

Fifteen minutes later, skillfully handled by the two sailors, the caique manoeuvered alongside a huge, grey painted ship lying outside the harbour. The heavy swell and surge of the water lifted the little fishing boat up and down like some new-fangled fairground ride, every now and then scraping and bumping against the side of the huge vessel.

"Right, lads," said one of the sailors, "get ready to jump onto those nets hanging over the side. The two matelows on the deck above will pull you over. Don't worry, you'll get the hang of it. But make sure you grab the nets, otherwise you're in for a soaking."

After this brief instruction on boarding proceedures, I had to gauge the rise and fall of the little fishing boat on the heavy swell of the water, against what appeared to me to be a smooth, grey wall the height of the India Buildings in Liverpool. The third time the boat reached the crest of a swell, the sailors shouted in unison, "Now, now. Jump for Christ's sake." With their forceful assistance I made a terrifying leap from the caique to the rope net hanging over the side. I scrambled up the last six or seven feet of the thick, slippery net very conscious of the rifle slung across on my back, hoping it wouldn't snag on the ropes, before I was hauled unceremoniously on board by two burly matelows.

I found myself on the "Calcutta".

If I had been free to choose to embark on any vessel of the Mediterranean Fleet taking part in the withdrawal, I would have selected H.M.S. "Calcutta". She was an anti-aircraft cruiser armed with 4.5 heavy ack-ack guns and numerous light, rapid-firing pom-poms. Her firing power was far superior to all the guns of the 106th Regiment put together. The "Calcutta" was probably the best ship in the whole of the Task-Force able to withstand the onslaught of the German bombers, which I was certain would arrive as soon as it was light.

Safely on board after my hair-raising climb up the scrambling nets, I was shepherded to one of the Ordinary

Seaman's Messes somewhere in the bowels of the vessel. Exhausted troops were lying everywhere: on and under the mess tables, in the narrow footwalks between the tables and even in the unoccupied hammocks slung above the mess tables of the sailors on watch. Most of the dog-tired troops were already in the sound and solid sleep of exhaustion.

The hospitality, kindness and friendly comradeship we encountered as soon as we set foot on "The Calcutta", confirmed all I had ever heard of the remarkable fortitude of the sailors in the British Navy. We were fussed over like long-lost relations and plied with food and hot drinks. More importantly, we felt re-assured by the casual calm of the seamen, who gave the impression that evacuating British troops was all in a day's work. Nothing to get excited about. Sadly, a few weeks later, the "Calcutta" was bombed and sunk carrying out the same dangerous, abortive mission, during the evacuation of Crete.

I had my fill of the welcome, hot, pea soup and thick, corned beef sandwiches and strong, sweet cocoa. It was the first palatable food that had passed my lips since leaving Larissa. I threw myself down under one of the tables. Despite the unaccustomed, claustrophobic confinement of the low deckhead and overcrowded mess-deck, and the stuffy, humid heat from unwashed bodies, I, too, immediately fell into the deep, dreamless, sleep of exhaustion.

It seemed as if I had hardly put my head down on the bare boards of the deck when I woke suddenly, to the muffled sound of exploding bombs. Instantly wide awake, I crawled from under the table, my heart pounding away and the half digested pea soup chasing the corned beef sandwiches violently round my stomach, just as a sailor climbed out of his hammock slung over the table above me.

"Did you hear those, Scouse?" he said to me as he caught my eye. "That was a string of fuckin' bombs goin' off. Just missed us. If I was you, I'd get up on deck, if you can, just in case. That's where I'm going."

He didn't say what it was "just in case" of. Picking his way through the sprawled sleeping soldiers filling the floor of the Mess, I saw him disappear up the companion way. I roused Lance Ferguson, who had been lying alongside me on the deck, and we followed the sailor up the stairway.

We arrived on deck just as it tilted to one side at an alarming angle, as the cruiser made a violent swerve to avoid another string of bombs which fell harmlessly in the sea alongside. We learned, later, that the captain of the Calcutta, lying on his back on the open deck during the attacks by the German planes, dodged the falling bombs by altering the course of his ship.

There was controlled pandemonium. The four big ack-ack guns were all firing at the same time. The regular rapid, distinctive boom-boom-boom, boom-boom-boom of the pom-poms was accentuated by the random crackle of dozens of Lee-Enfield rifles. Bren guns and ancient Lewis guns were being fired by infantrymen spread all over the deck. Lance and I still had our rifles and thought we would join in the fun with the few rounds of ammunition we were still carrying, but a burly Sergeant Major from one of the infantry units, stopped us.

"You can't stay up here, lads," he said, "there are too many on deck already. You'll have to go back down below."

Lance and I retreated once again, this time to the top of the companionway. We were still there when shortly afterwards the firing stopped.

Thankfully, there were no more air-raids so eventually we went down to the Seamans' mess again. I renewed my acquaintanceship with a long forgotten breakfast of beautiful, thick bacon sandwiches. The lucious bacon fat dripping from the freshly baked bread over my hand, swilled down with as much hot, sweet tea as I could drink.

I settled down, sleepily, to await our return to Alexandria, day-dreaming of the forthcoming luxury of a haircut, shampoo and head massage, followed by a much needed bath and a slap-up feed.

Of course a week or two of well-earned leave was long overdue!

Chapter 6

The sinking of the *Slamat*, *Diamond* and *Wryneck*

I didn't get to Alexandria.

Much to my regret I never again saw Egypt, Cairo or the Western Desert. Needless to say I didn't get my haircut, or my shampoo and head massage. My much needed hot bath also became another forgotten dream.

Instead, we were disembarked hurriedly and unceremoniously at Suda Bay on the island of Crete, the ack-ack cruiser returning with all the speed she could muster, to help to protect the last of the evacuation ships from Greece.

I staggered off the "Calcutta" still in a complete daze after the trauma of the panic retreat, under constant attack from dawn to dusk, on the flight from Larissa to Nauplion, with the nerve wracking, Stuka-dodging voyage across the Mediterranean. One of the thousands of bewildered, confused and bomb-shocked refugee soldiers dumped on the island without kit, bedding, transport or arms except for a few rifles. I was hungry, dirty, glad to be on shore again and free from the incessant air-raids, but at the same time cursing my usual good luck that I was not in the safe haven of Alexandria.

Unlike the Dunkirk evacuation of the British Expeditionary Force the previous year, there were no sympathetic, claps-on-the-back, or welcoming reception committees at Suda Bay for the remains of the spent, token force of British and Anzac troops from the fiasco of Greece. There were no British Red Cross marquees, staffed by understanding ladies from the Womens' Institute, to provide hot dinners, sausage rolls, meat pies, cream cakes and endless cups of tea. There were no hot baths. There was no issue of fresh kit to change our soiled underclothes, or new uniforms to replace our threadbare battle dress. There were no rail passes to take us on two weeks Home leave.

Instead, after sorting ourselves out on the quayside, from the motley collection of Australians, New Zealanders, Service corps drivers and clerks, engineers, pioneers, artillerymen and remnants from the battered, gallant Greek Army, the 106th were marched away.

A ragtag and bobtailed assortment of Liverpool Scousers, the cheerful, wagging tail having been left behind at Naplion (Argus).

We came to a halt at one of the many olive groves lining the road, somewhere between Suda and Canea. This was to be our new "Camp", and it did not take me very long in our new abode to realise that I had jumped right out of the overflowing frying pan of Greece into the smouldering tinderbox of the Island of Crete, which was about to blow up any minute.

There were no facilities of any sort in the camp among the olive trees, except the meagre protection the trees afforded from marauding Messerschmitts and Dorniers. After a few quiet days, they were to make their presence felt more than ever they did in Greece.

We were issued with old, thin Army blankets reeking with the pungent, disinfectant smell of de-lousing powder. One blanket between two men – if you were lucky. Rough, shallow trenches for makeshift latrines were excavated to windward of the camp.

A field "kitchen" made its appearance. A kind of ancient iron wash tub, or boiler, heated at the base by a little wood-burning fire, the smoke going up a blackened metal stove-pipe at the rear of the tub. Last used in the 1914/18 world war, this geriatric appliance produced for the now half-starved youngsters of the 106th, a thin stew of the much vaunted McConachies Meat-and-Vegetable. Howls of complaints about the water content of the pale brown mixture, brought the explanation that there wasn't enough food on the island to feed those who were already there, before the influx of the 10,000 or so rescued from the Greek mainland. We would have to lump it or like it. Didn't we know there was a war on?

Drinking water and washing facilities were provided by a shallow stream running through the olive grove, to which, after finishing my meagre ration of M & V stew, I made a bee-line.

The rivulet of water, babbling its way from the snow capped White Mountains of Crete en route to the blue Mediterranean, was only a degree or two above freezing. I revelled in the fresh, icy-cold water, thankfully washing away the dirt and stale sweat accumulated in my hurried and perilous journey through Greece. The weather was glorious and the warm, early summer sunshine quickly dried my shirt after I had used it to dry myself off.

Late arrivals joined us as the day wore on, but it was not until the following morning that we became aware that the Regiment had lost some 250/300 men during the evacuation from Nauplion.

We learned that the casualties were mostly from the Administration Staffs of the Regiment. Fitters, storemen of the Quartermaster Stores, cooks, medical orderlies and clerks from the four Battery Offices and Regimental Headquarters. Mostly they were non-combatants – if there was such a body in Greece and Crete – or temporary non-combatants.

The losses also included the few survivors of the bombing of Piraeus, where one of our batteries was part of the dock's defensive system. They had been blown out of existence on the first day of the blitz when an ammunition ship, the *Hellas*, moored to the quayside, blew up.

Among the casualties was a sprinkling of the inevitable column dodgers, to be found in any army. Also walking wounded with arms in slings and bandaged heads or nerves shattered by the endless raids of Stukas and fighters. There were men who had been on the sick list with minor ailments. Stomach aches, blistered feet or the griping, exhausting, and uncomfortable pains of dysentry, which had occurred in the latter stages of the retreat and which we were all to experience later.

Odds and sods were making their confused way to Casualty Stations or the Military Hospital at Athens. Among them were 61 attachments to the 106th from the R.A.S.C., R.A.M.C and the Signal Corps. They had been with us since our arrival in Greece and become part and parcel of the Unit.

This advance party of the 106th escaping from Greece had been put aboard a trooper, the *Slamat*, a former Dutch merchant ship. She was part of the hurriedly assembled evacuation Task

Force, comprising two troop transports, *Slamat* and *Khedive Ismail,* three destroyers, *Isis, Hotspur* and *Diamond* and the *Calcutta,* an ack-ack cruiser. They were attempting to rescue what was left of the Allied forces.

Unfortunately the *Slamat* delayed sailing at her appointed time. Apparently the skipper, Captain Lundinga, waited to cram on board even more troops making a late arrival at the evacuation point, thereby delaying the departure of the Task Force convoy. Tragically, she waited too long and it was after 4,30 a.m. when the *Slamat* eventually steamed away from Nauplion crammed from bow to stern with Allied troops.

About seven o'clock in the morning of that lovely spring day, the convoy, still making its way through the Gulf of Nauplia, well within reach of the Luftwaffe now based on the aerodromes and landing strips of Southern Greece, was attacked by successive flights of Stuka dive bombers.

Early in the engagement, despite the protective curtain of ack-ack gunfire from the destroyers and cruiser, the *Slamat* received two direct hits, disabling the ship and setting her on fire. She had to be abandoned. Miraculously, the other trooper, the *Khedive Ismail,* who had not picked up any troops that night, survived the dive bombing and escaped under the protection of the *Calcutta,* the *Isis* and *Hotspur.* The *Diamond* remained with the stricken *Slamat* to pick up survivors in the oil-covered waters, now being viciously sprayed with machine-gun and canon fire, without any mercy, by the Stukas.

That was by no means the end of the Greek Tragedy for the 106th and our Saviours, the Royal Navy.

The brave *Diamond* was joined at the scene of the carnage by another Royal Naval destroyer, the *Wryneck,* to assist in picking up survivors.

Gallantly following the age-old traditions of the British Navy, the two destroyers picked up nearly six hundred survivors from the burning *Slamat.* The struggling men had been battling to keep alive in the thick oil slicks slurping about on the surface of the water. Covered from head to foot in the glutinous, black, tarry oil still oozing from the stricken ships, they left their Carley Floats and scrambled up the boarding nets hanging over the steep, grey sides of the destroyers. Many without the strength to make the exhausting climb, fell back in the water and disappeared forever. The two heroic destroyers, hove-to in the swell of the oil-covered water and attempting frantically to get the men on board, became sitting targets. They were next to receive the concentrated attention of the German Messerschmitts and Stuka dive bombers.

The final blow struck about mid-day. Unable to resist any longer the renewed attacks of wave after wave of the unopposed Stukas, they, too, were sent to the sea bed.

We learned these appalling details of the bombing of the *Slamat* and the two destroyers, and their subsequent traumatic experiences in the water, from four 106th men, who survived. Sergeant Major Alf Daybell, Gunner Jimmy Brown (one of the Scots Militiamen who had joined us at Barlborough) Gunner George Caldwell and Gunner George Turkington were among the fortunate handful who were eventually plucked from the oily waters by the destroyer *Griffen*, and landed at Suda Bay.

They managed to keep themselves alive for some 28 hours by a combination of luck, sheer guts and an obstinate refusal to give in, clinging to the flotsam from the doomed ships, or hanging on desperately to a Carley Float (part of the ship's life-saving equipment) hastily thrown overboard by some well trained seaman in the last moments before his ship went down. The slatted, wooden, floating platforms – far too few in number, anyway, for the hundreds of men thrashing about in the filthy water – were overwhelmed and overturned by the desperate struggling men. Many of them were badly injured, or blinded with oil-filled eyes. Some were nauseous and spewing violently. A few had succumbed to panic and were threshing about wildly in their efforts to grab hold of the rope grips, or scramble aboard the float. They were all covered in black oil and beginning to feel the effects of the cold water.

Many years later George Caldwell, general manager of a commercial printers in Richmond Row, Liverpool, related his story one afternoon when I was placing an order with him at the shop. In his usual, soft spoken, self-effacing manner he told me of the nerve-wracking thirty hours or so he spent in the oily water of the sea and on the slippery, hazardous slats of the Carley Float.

Dazed, and unable to remember how he got into the water, he swam to the life raft and managed to get hold of one of the loops hanging down the side. The float kept rearing into the air with the weight of the struggling men trying to climb on it, one end going deep in the water spilling its desperate human cargo from the precarious, slippy, surface and breaking the hold of those hanging on to the loops of rope. Every time the Carley righted itself, he managed to swim back to it, as one of the diminishing band of struggling survivors to regain a grip. Eventually, there were only a few lucky ones left to haul themselves back on to the float. They were eventually rescued and taken to Suda Bay. Alf Daybell was one of them and he couldn't swim a stroke.

Hundreds were lost in that disastrous, unnecessary calamity in the Aegean Sea. But for a quirk of good fortune, I and many more of the 106th could have suffered the same fate and been crammed aboard the *"Slamat"*. The Finger of Fate was raised once again, when last minute exchanges of men destined to depart on the trooper replaced men on the guns, whose nerves had gone or were slightly injured. Some responded voluntarily, some with a casual command. Fortunately for me, the crews of the ack-ack guns were kept at Nauplion as a rearguard defence, helping to protect the evacuation ships.

I lost some very good mates in those dreadful 24 hours. Arthur Taylor, my closest friend, who had joined the T.A. on the same evening and was my constant companion until his transfer to the Battery Stores because of his deafness. "Tinker" Bell, Tony Gould's driver/mechanic in my section in the desert, always had a cheery word and a smile on his face. Frank Young the ex-boxer, known professionally, as Kid Shepherd at the old boxing Stadium in Liverpool before the outbreak of war. Frank was both mentor and trainer in my one and only foray into the world of boxing, when I became a member of the 106th boxing team in Palestine. Somewhat punch-drunk, he was unable to put a pen to paper, and for a while I wrote his letters home. Chrisy Wishart, the Middle-weight contender in the same team, was never to box again. Dougie Matson, a salesman in the Electrical Department at Baxendales, where I worked until the outbreak of the war, was among the missing.

Most of the casualties were all familiar faces. Aquaintances, friends, comrades and sometimes close relations. Everybody in the Unit was affected in some way or other by the tragic deaths. Particularly those from the densely populated back streets off Scotland Road, Great Homer Street and William Henry Street, who volunteered a few months before the declaration of war. Pals lost pals, neighbour lost neighbour, cousin lost cousin, uncle lost nephew, brother lost brother and there was even a son who died of a broken heart in a German Prisoner-of-War Camp who lost his father in those awful twenty-four hours.

The Slamat

I believe the Ministry of Defence Official Records of this disaster, baldly state that:
"The S.S.Slamat was lost off Nauplion on the night of the 26/27th April, 1941 at 7 a.m. Survivors were picked up by the Destroyers Wryneck and Diamond but these two ships were also sunk at noon. From the three ships there were tragically only 50 survivors. 1 Naval Officer, 41 Naval Ratings and 8 soldiers."

I was to learn eventually that, in the weeks following the disaster, the War Casualty Notices in the Obituary pages of the

"Liverpool Echo" were filled, night after night, with brief details of the men who died. These tributes were usually accompanied by a tiny, one inch square photograph which was too indistinct to do justice to the man who perished. I do not think the true story of the terrible losses in the evacuation of Greece has ever been told, except perhaps, as stark figures in history books. The debacle becoming just one of the many forgotten campaigns, of one of the forgotten armies, of the war.

Many, many years later Sergeant Major Daybell after a successful career in the catering industry and completing his full term of service in the Territorial Army which he rejoined on his return home, died of cancer in Clatterbridge Hospital. I visited him a day or two before he died.

In 1997 I was invited to a surprise birthday party on the occasion of George Caldwell's eightieth birthday. It was hosted at the home of his daughter and attended by twelve Old Comrades of the 106th. A special guest, was the Scot, Jimmy Brown, George's fellow survivor from the oily waters of the Mediterranean. During the celebrations, Jim told me that, he was in the overcrowded hold of the "Stramat", just before she was bombed. He owed his life to the fact that he had an urgent call of nature, and made his way up the companionway to the "heads" on the deck. He had just made it there when the first bomb exploded in the hold he had just vacated.

When Regimental Records were eventually completed it was found that 170 men of the 106th R.H.A. were killed during the evacuation of Greece in April, 1941. A Memorial Tablet inscribed with their names stands in the Military Cemetery at Phaleron, Athens. A wreath of Remembrance is placed at its foot, every year, by the Old Comrades Association of the 106th (Lancashire Yeomanry) Royal Horse Artillery, TA.

HERTS. YEOMANRY
LCE. BOMBARDIER   CLARKE P.E.

LANCASHIRE HUSSARS YEOMANRY

CAPTAIN   HAUGHTON J.C.   PINNINGTON J.C. M.C.   LIEUTENANT   DOMVILLE K.
COUGH B.C.   MOSS F.E.   MOWNSEY A.   SECOND LIEUT.   KRYACK E.L.
WARRANT OFFR.I   ELSLEY W.   WARRANT OFFR.I   ANDREWS E.R.   RASFORD T.
DUGGAN F.F.   HARRIS W.   HARTLEY J.A.   JEREMY J.E.   WALKERLEY R. G.
WARRANT OFFR.II   BARISH W.   STAFF SERJEANT   DARK S.E.   SMITH H.
SERJEANT   JONES W.A.   LACEY T.C.   LANCE-SERJEANT   BARCOCK J.W.   OWEN R.A.E.
BOMBARDIER   BYRNE W.   CORRIGAN G.   DAVIES H.A.   EWING A.   FOWLER J.G.
GREENHALGH J.H.   MACDONALD A.   NETHERWAY W.H.   NUTTALL E.G.   TRAVERS W.G.
WALKER S.A.A.   LCE. BOMBARDIER   BENNION G.R.   CONNOLLY W.   MACKINTOSH A.
MAGUIRE W.   OSCROFT S.   RUSTELL N.W.   TAYLOR J.T.   WADDELL A.C.   WILLS A.A.
GUNNER   ACKRILL P.   ARMITAGE J.W.   ASPINALL S.   AYERS A.H.   BELL J. 877191
BELL J. 936918   BELL R.   BISWICK P.S.   BLANE-HOWARD   BLOW R. J.J.   BOOTH G.J.
BROWN J.E.   BROWNING W.   CARR J.   CARR J.E.   CARROLL E.   CARTER T.A.
CHRISTIAN T.E.   CHURCHILL T.   COOK F.R.   COTTER J.T.   CROSTON D.R.   CUTLER T.
DAGNALL V.E. M.M.   DAVIES W.   DAVIS C.S.   DEMPSIE T.R.   DEVITT J.   DICKENS C.F.
EASDON V.J.   ELMS F.   EYRES R.H.   FORD S.G.   FULLER J.   GING P.   GRAHAM E.
GREEN J.H.   GUNN E.   HALL J.T.   HALLAM H.   HARRIS H.   HARRISON R.   HARRISON T.T.
HEYES J.   HODGE F.C.   HODGSON J.   HODSON J.   HOEY J.A.   HORDER J.   HORNER F.
HUGHES J.W.   HUGHES R.   JOHNSON T.C.   JOHNSON V.J.   JONES F.J.   JONES J.
JONES J.J.   JONES S.   JONES T.   KELLY E.   KENNEDY A.   KILVERT H.E.   KING J.P.
KIRK T.   LAIRD A.H.   LEACH D.   LLOYD C.   LLOYD J.   LOMATH T.R.   LOWIS P.K.
McBRIDE J.   McGINTY W.H.   McGOVERN L.   MATSON R.   MATTHEWS C.T.   MATTHEWS P.
MAYND G.R.   MELLOR H.   MILLS R.T.   MOORE E.A.   MOORE W.R.   MORRIS L.   MILLARD G.F.
MULHOLLAND D.   MURPHY W.   MURRAY P.   NASH A.E.   NEEDHAM W.   OSCROFT E.
O'SULLIVAN D.   OWENS E.   PALMER A.   PARKER D.   PEARCE D.   PEARSON R.J.
PEERS A.E.   PELLESCHI V.   PENNOCK T.   PERRY G.   PURCELL W.F.   QUINN H.   RADFORD E.
ROBERTS E.   RYAN J.   RYAN R.   SHAW R.V.   SIMMS D.   SIMPSON J.   SOUTHERN F.
SOUTHWORTH H.   SPENCER H.J.   STENSON W.   STIRLING D.   SULLIVAN T.   SUNSHINE R.
SWIFT R.   TAYLOR A.B.   THOMAS J.R.   THOMPSON J.   WARREN W.J.G.   WEALTHY E.J.
WELSH G.E.   WHELAN J.J.   WISHART C.   YOUNG F. 832736   YOUNG F. 900912

GLAMORGAN YEOMANRY
BOMBARDIER   MORRIS W.

Memorial at Phaleron, Athens, Greece

LANCASHIRE HUSSARS YEOMANRY

CAPTAIN Haughton J.C. Pinnington K.C.(M.C.)
LIEUTENANT Domvill R. Gough R.C. Moss F.E. Mounsey A.E. **SECOND LIEUTENANT**. Kissack E.L.
WARRANT OFFICER I. Elsley W.
WARRANT OFFICER II. Andrews F.B. Basford T. Duggan E.T. Harris W. Hartley J.A. Jeremy J.D. Walkerley C.G.
WARRANT OFFICER III Barish W.
STAFF SERGEANT Dark S.E. Smith H.
SERGEANT Jones W.A. Lacey T.C.
LANCE SERGEANT Barcock J.W. Owen R.A.T.
BOMBARDIER Byrne W. Corrigan G. Dawes H.A. Ewing A.
Fowler J.G. Greenhalgh J.H. MacDonald N. Netherway W.H.
Nuttall E.C. Travers
LANCE BOMBARDIER Bennion G.P. Connolley W. Mackintosh A.
Maguire W. Oscroft S. Rustell N.I.W. Taylor J.T. Waddell A.C. Wells A.A.
GUNNER Ackrill F. Armitage J.J.W. Aspinall B. Ayers A.G. Bell J.877191 Bell J 936918 Bell R. Beswick P.S. Blane H.MacD Blower E.J. Boote C. Christian T.E. Browning W. Carr J. Carr J.T. Carroll F.J. Carter T.A. Dagnall W.E.(M.M.) Davies W. Davis C.S. Dempsie T.R. Devitt J. Dickens C.E. Easdon V.I. Elms P. Eyres R.H. Ford S.G. Fuller J. Ging P. Graham E. Green J.H. Gunn F. Hall J.T. Hallam H. Harris H. Harrison R. Harrison T.F. Heyes J. Hodge F.C. Hodgson J. Hodson F. Hoey J.A. Horder J.J. Horner F. Hughes J.W. Hughes R. Johnson T.C. Johnson W.I. Jones F.J. Jones J.E. Jones I.J. Jones S. Jones T. Kelly E. Kennedy A. Kilvert H.L. King J.P. Kirk T. Laird A.H. Leach D. Lloyd C. Lloyd J. Lomath T.D. Lowis P.K. McBride J. McGinty W.H. McGovern L. Matson D. Matthews C.T. Matthews P. Maund G.R. Mellor H. Mills R.T. Moore E.A. Moore W.R. Morris L. Mullard G.F. Mullholland D. Murphy W. Murray P. Nash A.E. Needham W. Oscroft F. O'Sullivan D.

Owens E. Palmer A. Parker L.J. Pearce D. Pearson R.J.
Peers A.E. Pelleschi V. Pennock T. Perry C. Purcell W.T
Quinn H. Radford E. Roberts E. Ryan J. Ryan R.
Shaw R.V. Simms D. Simpson J. Southern F. Southworth
H. Spencer H.J. Stenson W. Stirling D. Sullivan T.
Sunshine R. Swift R. Taylor A.B. Thomas J.R.
Thompson J. Warren W.J.D. Wealthy E.L. Welsh G.E. Whelan
T.E. Wishart C. Young F. 832738 Young F. 900912

Chapter 7

The Hidey-Hole on Crete

The stuffing was knocked completely out of us by this terrible news. Incredibly, we had a few days of rest and comparable quiet in the doubtful shelter of the trees of the makeshift Camp in the olive grove. For a few blissful days we were, more or less, left alone to recover, and catch up on some very much needed sleep. I made up a "Solo" school with Jack Mooney, Lance Ferguson and Dick Higgins. I braved the icy waters of the mountain stream twice a day, and managed to get some of the grime out of what was left of my tatty battledress and threadbare underclothes.

As the possessor of a Lee Enfield rifle – the same one that almost became entangled in the scrambling nets of the "Calcutta" – I was issued with a bayonet. At a brief lecture by Sergeant Christie – one of the older 106th Terriers and an ex-regular army infantryman – I learned how to fix it on the end of my rifle and, in theory, how to thrust it in a German stomach, "and remember to twist it as you pull it out".

At first, I was somewhat embarrassed by this new weapon of war, for the combined length of the rifle and bayonet was almost as long as me. I was completely horrified at the thought of sticking this fearsome implement into someone's stomach. But I was even more horrified at the thought of some burly Prussian, his cheeks marked with duelling scars, floating down from the skies and poking into my stomach the dagger-like bayonet I had seen on the end of Italian rifles back in the desert. So I carefully honed the twelve inch bayonet and polished it, and oiled it with the scrap of oily 3" x 2" kept in the stock at the butt end of my rifle.

Luckily, I never had to use it for its intended purpose, as I never really got the knack of fixing it correctly on the end of my

68

rifle.

Rumour and counter-rumour, in the usual 106th fashion, fuelled no doubt by the unusual inactivity, bounced about from tree to tree in the olive grove.

We were to reinforce our Sister Unit, 149th R.H.A. (The Hoylake Horse) who had just arrived in Egypt; we were being sent home in time for August Bank Holiday, a refit and re-training as a heavy anti-aircraft Unit for ack-ack duty on the docks in Liverpool and Birkenhead; we were going to India after a month's leave in Durban, South Africa and then getting our 4.5. howitzers back for "peacekeeping" on the Khyber Pass; we were returning by the next ship to Egypt, where the Unit would be made up to full strength and join two new divisions fresh out from Home, to take part in a forced landing to re-occupy Greece.

There seemed to be a grain of truth in this last item of pie-in-the-sky. One day, Sergeant Major Daybell approached me and asked if I would take on the job of Regimental Clerk when we got back to Alexandria. He had been informed that he was to be promoted to Regimental Sergeant Major on our return to Egypt, where he had to establish a new Regimental Office. The job for me would carry three stripes. Like the offer of promotion by Mr Beckett at Baxendales in September, 1939, I had no doubts or hesitation in accepting.

However, like my first abortive chance of promotion back in the good old days, fate, circumstances, or whatever you like to call it, decreed otherwise. With my unaccustomed shiny bayonet dangling from my belt and twenty rounds of 303 ammunition in my haversack, I was on the move the following day, yet again. A detachment of hurriedly trained 106th artillery/infantrymen was given the job of guarding Crete wireless station. Apparently it was the only means of communication with the people controlling our destinies from the other side of the Mediterranean in Alexandria.

We were to await, with much apprehension, the invasion of the Germans.

This, we were informed, was imminent.

Indeed it was, for we barely had time to dig the shallow slit trenches in our new position. Without warning, we were subjected to a "softening up" by the Luftwaffe which made the

69

blitz in Greece seem like a thunder storm in North Wales. The Messerscmitts and Stukas recommenced the daily forays which they had practised in Greece, strafing and dive-bombing us unceasingly from first light of that beautiful, cloudless, sunny day until darkness fell. And the troops concealed in the trees were the target. The attacking planes purposely, seemed to avoid the radio station.

Lance Ferguson and I squeezed into the shelter of the hollowed-out bole of a huge, gnarled, ancient olive tree. Its girth was almost as wide as its height. Judging by the deposit of old bones left in the dry soil, it had been the lair of many a wild animal for decades. Lying curled up in the bottom of our natural hidey-hole, we persuaded ourselves that we were better protected than in the hastily dug slit-trenches.

Attacking in flights of ten or twelve, the yellow-nosed Stukas, diving almost vertically one after the other, their howling, frightening klaxons screaming above the whine of the engines and the hammering of their machine guns, dropped their bombs unhindered. Each plane seemingly making its terrifying attack on me personally as I lay directly beneath its vertical flight path. And immediately each flight had finished trying to blow me off the face of the earth, Messerschmitts fighters circled the wireless station strafing the area continually.

Without really being aware of the fact, we had become battle-hardened by our harsh months in the desert culminating in the bloody Battle of Beda Fomm outside Bengazi, followed by our harrowing experiences in Greece. So it was not too surprising how Lance and I, in the make believe safety of our funk-hole, became almost "accustomed" to these attacks. At least, we became sort of street-wise, aware that the strafing Messerschmitts were firing indiscriminately, and that if they were not heading in a direct line for us we were in luck. The Stuka pilot directing his plane on his seemingly suicidal dive wasn't always aiming at us, personally, and more often than not the bombs exploded well clear of their target.

Dawn on my second day at the wireless station heralded another dose of the frightening medicine. A double dose, in fact, when it became impossible to lift a head out of a slit trench or, in my case, to crawl out of the base of the tree to obey a call of nature urgently increasing with each visit from the enemy planes. Until, around about mid-day, the terrifying raids ceased, abruptly and unexpectedly. Lance and I poked our heads out of our lions' den in disbelief as everything became eerily and unnaturally still and deathly quiet.

But not for long.

After a short, apprehensive interval, the unusual, pregnant, breathless silence was broken by the sound of a different engine from that of the Messcersmitts and Stukas, which had become so familiar. Then my stomach churned once again. From the direction of the sea beyond Suda, I could see dozens of aeroplanes flying towards us in close formation, wing to wing. Trundling and rumbling along at a slow, steady pace, the black cross insignia of the German Luftwaffe on the wings of the lumbering planes was clearly visible. We could see, also, that the huge, transport planes were pulling gliders attached by long tow ropes. Passing directly over us, we watched fascinated, as strings of little doll-like figures fell out of the planes and floated earthwards under brightly coloured red, blue, green and white parachutes. From some of the descending, floating canopies, swaying from side to side, dangled a long, thin canister or a round barrel and, on one or two, the wheels of what appeared to be small field guns.

As we watched, open mouthed, we saw most of the falling parachutes overshoot the wireless station. Bursts of machine gun fire startled us out of our trance. Raising our rifles we fired at the few figures floating gently downwards towards us. I fired half of the twenty 303 bullets which had been allotted to me, blindly taking pot shots at the floating figures until someone shouted "hold your fire, hold your fire."

My luck had held once again. The bulk of the group of parachutists designated to take the wireless station, overshot their target and dropped instead directly onto one of our infantry battalions. The lucky ones, not killed as they dangled helplessly from the end of their parachutes, were taken prisoner, but the majority of them were killed before they even reached the ground. So were most of the German paratroops dropped on Crete that morning.

We knew little of that, of course. We knew little of

anything, because nobody bothered to tell us. The rumours had already begun. The only thing we actually knew for certain was that we had had nothing to eat or drink for 48 hours, except for a limited issue of "biscuits and bully".

As darkness fell, it was no surprise to find we were on the move once again. In typical Army fashion, the order-of-the day was that we were to leave all our gear, except rifles and ammunition, as we would return to the wireless station next day. So Lance and I reluctantly departed from our coveted hidey-hole-in-the-tree, leaving behind our few belongings including the single blanket and our side packs containing shaving gear, and the few bits and pieces of our personal possessions. We left them hidden in the roots of the old tree and for all I know they may still be there.

At a road junction somewhere on the main road midway between Maleme and Suda Bay, we reinforced a mixed collection of gunners, sappers, privates, office clerks and storemen. Odds and sods from various Units and odds and sods without any Unit.

At Maleme there was a small landing field which was the home of the half dozen remaining planes of the Royal Air Force in Greece and Crete. I believe the original "squadron" comprised a mixture of Hurricanes, Gladiators and Fulmars, although I saw nothing at all of the planes during my time on Crete. I heard later that they had all been shot down on the first day of the attack, when trying gallantly to get airborne from the landing field.

On arrival at the crossroads, we learned that the bulk of the German parachutists dropped on the island that first day had been disposed of, except for small isolated pockets which were being eliminated. A number of enemy gliders, however, had successfully landed at Maleme, and despite fierce opposition from the defending New Zealand infantrymen, had gained a precarious hold on the little air-strip. Ominously that afternoon, Junkers troop carriers had crash-landed at Maleme, reinforcing the few surviving Germans from the grounded gliders.

So with the rest of the 106th lads from the wireless station, I joined the motley collection of sparsely armed troops at the crossroads, to nervously form part of a second line, or reserve line, in case the Germans broke through at Maleme and advanced along the road toward Suda Bay.

In the darkness we set-to to make the ditches at the sides of the road junction deeper and wider. We enlarged slit-trenches to provide us with some protection against the marauding flights of fighter planes and Stukas, which we knew would be on us from first light next day. There was no time to wash or put together a hot meal, food being again restricted to water and corned beef and not much of that, either.

I had little sleep that night. In the early hours I was disturbed by the thunderous sound of distant gun fire, and could distinctly see their vivid flashes and then the glow of fire out at sea beyond Suda. It was the British Navy repulsing a convoy of crack German troops carried in small Greek fishing boats and caiques, attempting to make a seaborne landing on Crete in support of their airborne invasion of the previous day. We stood around, excitedly watching the illuminated display, like Bonfire Night in Stanley Park, until exhausted, I got my head down under an olive tree. I managed to get some sleep before the dawn visit of the Messerschmitts woke me, bringing on the usual sickly feeling in my stomach, and sending me helter-skeltering to the uncertain protection of the ditch at the side of the road.

I spent the rest of that day cowering in the muddy ditch, as the German fighter planes roared up and down the road. Up and down, up and down, their machine guns spraying us continually, completely oblivious of the sporadic rifle and Bren-Gun fire directed at them from our slit trenches. Sometimes there would be a slight lull and my spirits would lift, as I thought that they had decided to leave us alone, Then they would reappear. We had nothing at all to eat. The only water I had to ease the dryness of fear in my mouth, was the pint of lukewarm liquid in my water bottle.

The relief was indescribable as towards the end of the day, with the light beginning to fail, the attacks ceased and the shaken, pseudo-infantrymen crawled out of the muddy slit trenches. Then I witnessed an act of bravery I had only seen before in cowboys-and-indians films before the war. It was one of the bravest, individual acts of calm courage I ever saw during the whole of my service.

It occurred when one of the young Engineer sappers

73

climbed out of the trench, ranting and raving at the top of his voice, uncontrollably mouthing hysterical obscenities against the German Luftwaffe and his British comrades alike. Brandishing his rifle with his finger hooked around the trigger, he threatened to shoot anyone coming near him. As if confirming his threat, he fired two or three shots indiscriminately in the air. Those near him, like me, promptly sought the safety of the recently vacated slit trenches. Then I saw a solitary figure walk casually towards him, his hands in the pockets of his shorts, calmly talking all the time. Telling him not to be such a fool and to put the rifle down, and come and get a mug of tea. Disregarding the rifle which the deranged sapper was now pointing at his chest, he coolly carried on walking until he was able to grab hold of the weapon and wrest it from him. The young sapper was led away sobbing bitterly and I never saw him again.

It was about that time, too, that Frank Smith, one of the 106th diehards, decided that he was going to do something about the grub, or lack of it, and lit a fire to brew tea and heat some, M & V tinned stew. The smoke from the fire, rising into the fading twilight brought howls of protests from some of the late occupants of the slit trenches, as they voiced their opinion that the smoke would attract more of the marauding enemy planes. Frank took no notice of the dissenters. Half an hour later I partook of my last hot meal of any substance for some considerable time.

Chapter 8

Across the White Mountains on Potato Water

Early the following morning, well before dawn and the return of the Luftwaffe, we abandoned the position on the crossroads.

Split into groups of twenty or thirty, each group in the charge of an Officer, we learned that we were to make our way across the mountains, on foot, to the little fishing port of Sphakia on the South Coast, the other side of the island. My chaperone was Captain Darling who gave us a little pep talk saying we were all to keep together, and there were to be no stragglers. The sooner we got to Sphakia the sooner we would be taken off the island by the Navy.

Water bottles were filled with the brackish, dirty water from the ditch and "emergency rations" were distributed. My allocation of this lucky dip, was a rusty, dinged tin, contents unknown, as the label was missing. One or two lucky ones were given a tin of corned beef, or meat-and-vegetable stew, However, the lugubrious ex-regular, Yorkie, raised his voice in protest when he found he was expected to hike across the White Mountains of Crete on a tin of Hartleys raspberry jam. Meagre fare to cross the snow-capped mountains of Crete, for young men who had been on skimped, iron rations for months.

The only road between Suda Bay and Sphakia meandered, agonisingly, across, around and up and down the towering mountains of central Crete. It proved to be little more than a cart-track. We joined the motley collection of slowly moving soldier-refugees trudging their way up and down the steep inclines until dawn. Then the first raids of the fighters drove us away from the easy walking of the track. In the lulls between the attacks we stumbled across the open mountainside. When the planes were overhead we dived for whatever cover we could find in the rocks and boulders.

To add to our misery, the weather was glorious. At midday, as the sun climbed the cloudless, blue skies, it became unbearably hot, and the walking and scrambling became even more difficult and exhausting. Water had long since given out. The only water to be found was in the circular, stone wells on the outskirts of the villages on the road, Captain Darling was hard put to keep his little group together, as one or two of us were for going back to fill the water bottles. The strafing was now almost continuous. The enemy fighter planes were scouring the mountainsides in formation, like a gigantic airborne tooth comb in their search for the fleeing troops. In mid afternoon, during a particularly vicious assault by the Messerschmitts, we found shelter in the overhanging rocks of a steep gorge cut into the side of a mountain.

By this time some of the lads were on the brink of exhaustion. Thankfully, Captain Darling decided we would halt there for a while to rest and eat.

Using my newly-issued bayonet for the first time, I satisfied my curiosity and opened the mystery tin of emergency rations. The battered tin contained tiny potatoes immersed in a warm, dirty-grey liquid. I promptly quaffed the salty water in a futile attempt to ease my now raging thirst, swallowed a couple of the unappetising, half raw potatoes, followed by a thin slice of corned beef and a spoonful of Yorkie's raspberry jam.

I was to regret drinking that Hartleys potato liquid. Later in the afternoon, taking cover again from the strafing, I suddenly and violently threw up. Whether my projectile puking was due to the potato water, exhaustion, thirst and hunger, or sheer terror of the continual harrassment of the enemy planes, I can't honestly say. I suspect it was the fright and terror. I had never been ill since being called up, except for New Year's Eve at Barlborough when Lance Ferguson, now sheltering by my side on the mountain, had spiked my bitter with whiskey.

Anyway, I wasn't for going on. And I said so when Mr Darling stood up and said "come on lads, it's quietened off a little, let's get on."

"I'm not going on," I said. "I'm knackered and I'm sick." And in true Beau Geste language, "I'll only hold you back. You go on and I'll catch up later."

The Captain was not having any heroics.

He planted his feet apart in the stance of Military Authority and said, firmly and loudly, "You can't stay here, Arthur, get on your bloody feet before the Germans catch up with us."

I replied by being violently sick again, spattering his scuffed, dusty boots with flecks of vomit. This seemed to have the surprising effect of changing his attitude, when he reverted back to that of the pre-war, trainee chartered accountant from Water Street. He then said, "Come on Doug. You can't stay here, lad, sick or not and I can't let you stay. You'll have to move, and quick."

"Come on, Doug," he said again, persuasively. "Get on your feet and I'll try to get you a lift on one of the trucks on the road."

Lance, and some of the others, weren't so polite. "Come on for Christ's sake, Doug, let's piss off while we've got the chance."

I got back on my feet still vomiting bits of grey potato, and grey bile and staggered after them down the hillside. The road was now carrying traffic again as the failing light heralded the end of the non-stop ariel attacks.

On the road, packed once again with weary, foot-sore, retreating troops interspersed with a few slowly moving trucks and motor cycles, Captain Darling stopped an open 15cwt Morris truck. Already heavily overloaded with what looked like office personnel from some defunct Service Corps Office, he asked a Major, sitting in the passenger seat, if room could be found for me. There was a muttered exchange of words between Mr Darling and the Service Corps Major, then I was hauled up over the side of the truck. After some reluctant budging and shoving amongst the men crammed in the back, space was found for me against the tailboard of the vehicle. I was promptly sick again. This time I had the presence of mind to take off my tin hat and vomit into it. There was no comment from my new-found fellow travellers, but I had the feeling that they were objecting, silently, that I was the cause of another annoying delay in getting to Sphakia.

The rest of the journey in the Morris passed off without incident. We never made Sphakia, however. The few trucks and motor cycles, and the thousands of troops who had made their painful way on foot over the mountains, were halted at the top of the steep and rugged cliffs overlooking the little harbour. All wheeled vehicles were then tipped over the top into one of the gullies or ravines. Included was the abandoned B.S.A. motor bike that the indefatigable Ossie Whitehead had dragged from a ditch just outside Suda. He got the engine running after five minutes tinkering, stuffed grass in the tyres to replace the bust innertubes, then with Frank Smith on the pillion bumped his way to Sphakia. Ossie and Frank Smith were two of the few 106th men to get away from the island.

Purged of the potato water and rid of my belly-ache but tired, hungry, thirsty and confused, I met up with what was left of the 106th Regiment on the road at the top of the escarpment. We tagged on the end of a long queue of thousands of exhausted troops, kicking their heels in frustration at the unexplained hold-up. My thoughts were alternating, again and again, on when I was going to get something to eat and when the Navy would get us away, as they had already done from Nauplion in Greece a few short weeks before. The long line of impatient men started at the embarkation point on the beach at Sphakia, and wound its way up the mountainside to where we had joined it at the top. The invisible tail-end of this snaking column continually lengthened as other fleeing troops arrived.

When darkness fell there was renewed activity in the column of men ahead of us. With a surge of optimism we started a reasonably disciplined march down the hill towards the harbour, only to come to an abrupt and disappointing halt after 50 yards. Nobody knew why we had stopped or what was happening. In utter frustration the exhausted men threw themselves down where they had halted. I lay down on the dusty road still warm with the heat of the day's sunshine, my rifle between my legs and my knees drawn up under my chin. I had just dropped off to sleep when the shout went up, "On yer bloody feet, on yer feet, we're off again. Come on lads, get yerselves in fours."

We didn't take much urging but the excitement of this new movement was short lived as we halted yet again after a few faltering steps, this time to be told to move to one side of the road to clear the way for, unbelievably, a battalion of Aussie infantrymen who marched smartly past us, silently, heading down the hill towards the embarkation point. Many years later, I was to learn that the presence of the Australian and New Zealand troops on Crete had become a political issue between the U.K. and ANZAC governments, and belated efforts were made to evacuate the Colonial troops from the island for their return home. Many were taken off Crete in preference to the British troops. There were thousands of these wonderful Aussies and Kiwis, all volunteers from the other side of the world, who were waiting to get off the island. Like us, they had been in almost continual action for the past eighteen months in the Western Desert, Greece and Crete.

The pantomime of false starts and stops on the road, went on until well into the middle hours. Long before we were anywhere near the beach, we were told there would be no more evacuation that night. We were to make ourselves scarce in the rocks and caves of the escarpment and return to the road at nightfall.

The escarpment was honeycombed with caves, gorges and ravines, which, with the rocks and boulders on the plateux provided adequate shelter against the enemy planes. Thankfully, on that first day of anxious waiting, the attacks eased off and then petered out altogether. The German Luftwaffe switched its attention to attacking the struggling rearguard somewhere back on the Suda road, and sinking the gallant ships of the Royal Navy valiantly attempting to evacuate the thousands of Allied troops from the Island.

There was no issue of food of any kind and the only water available was from roadside springs, which were little more than running ditches. Lance and I "volunteered" to go on a scavenging party led by Sergeant George Lunt, with Frank Smith and Bill Copland. Apparently, there were tinned rations to be found down on the beach, the remains of supplies brought in by one of the evacuation ships and dumped near the embarkation point.

We didn't have much luck.

Scrambling down down the cliff face, lying low when the occasional Stuka or Messerschmidt flew over, we came to the spot where the rations had been dumped at the edge of the water.

It did our hearts good to see the familiar labels on tins of Fray Bentos corned beef, Machonacies meat and vegetable stew, delectable-looking Princes' tinned pears and pineapple and other forgotten luxuries scattered about in the shallow water and pebbles of the beach. Our excitement was short lived, however, when we found that these hastily deposited provisions had been subjected to aerial machine gunning and dive bombing and all the tins were "blown", the contents useless.

Struggling back up to the road at the top of the cliff to rejoin the Unit, we came to a group of noisy, exuberant, resourceful, Australians in the process of slaughtering the ancient, decrepit donkey we had seen on the way down, foraging in the sparse vegetation of a stony paddock adjoining a derelict farmhouse.

Attracted by the gruesome sight Lance and I stopped to watch the bloodthirsty proceedings, hopeful that we might get a piece of the action, so to speak.

The scene reminded me of Brennan's knackers yard in Cherry Lane. As an inqisitive ten year old, I used to sneak in to watch, wide-eyed and indignant at the injustice of the poor old, exhausted horses from the Co-op Laundry or the redundant boat-horses from the Leeds and Liverpool Canal, being slaughtered.

A gory Aussie, stripped to the waist, his sunburned torso spattered with blood from beneath his wide broadrimmed bush-hat to his web belt, was standing astride the beast wielding one of Sergeant Lucas's twelve inch bayonets. He had made a deep cut down the length of the animal's belly. I watched fascinated as he reached inside the carcass and expertly cut off a slab of dripping meat, which, to me, looked just like the thick frying steak in the window of Costigans the Butchers in Breck Road. Matter-of-factly, as if he was carrying out this operation every day, (which he probably did, in the outback of his Homeland) he passed it to his bronzed companions who had already got a fire going.

The Aussie butcher bent to his task again and then pulled out another slab of bloody meat. His eye caught the hungry look in mine as he looked across and he said, "'Ere y'are, Pom, put this in your tin 'at and make sure yer cook it well."

It was the large, round, blood-red liver of the poor old,

pensioned off beast-of-burden. I couldn't believe my luck as I carried my bloody prize away to show the other members of the combine.

I cooked this totally unexpected windfall in my tin hat balanced on stones over an open fire. I stripped away the inner lining of the metal hat, and cleaned off the remains of my sudden puke of the previous day as best as I could. I fried the dripping liver in a few drops of olive oil left in the bottom of a bottle Lance had found that morning in the empty farmhouse.

Five of us shared that never to be forgotten "hors d'oeuvre", although, regrettably, there was nothing to follow it. We divided it, meticulously, into five equal portions. The greyish, dirty-looking, half cooked liver and the gravy of olive oil and donkey blood, went down very well.

It was delicious. No salt no pepper. no onions, no chips, no buttered cob... but it was delicious.

Unlike the potato water, my stomach accepted it without demur.

I was to learn, later, that the Australians in the outback, habitually threw away the liver of any animal they were butchering, because that was the dubious part of the carcass harbouring any infections or poisons.

We had also experienced our first comradely taste of the share-and-share alike principle of the Prisoner-of-War by forming a stick-together "combine" or family. Myself, George Lunt, Lance Ferguson, Bill Copland and Jack Mooney.

Chapter 9

"GOTT MIT UNS"?

I slept uneasily that night in the dubious shelter of the abandoned farmhouse. Without blanket or greatcoat, or even a battledress blouse, I was glad of the meagre protection the old walls of the semi-derelict house gave me, from the piercing cold which grew worse as the night progressed.

It was barely light, the next morning, when I stumbled out to join the rest of the 106th, to learn from one of our Junior Officers the not unexpected news that the Battle of Crete was over. We had capitulated and there would be no further evacuation from the island that night, nor any other night. I was therefore shortly to become a Prisoner of War. One of some ten thousand Allied Troops from the United Kingdom, Australia and New Zealand left on the island that day.

The never-to-be-forgotten day. The First Day of June, Nineteen Hundred and Fortyone.

We were instructed to destroy any arms we were carrying. I went to great trouble to bury in the thin stony soil of the paddock, the bolt of my 1914 Lee Enfield rifle and the five rounds of 303 I still had in the breach. After breaking the wooden stock and bending the barrel on a rock, I chucked the battered remains over the edge of the escarpment into the sea.

Shortly afterwards, I was in a state of total bewilderment, numbing shock and humiliation, a terrible feeling of being let down and letting others down, but, at the same time, thankful and relieved it was all over. There would be no more frightening attacks of the screaming Stukas and Messeschmitts. I saw for the first time at close quarters, my first German.

A tall, heavily built, bronzed, older-looking man, dressed in shorts and grey shirt and wearing solid-looking mountaineering boots, he picked his way carefully down through the boulders and rocks on the incline from the road. The first thing I noticed about him was the large revolver he carried in his right hand, dangling down by the side of his knee, his forefinger curled around the trigger. On his head was a blue/grey cap with a long peak and a Swastika cap badge pinned in the centre. Binoculars were slung around his neck, hanging just below a black, Iron Cross decoration fastened on his shirt.

As he passed by, close to me, I couldn't help but see the heavily embossed words on the clasp in the centre of the broad, black leather belt he wore round his middle.

"GOTT MIT UNS."

Although I had no knowledge of German, the meaning was immediately plain to me. I wondered, then and there, "If God was on his side, then who was on ours?"

Clean shaven and smart, he showed no fear as he walked alone among the crowd of silent, demoralised Allied troops who had been told only a few minutes before, by our Officers, that the Powers-that-Be had decided to give up the island due to the terrible losses of the Navy attempting to evacuate our troops. I looked about me and although there were many downcast heads there were no hands raised in the humiliating act of surrender. And there were no film crews to record our inglorious defeat nor his narrow victory. The German officer's first words, though, I was to hear time and time again.

"For you the war is over," he said, almost conversationally, as he strolled amongst us. "Come on lads," he said, "for you the war is over. You are now Prisoners of War. Guests of the German Reich. You will find that the German Army will treat you well if you behave yourselves and do as you are told." Then he said with seemingly unconscious irony, "You've missed the boat, lads, you've missed the boat."

Waving his revolver in the air pointing in the general direction of the road, he said "Form up on the road at the top, right away. You will be marching back to Suda Bay. I know you are all hungry and I promise you will get something to eat when you get to the first village on the road."

His English was almost without any accent.

On the road at the top of the escarpment I joined the growing number of dejected Allied troops coming out of the caves and hidey-holes of the cliffside, and being shepherded into line by a surprisingly small number of German soldiers. They looked fit and bronzed and all were carrying, cradled in their arms, small sub-machine guns the likes of which we had never seen before except in old gangster films. Although most of them seemed to be able to speak English they proceeded immediately to give us our first lesson in German with their raucous "gemma, gemma" and "raus, raus", phrases which we were to hear many times. Accompanied by threatening gesticulations of their sub-machine guns they prodded and bullied us into line on the road. All our commissioned officers were separated from the main body and taken away immediately. I never saw any of them again.

I was thirsty even before we started to dejectedly trudge our way along the dusty, mountainous road back to Suda Bay, and it very soon became clear to me that water and food, a problem that had been a part of my life since my first days in the desert back in September, 1940 was going to be an even greater problem. Particularly water.

It soon became apparent, also, to the German guards walking alongside the slowly moving column that we had to have water. At the first of the villages we came to they let us stop at the village well. The circular, stone-walled well was the only water supply for these little clusters of houses of the remote mountain villages of Crete. Normally the water was drawn up in a chain of buckets by a donkey or mule, endlessly circling the stone walls of the well. But the animals had vanished, as had the occupants of the village. So I pressed into service once again my ever useful steel hat, by lowering it down to the water on a length of string tied to the chinstrap. To the repeated shouts of "Gemma, gemma" I hurriedly pulled the unwieldly half-round, metal hat to the surface, frustratingly spilling some on its journey, and emptied the contents, weeds, soil and all, into a discarded 4 gallon aluminium petrol container. Lance Ferguson and I had converted the dented petrol tin into a bucket by inserting a stick through two holes across the top, to carry it slung between us.

Our portable water bucket proved to be a life saver as there was no water or food issued to us by our captors either at that village or the next one. Or the next. Our Combine of five survived on the water in the petrol tin, dipping into it frequently as we trudged along and refilling it at one of the wells whenever we got the opportunity. The water, dirty and cloudy with the dust and sand kicked up from the road by the column of moving men, and luke-warm to boot, kept us on our feet.

By now, I was beginning to feel the terrible pangs of hunger which was to haunt me, on and off, for the next few years. Desperate for food of any sort, I gladly picked up orange peel thrown away by of one of the guards as he walked along just in front of me eating a large mouth-watering orange. In desperation I plucked stems of a thickish green, reed-like grass, growing at the side of the road and chewed and sucked on them as I staggered along. Eating was to occupy my thoughts almost the whole of my waking hours for many weeks ahead and was to become the main topic of conversation amongst the prisoners.

The whole of that awful day was spent trudging, despondently, along the road threading its way over the White Mountains, urged on by the bullying and threats of our new hosts. At long last we passed Suda Bay to arrive at Lower Galatas, near Canea, in the late afternoon, beaten, foot sore and exhausted.

We were herded into a compound the Germans had hurriedly prepared by the beach. One of many they had placed all over the island. (The same beach, today, is a luxury complex of holiday hotels, with swimming pools and restaurants). Four or five strands of barbed wire formed a six foot high fence on three sides of a square, the fourth side being open to the beach and sea. Guards were posted at intervals on the outside of the fences. The main road from Maleme to Suda ran through the top of the square, alongside which had been dug a deep, wide latrine trench just inside the wire. This makeshift lavatory became a scource of acute embarrassment to me. Later, struck down by the dreaded squitters of dysentery, I had to squat over the ghastly, foul smelling trench, my backside exposed to the sympathetic gaze of the passing Cretan populace.

There were no facilities of any kind in this hastily erected barbed wire compound. No huts, no tents, no blankets, absolutely nothing. We slept, or tried to sleep, huddled together to keep warm, on the bare sandy soil.

The lucky ones who had not made the abortive hike to Spharkia and back, with a few cigarettes still in their pockets, were able to barter for food with one or two of the guards. As did the fortunate few who owned wristlet watches or signet rings or jewellery – going away gifts from family or sweethearts or wives. The war-time black market had its origins in the prisoner-of-war Stalags of Nazi Germany.

Even the rubbish tip in one corner of the field became an overnight goldmine. So it was very quickly cleared of usable rubbish like empty jam tins to be made into drinking mugs or cooking utensils. Scrap paper, bits of wood, dried grass, anything that would burn, were commandeered to provide fuel for cooking fires.

Shortly after our arrival, the Germans issued the food they had continually promised us from the dawn of that day. Part of the booty they had taken over from the RASC dumps after the capitulation, it was a 12oz. tin of Libby's corned beef to be shared beween 10 men. The hot sun of that lovely early summer Cretan day had rendered the contents into an oily thick mess, impossible to slice with a knife. So it was doled out carefully by the spoonful, each man gathering round to watch the proceedings and make sure he got his fair share. A spoonful each. When it came to my turn to partake of the repast, I found I couldn't chew it. My tongue, the inside of my mouth and the back of my throat were swollen, and stung alarmingly when I tried to swallow the salty, gravy-like mixture. I had to let it mix slowly with my saliva and slide painfully down my throat.

The following day a field kitchen was provided by our captors. Thereafter we queued impatiently, each day at noon, to receive a cupful of a watery mixture of rice and biscuit containing traces of Crosse and Blackwell's tinned meat-and-vegetable stew. If you were lucky, there were also shreds of corned beef. Some days it was just boiled rice, but not much of that. It was the only food of any sort we received.

The unenviable task of receiving the daily ration from the Germans, and the fuel to cook or heat it, fell to Troop Sergeant

Major Alf Daybell of the 106th, one of the senior NCOs in the compound. Supervising the first issue of the stew, at the head of a long queue of starving men more than anxious to get their first taste of food for over a week, the Sergeant Major soon realised he was seeing faces of men who had been in the queue and already received their ration. Faces of some of the 106th men. Faces familiar to the Sergeant Major.

He went purple with rage, stopped doling out the miserable concoction and, recruiting some of the senior sergeants, called a parade. He harangued us for ten minutes, telling us that we were not to behave like savages. He reminded us that, although now Prisoners-of-War, we were still in the British Army, under the Army's discipline, and could still be "put on a charge". We were all in the same boat, and would have to all pull together. I have to say that the "doubling-up" was never repeated, except when the Germans themselves were in charge, when it became a matter of honour to do so if you could.

And it wasn't very long before the comradeship of the Prisoner-of-War established itself. Broadly speaking, cadged or filched food, fuel, water or cigarettes were shared as a matter of course.

It wasn't very long, also, before a Concert Party was put together by Ernie Mack (Ernie McGrae) of the 106th, a gun-layer on the other gun in my section in Greece. Ernie was, and still is, an excellent stand-up comedian with a never ending repertoire of jokes, songs, and parodies of songs, accompanied by his expert playing of his banjolele. He had retained his banjo, somehow, in the evacuation of Greece and the abortive evacuation of Crete, ignoring orders to throw away, or destroy, all personal belongings. Now he put it to good use.

The parody of the St. Louis Blues, "The Liverpool Blues", sung by Ernie Mack at that first morale building concert-party is still remembered and sung by his old comrades, to this day.

"Oh! I've got the Liverpool Blues,
I've got the "Hey Whack, how yer gettin'
on Wack, Liverpool Blues
It's just a little song I never want to lose.
I don't wannerbe down in Tennessee,
Scotland Road, that's good enough for me.

I don't wanner see the Mammas picking melons
Give me the "Mary 'elens" shouting
"two-a-Penny lemons

Oh! I've got the Liverpool Blues
It's just a little song I never want to lose.
Now over in America there's a big White House,
But give me Saturday night with the old
pan of scouse.
Oh, I've got the Liverpool Blues.

Ernie, and many others like him, did a marvellous job in that grubby compound, and in the years to come. Helping to keep up the spirits of his fellow comrades some of whom were still finding it extremely difficult to come to terms with the shattering, irreversible change in their lifestyle.

Chapter 10

The Ju-Jube Tree

A few days after our incarceration in the compound, we began to hear accounts of the remarkable support and assistance the Crete people were giving to Allied Troops, who had avoided being rounded up and were still on the loose, hiding in the vast orchards of olive trees and the remote villages of the White Mountains. We also heard that men had escaped from our barbed-wire compound and returned with their pockets full of rice and raisins, which they had bartered, bought or begged from the local population. So, spurred on by these tales of derring-do and our now ever-present hunger, Lance Ferguson and I decided we would try our luck at escaping through the wire.

We had already noticed that the number of guards on the track on one side of the camp from the main Suda road to the beach had been reduced, and that only two or three were protecting that side. We watched the sentries, each patrolling up and down their section, pausing to chat with each other for a minute or two when they met.

So, one hot, sweaty afternoon, my stomach rumbling for more of the thin Oliver Twist gruel for which I had queued all morning, Lance and I squirmed under the bottom strand of the barbed wire fence and lay on our bellies in a shallow ditch at the side of the road. My left arm was bleeding rather heavily from a long scratch received in the struggle. My heart thumping rapidly and my bowels rumbling uncontrollably, we watched the two sentries patrolling towards each other. When they stopped to chat, with their backs to us, a cigarette changing hands, we dashed across the dusty road to fling ourselves in a ditch on the other side beneath the prickly protection of a clump of gorse bushes. We lay quiet for a moment or two, my heart still going ninety to the dozen, until we made sure we had not been spotted.

They were still chatting when we climbed out of the ditch into the protection of the thickly growing trees of an olive grove, and ran out of their sight.

We found ourselves on a footpath running parallel with the shore heading in the direction of Canea. The sandy, narrow path was lined with olive trees and overgrown with vegetation and weeds. After a while we came to a fruit tree. Or, to our townee eyes, a huge, overgrown bush. It was heavily laden with some sort of fruit. Large, purple berries, some of them just within reach and, in our state of near starvation, invitingly ready to be picked and eaten. To this day I don't know what the berries were. Twice the size of a raspberry, a deep purple colour, they were absolutely delicious. Sweet, ripe and juicy. Greedily, we stuffed the lucious fruit into our mouths as fast as we could like four-year-olds given jujube sweets for the first time. We soon stripped the lower branches of this heaven-sent manna and climbed for more of the forbidden fruit hidden in the thick leaves of the higher branches. We paused for a moment when I reminded Lance of the Combine back in the compound.

"How can we get some to the lads, Lance?" I asked.

"We can't, can we?" replied Lance. "So let's fill our bellies while we've got the chance."

For without containers or bags of any sort it was impossible to carry any of the soft ripe fruit. So we silently went on with the beautiful job of harvesting and eating as many berries as we could, cramming them into our mouths, with the purple juice running down our chins. Suddenly we heard voices, jabbering away in German, coming towards us along the footpath from the direction of the camp. Instinctively, we froze and held our breaths. Lance's normally florid face, heavily freckled and outlined by his carroty red hair with a three-day growth of ginger stubble on his chin, went a sort of dirty white. I felt the colour in my face change to a similar hue when I slowly turned my head to look down at the approaching glider men. Then I saw, to my consternation, that one of my boots attached to twelve inches of my right leg was standing in the fork of the lower branch of the tree, and plainly visible to any passer by.

Engrossed in their conversation, they didn't see my exposed limb, and I heaved a sigh of relief as the two Germans passed beneath me. Their sub-machine guns slung on their shoulders, almost touched my boot as they went by with their heads down, chatting away as if there was no war on.

***

The footpath ended among the little houses of the fishing harbour of Canea. The town was completely deserted, nobody at all to be seen on the dry, dusty, unpaved streets, neither residents nor German soldiers. We wandered aimlessly along, until, in a narrow lane, little more than a back alley, a door suddenly opened and a harassed looking, elderly woman, after looking up and down, beckoned us to enter. We didn't need much encouragement. After she hurriedly closed and bolted the door we found ourselves in a sort of walled, garden-cum-backyard occupied by a few scraggy hens, an old donkey standing in the limited shade of an olive tree in the centre, and two black, bearded goats, tethered to a stake by a piece of rope. The untidy yard reminded me of the back yards of the terrace houses of Waltham Road, way back in the late twenties where some of the tenants kept hens.

She greeted us with a babble of unintelligible Greek, punctuated with the frequent passing of her forefinger across her throat in a slashing motion and then disappeared through a door at the back of the yard. A minute or so later she came out with a bowl of water, a grey looking towel, a bandage, and proceeded to clean my barbed wire wound and then dress it deftly with the bandage. My brief knowledge of the Greek language was limited to the few words of polite greetings I had picked up during the seven or eight weeks of the campaign in Greece and Crete. So, after my hestitant thanks, in the form of "cali mera" and "endaxie", I was able to indicate in the universal sign language of the Middle East that we were thirsty and hungry and that we wanted to buy food.

Without more ado, this wonderful lady, this Florence Nightingale of Canea, hitched her black, voluminous skirts above her knees, straddled her skinny legs across the back of one of the goats facing its rear end, held a round earthenware bowl under the animal's swollen udder and squirted milk vigourously, into it. Without moving from the now protesting goat, she handed the bowl of warm milk to me, and after I had quaffed the delectable nectar, she went through the same proceedure for Lance Ferguson.

Then, releasing the goat from her cowboy grip, she vanished into what seemed to be a covered extension, or lean-to, attached to the house over the back door. Sparsly furnished, with a rough wooden table, two rickety chairs and a store cupboard standing on the baked clay floor, it appeared to be the kitchen of the humble dwelling. She delved into the cupboard and emerged carrying two small hessian sacks. One held rice, the other raisins, and she indicated that we could fill the pockets of our battledress trousers from the contents. Despite our entreaties she firmly refused our offer of the few drachmas we possessed, left over after seeing Errol Flynn back in Larissa. Placing her forefinger across her lips, in the time honoured way of indicating silence, she unbolted the door. After looking swiftly up and down, she ushered us outside into the deserted alley.

We were to learn, later, the reason for her caution, apparent haste, and anxiety to get us out of the yard. The Germans were showing no mercy to any Cretan man, woman or child, caught helping or assisting Allied servicemen on the run or begging for food. We also learned, to our horror, that they were shooting them, out of hand, without trial or argument. Everybody met the same fate, young children, old men and women alike. The whole population of some of the Cretan villages were slaughtered by the Germans after they had been discovered harbouring escaped prisoners.

***

Satisfied with the results of our begging expedition, we returned along the footpath; again choosing a suitable moment when the guards' backs were turned, we wriggled under the barbed wire back into the compound.

The Combine spent the rest of the day, slowly and painstakingly boiling rice in a 2lb Hartleys jam tin rescued from the rubbish dump, over a meagre fire of carefully hoarded bits of wood, dried grass, and scrap paper comprising the best part of Lance Ferguson's Pay-Book. It was a slow process, requiring the attention of the five of us for the rice had to be stirred continuously to prevent it sticking to the bottom of the tin. So the chief cook had to keep stirring while the others kept looking for the tinder for the fire. It was well worth the effort after it was more or less cooked, and we had added some of the raisins.

We used about half of that wonderful gift from the Lady of Canea. A precious gift of food which she could ill afford given unhesitatingly at great risk to herself and her family. I have never forgotten her.

Many years later, on a visit of nostalgia to Crete with a party of veterans of the 106th Old Comrades Association, I tried to find that Good Samaritan. Without success, unfortunately, for with the passing years Cania had changed. I could not find the back alley. The footpath with the jujube tree had become part of a chalet holiday camp, built on the site of the barbed wire compound.

Emboldened by the success of our escapade and spurred on again by our hunger pangs, Lance and I broke out of the compound three times altogether. The second time, we did not have the same good fortune, although we grew bolder and decided to try the shops and tavernas on the main road in the centre of the harbour. The road was deserted except for a solitary British 15cwt. Morris truck, parked outside what appeared to be a bakery or grocers.

Curiosity getting the better of us, we approached the truck to find a Royal Army Service Corps driver sitting at the wheel.

"I'll bet you haven't had much luck, lads," he said, as we drew level with his cab. He knew we were out on the scrounge.

"You won't get much around 'ere, anyway," he went on. "I'm drivin' this for a fuckin' Jerry Feldwebel who's pinchin' any grub or anythin' else he can lay his hands on."

And with a smirk of triumph on his face, he went on, "He hasn't had much bloody luck either, as you can see from the back of the truck. I think the civvies have stashed all their stuff away and most of them have buggered off to the mountains."

There was nothing in the truck except a few empty sacks

and boxes, a spare wheel and a tarpaulin cover.

"I tell you what, though," our new friend said, "he's not a bad sort of a geezer for a Jerry bastard, and he'll give you a lift back to the barbed wire if you ask him. He speaks a bit of our lingo."

Lance and I looked at each other with doubt in our eyes. We'd been out most of the morning and for our pains had only been able to scrounge a handful of raisins and a cupful of rice. We didn't want to hand that over to any German. But we were tired, fed up, hot and hungry. A ride back to the compound would be a relief. Hesitating, because we knew blokes who had been caught outside the compound being belted around the ear with a rifle butt and then locked up for three days without any food or water in the dreaded "bunker". The civilian gaol in Cania.

Before we had time to say anything, however, the German three-striper walked out of the shop and the quick thinking driver made up our minds for us before we had a chance to open our mouths.

"A'right for a lift, for these two, Boss," he said to the Sergeant, jerking his thumb in our direction, "they wanna go back to the compound."

Much to our surprise and relief the Sergeant, without saying a word nodded his head in the direction of the back of the truck. Ten minutes later, passing the two sentries at the gate of the compound, we had successfully "escaped" back into the prison camp.

***

Our third escapade proved to be the most exciting although, again, we weren't befriended by a Florence Nightingale nor any other Good Samaritan in the deserted streets and alleys of Canea. Luck had run out in our search for any sort of food. There were no more berries on our jujube tree either, and we searched in vain for its mate as we walked along the path. But, luck came our way in another form. Somewhere on the other side of Canea we stumbled on what appeared to be a warehouse, lately occupied by the Royal Army Service Corps.

It was a disused church or church hall. We found a veritable pyramid of discarded British Army clothing, piled high in the centre of the floor. Torn shirts and underclothing, worn-out battle-dress trousers and blouses, old boots and smelly socks.

Lance and I rummaged in this rag-and-bone collection and we exchanged the filthy shirt and trousers we had worn since landing in Greece. I found a reasonably servicable battle-dress blouse, an Army pullover, a pair of dirty, but holeless socks, and marvellously, a pair of boots. One was a size six and the other a seven, but they were in pristine condition compared with mine, worn out crossing the mountains during the scramble to Sphakia.

Triumphantly wearing our booty, we made our way back to the compound by way of the ju-jube tree footpath.

As we reached the road at the end of the path, which we had to cross to get back into the camp, we heard a hullabaloo of German voices. Excited, high pitched commands of "Halt, halt..." "Los, los" and other unintelligble shouted orders were followed by two rifle shots. The loud reports scared the life out of me for I thought, for one panic stricken moment, they were directed at us. Squirming under the gorse bush, we poked our heads over the edge of the ditch to see Germans all over the place, running up and down the track. We also saw a khaki clad figure lying on his back in the road and two of the Jerry guards, nearest to us, running towards him.

"Come on, Lance," I said, "let's chance it now."

Taking advantage of the diversion we scurried across the track to fling ourselves under the lowest strand of barbed wire, helpfully held up by one of the many prisoners lining the other side of the fence, shouting encouragement to us and insults at the German guards. The sentries had shot and wounded a young Kiwi as he attempted to cross the road from the camp, as we had done earlier in the day. A guard had spotted him, shouted a warning which had been ignored, and then fired two rounds, one of which hit the young lad in the leg. His misfortune was our good luck; we would not have got back into the camp that day without the kerfuffle he had caused when he was shot.

By any stretch of imagination, our "escapes" couldn't be included as one of the "Great Escapes" featured in films years later. The risks we took in our search for something to eat were double risks, because we had to "escape" back into the compound to take what food we had managed to obtain to our mates, risking a sadistic beating with a rifle butt, and a spell in the bunker for a few days without any food at all.

Remembering the unfortunate Kiwi lying in the road, blood pouring from his leg, and learning later that he would more than likely lose the limb, made Lance and me think again about attempting any more fruitless foraging expeditions. In the three weeks since the capitulation a few hardy souls had decided to chance their luck, whilst it was still comparatively easy, to break out of the compound and seek the assistance of civilians in the remote mountain villages who unhestitatingly gave their help. The Germans had consequently strengthened their guards around the camp, sapped the energy of the inmates by keeping them on starvation rations, and ruthlessly killed on sight civilians caught harbouring or helping escaped prisoners.

We had all discussed time and time again, the pros and cons of breaking out and going into hiding, or just waiting to see what fate had in store. The Germans had also let it be known that we were to receive post-cards to enable us to write home. It was many weeks since I had written home. As I knew my Mother was far from well I realised that it would not be possible to relieve her anxiety if I remained in hiding. Rightly or wrongly Lance and I decided that the rewards were not worth the effort or risk. We didn't try to escape again.

However, five men from the 106th broke out of the compound and went on the run.

Alec Drillsma, Jim Baxter and Johnny Barclay were hidden by Cretan families for months, but gave themselves up to the Germans, after they had decided that the risk to the families sheltering them was too great. They didn't want to see them shot out of hand if they were discovered. Also, with the approach of winter, conditions in the mountains were becoming extremely rigorous. Food was scarce and came only from the paltry rations, shared willingly, of the wonderful Cretans.

Jim Casey, one time driver/batman to Tim Hely, the 106th's Commanding Officer, and Peter Savage, were on the run for some two years. During this time they made contact with Allied Agents who were landed by boat on the island to reinforce the civilian Resistance Movement. Jim Casey had a part in the successful expedition to kidnap the General commanding the German forces on Crete, Major-General Kreipe. Years later, this incident was made into a film.

Gunner Casey was awarded the B.E.M.

Chapter 11

Twenty-one today, twenty-one today

In the third week of my captivity, to add to my already abject misery, I became infested with body lice, like everyone else in that dreadful compound. I don't mean one or two head nits which had already made their itchy presence felt. I mean a veritable plague of the horrible parasites. Appearing out of thin air, my first sight of these unwelcome visitors were the eggs of the creature lining the seams of my battledress trousers, and the creases in the shirt I had rescued from the rag warehouse. They proved very difficult to dislodge from their sticky hold on the material. Luckily for me few of them developed into the grey, wriggling vermin I saw on other men.

Our only means of fighting these new invaders was with the salt water of the Mediterranean. It was a strange spectacle indeed, comical in other circumstances, to see hundreds of totally naked young men, taking advantage of the hot mid-day sun and sitting in the shallows on the beach, washing their body hair in the salt water and rubbing wet sand in the crevices of their clothing, to rid themselves of the lice and their horrible, white eggs. The Germans appeared to encourage this community delousing, but if a couple of energetic, or foolhardy desperados swam out into deeper water, the guards were quick to fire warning shots over their heads. A timely reminder, that they were not to consider swimming across the Mediterranean to Egypt and freedom.

Despite the valiant efforts of Ernie Mack, Jack Mullins, Ted McShea and other stalwarts of the amateur stage, to boost the fast disappearing morale of the ragged inmates of the camp with hastily arranged "concert parties", the spirit in the compound went from extremely bad to extremely worse.

Most of the men had diarrhoea or, worse still, dysentery.

The stinking latrine trench alongside the road had been filled to overflowing, and then covered with the soil excavated from a second trench, further encroaching on the already crowded area occupied by the prisoners. Protests made to the Germans by the Senior N.C.O. Sergeant Major Daybell had little effect, although a few of the more chronically sick were moved to the hospital in Canea.

Not, however, in time to save the life of Frank Kinsella, another 106th Territorial who died there early in June. Jack Mullins also died later on from the effects of prolonged chronic dysentery, shortly after our arrival in Wolfsburg, Austria. Frank Kinsella's terminal decline started the day he had been dumped on Crete to learn that his Uncle, Joe Hoey, had been lost on the Slamat. Early in 1939 Frank had, apparently, persuaded his Uncle to join the 106th, and never forgave himself when he learned of his death. He went into a state of deep depression and despite the efforts of all his mates nothing could bring him out of his state of mind. It was said he died of a broken heart.

We were always hungry. Food was cut down to a small slice of bread, or a hard biscuit, in the morning; followed by half a cup of a thin, boiled rice, flavoured if you were lucky, with shreds of corned beef, in the afternoon. It was obvious that the Germans were deliberately trying to weaken our spirit by keeping us short of food.

Eating and food became the sole topic of conversation. A kind of self torture developed, with dreamlike descriptions of the wonderful meals Mother used to cook in days gone by. Sometimes, silly, minor quarrels would break out among close friends about the best way to boil an egg or make a brew of tea. Once I overheard a heated argument about the true ingredients of scouse and blind scouse.

So it was small wonder that even the spell-binding rumour flashing through the compound that Hitler had declared war on Russia on the 22nd June, l941, took second place to conversation, and thoughts preoccupied solely with food.

The 22nd June, 1941 was my 21st birthday.

No one was very interested in that however, not even myself. But the day was highlighted still further when, endeavouring to find a suitable spot to spread out my trousers to dry after my morning delouse in the sea, my fingers made contact with grains of rice in the sandy soil. In next to no time the five of us were on our knees, sifting through a rectangular area which at one time must have been the site of a store shed or hut.

Undeterred by the black rat droppings mixed in with the rice and earth, we separated each grain from the sandy soil and the shiny rat muck, and washed them carefully in water from our petrol-tin water-carrier. We boiled the precious gleanings with a few raisins still left from our foraging expedition to Canea, and carefully divided the end product amongst the five of us. As a special 21st birthday gift, I was given the honour of cleaning the can we had used to cook the mixture. I rescued every last grain of rice sticking to the sides. I have never forgotten my Twenty-first Birthday Party.

***

My sojourn in the compound at Galatas, and my unfortunate and unwelcome visit to the Island of Crete, came to an abrupt end when, without warning, we were told we were to leave the island. Carrying our pathetic bits and pieces of belongings we formed up on the road. With mixed feelings, again, of apprehension at what lay ahead, yet glad to be leaving the awful conditions in the compound, and still wondering whether it would have been better to go on the run with Lance Ferguson when I had the chance, I marched to Suda Bay to board a rusty old cargo ship, the "Yalova" of Hamburg, tied up at the quayside.

In the reluctant queue to file up the gang plank, someone saw lice on a young Service Corps lad just in front of me. Despite the heat of the noonday sun he was wearing his Army overcoat, no doubt thinking of the winter ahead and determined to hold on to his coat at all costs. But the sight of the greatcoat, covered in crawling lice, brought howls of protest from his fellow prisoners. I'll never forget the expression on the lad's face as he was forced to throw his prize possession over the side into the water.

It was soon obvious we were not embarking on some sort of Mediterranean cruise. The guards herded us like cattle on the ramp of a Dublin-Liverpool cattleboat down a makeshift, wooden stairway rigged up on the walls of a cavernous hold which disappeared into the bowels of the vessel. By the dim light of a few electric bulbs I could see condensation running down the steel walls, the rivulets forming ordnance survey maps in a fine grey dust, remnants from a previous cargo, covering the metal deck. Sorting ourselves out as best as we could on the bare, dusty floor, Lance and I were lucky to get a space near the Heath-Robinson stairs, down which came the only fresh air into the hold.

There was also another weird and wonderful wooden contraption, which had puzzled me as to its purpose as I queued to board the ship. Lashed to the rusty, sheering walls of the stern of the vessel, level with the deck, was a flimsy looking wooden platform which proved to be the "heads" or toilets for the exclusive patronage of the prisoners, the frightening use of which, when poised with your pants down on two narrow planks spaced six inches apart over the seething water of the ship's propellers, was enough to open anyone's bowels. Not exactly a new invention for waste disposal being patented by Twyford/Shanks or Mr Crapper himself. The idea was that the excrement from the p.o.ws, most of them suffering the pangs of diarrhoea or dysentery, would fall thirty feet into the waves and be automatically flushed away in the waters of the Aegean Sea.

But of course it didn't quite work that way. The wind and the roll of the ship caused a glistening cascade of crap to form on the side of the ship, almost before we lost sight of Crete. Frightening or not, a queue formed as soon as we had sailed out of Suda Bay. Waiting in line in the fresh air to use the trapeze-like heads, became preferable to the foetid atmosphere of the overcrowded hold.

The guards, posted at intervals along the line of waiting troops to deter anyone from jumping off and swimming back to Crete, soon got fed up with jostling the men to "gemma, gemma", and retired a safe distance from the slowly moving line.

Ted McShea tells the story of when he was waiting his turn

to do his balancing act on the flimsy heads. He inquisitively tried the handle of the door he was leaning on. To his surprise it opened to reveal a storeroom or glory-hole containing cleaning materials and ship's chandlery. Taking advantage of the guards' reluctance to get too close to the unsavoury heads, he slipped inside. Rooting around, he found tins of British issue corned beef hidden behind cans of grey paint stacked on a shelf. No doubt stashed there by a light-fingered member of the crew to take home to his family in Hamburg. Ted couldn't believe his luck and quickly stuffed the three tins of Fray Bentos down his trousers.

Mid-way through the afternoon, a German three-striper came hurrying along the deck with cries of "unter see boot, unter see boot", accompanied by a tirade of orders to the guards. It did not take a great deal of knowledge of German to interpret the meaning and the flurry of activity. We were all hurriedly forced back down the makeshift stairway into the hold, including those who had only just made it to the perilous heads. The hatch at the top of the stairs was drawn over the top and battened down, blocking off the sunshine and the only real scource of fresh air, frighteningly, the only means of escape from our maritime dungeon, should we need to get out in a hurry.

We were all well aware of what would be the outcome if we were torpedoed. Although the general opinion in the overcrowded hold, for some strange, over-optimistic reason, seemed to be that a British submarine would be bound to know that Allied prisoners were on the ship! There was absolutely no panic of any sort, and it wasn't long before the subdued murmur in the crowded hold swelled into a crescendo of glorious sound, when someone started to sing "Land of Hope and Glory".

Almost immediately the emotional refrain was spontaneously taken up by every single man of the hundreds in the hold of the ship; as if in defiance of the threat of friendly fire from our own submarines and the battening-down of the hatches by our captors. English, Scottish, Irish, Welsh, Australian and New Zealanders were all lustily singing in one voice.

The acoustics of the steel-clad hold amplified the singing far better than the lofty nave of Liverpool Cathedral could do, for a well rehearsed choir leading a packed congregation singing carols on Christmas Eve. The stirring anthem was followed by other National songs and hymns. "Danny Boy" and "Saucepan Bach", "Onward Christian Soldiers" and "Abide With Me", "Hang out the washing on the Seigfried Line", and "It's a Long Way to Tipperary". There was no conductor or concertmaster, nor padre nor priest to lead the captive congregation. There was no illuminated electric organ rising out of the floor, nor any other musical accompaniment, and there were no splinter groups breaking off to sing their own choice of song.

From an early age, I have enthusiastically joined in community singing, and can remember, vividly, the exuberant hymn singing of the childrens' services, led by a Salvation Army brass band, in the Evangelical Great Tent in Liverpool. The Great Tent, an annual event in Anfield in the late nineteen-twenties, was erected on a piece of waste ground in Breck Road for two weeks every summer. It was a great favourite with the children.

I can remember Saturday afternoon matinees at the "Clubby". Clubmoor cinema, packed with youngsters singing in time to a ball bouncing over the words of, "When The Red Red Robin Comes Bob Bob Bobbing Along" on the screen, before the start of the Big Picture with Tom Mix.

More recently I can remember the community singing at F.A. Cup Finals at Wembley and El Alamein Reunions at the Festival Hall in London and the Winter Gardens in Blackpool.

But never have I heard anything to compare with the singing in the dreary ship's hold that afternoon. Neither have I ever experienced the charged, emotional atmosphere the singing created. There seemed to be some unspoken prayer in the rhythms, familiar words and melodies of the old National songs and hymns. It was truly a never-to-be-forgotten experience.

This unpremeditated, unrehearsed, full-throated, male voice choir had just reached the climax of "Sons of the Sea, we're all British Boys", when the hatch cover was suddenly pulled to one side. A flood of sunshine gushed like a mountain stream down the makeshift staircase, accompanied by a lung-filling draught of welcome fresh sea air.

A bearded figure in Naval uniform walked to a point halfway down the staircase. He turned towards us and raised his hands to indicate silence.

"I am Captain Schmidt," he said, "and I want to say how sorry I was to be forced to close the only exit from the hold for you men. I received a message that there were British submarines in the area and I had no option but to obey my orders, to imprison you down below and take evasive action."

His English was perfect and we could hear every word he said.

"But," he went on, "I also want to say that I have never in my life heard singing like the wonderful singing coming from this hold today. You are all to be congratulated. The whole of my ship's company join with me in thanking you for a very moving concert. You are very brave men."

He went on "I am pleased to tell you that we have had the all clear and we shall be docking shortly. Thank you, again, for your moving concert and I wish you all the very best of luck."

Chapter 12

Salonika Concentration Camp

It was the next day when, desperate for food and water and gasping for fresh air, they let us out of the stinking hold of the ship.

We found that the young German paratroopers and glidermen who had been guarding us since our capture had been replaced. The guards bullying us through the streets of Salonika were a different breed of German from the young, crack troops who had dropped out of the skies on Crete, who for the most part after our capture, had treated us with a certain amount of respect and cameraderie.

Our new guardians were older men, apparently recruited from the Berlin area of Germany. Grim-faced and surly, they appeared to blame us for the fact that they were so far from home, and took it out on us at every opportunity. Any sign of lagging in the column, of dumb insolence, or attempting to speak to any of the few silent citizens on the pavements watching our dispirited progress, was met with a torrent of abuse, and sometimes striking the offender with the butt of a rifle in the back. I saw one heroic, steel-helmeted six-foot-two guard, or blackguard, violently using the butt of his rifle on an obviously heavily pregnant young woman, who was handing bits of bread to the passing prisoners. She staggered and fell heavily on her stomach. The loud protests from the prisoners were met by the stony-faced guard with cries of "ruhig, ruhig", "quiet, quiet", with pantomimed threats to use the butt on us. There were many similar instances when those brave Greek women of Salonika tried to pass us food.

Salonika prison camp, disused for years and dilapidated, dirty and vermin infested, had been at one time, a Greek Army Military Base. It was being used by the Germans as a transit camp for Allied prisoners-of-war captured in Greece and Crete who were due to be transported to Germany. 12,000 prisoners-of-war passed through the dreadful Salonika Concentration Camp in the summer of 1941. British, Australian, New Zealanders, Cypriots and Palestinians. I was held there for four weeks. The worst four weeks of my entire life.

The Germans took no chances with security. A high, impenetrable, double coiled, barbed wire fence completely surrounded the prison. At each corner was a lofty wooden tower manned by two guards with a machine gun, from which, after dark, beamed two moving searchlights.

Ancient, semi-derelict brick barracks occupied three sides of a dusty parade ground the size of a football pitch. Devoid of windows and doors – even the wooden frames were missing – these old barracks were home to vermin of all kinds. Rats, spiders, cockroaches and creepy-crawlies I had never seen before. Worst of all, were huge, red, stinking bed bugs. These blood-sucking parasites with their peculiar, obnoxious smell, came out of the cracks of the crumbling plaster walls in their thousands as soon as darkness fell. It was almost impossible to sleep. If you were foolish enough to squash one of these marauders, it left a splodge of dark red blood the size of a thumb-nail. We were packed like sardines into these filthy ruins, until they couldn't squeeze in any more. The fortunate overflow had to doss down on the parade ground outside. At the first opportunity Lance Ferguson and I joined them.

At one end of the barrack were the ablutions, a partioned room with a few brass taps on one wall emitting a trickle of lukewarm water and, horror of horrors, a bank of four foul smelling "oriental closets" against the other wall. I had seen these unsavoury closets many years before, illustrated in old Plumbers' Merchants catalogues. They were sold to Merseyside ship-repairers, or were exported to the Middle East and Far East. This was the first time I had ever seen them as a fixture. They were like a white porcelain shower tray with a four inch hole at one end and imprints of two feet. Each was complete with five toes, set at an angle to each other at a squatting distance from the hole. The flushing arrangements had long since vanished. The foul, cracked trays were encrusted with dried excrement, attended by hundreds of buzzing blue-bottles.

The indefatigable George Lunt had produced from out of thin air a battered old yard brush and a rusty bucket. Struggling with the intermittent supply of water from the taps, I helped him to clean some of the muck off the loathsome trays.

The food the Germans doled out in Salonika was almost non-existent. In the morning, after the first of the four or five parades each day, when our numbers were checked and rechecked and checked again, we received a small wedge-shaped portion of bread or a single round, hard biscuit. In the late afternoon we got the main meal of the day. We queued in a long agonising column to receive a cupful of watery soup. The contents became a sort of lottery, depending on whether the bored German guard dishing it out bothered to give the vat of repulsive looking soup a stir with his ladle, or just dipped it in and gave you the oily scum from the top. Sometimes you received coloured water with maybe a few grains of barley and one or two strands of half-cooked meat. If you were lucky the portion would be half full of the dubious solids. To this day I cannot bear to eat barley, the very smell of which takes me back to those vile tubs of so-called soup. Horse meat was the basic ingredient of the soup. The bones of the animal, boiled bare of any vestige of meat or gristle, were thrown into waste bins outside the "cook-house".

I can remember, sadly, witnessing a degrading scene and complete loss of control among my fellow prisoners at the waste bins. I saw a group of Glaswegians fighting among themselves over possession of the discarded bones, the victors retiring into a corner like dogs in a Liverpool back jigger to split the bones open and suck at the marrow inside. This animal behaviour was unusual and I never ever saw squabbling or fighting over food again during my time as a p.o.w. In fact the opposite was the norm and precious food was nearly always divided scrupulously and honestly.

Other desperate ways were used to obtain food. A black market was established with some of the guards, who were not averse to stealing our few belongings, for that is what the bartering amounted to. Valuable gold rings and watches, trinkets, family keepsakes and heirlooms were traded for unbelievably small pieces of stale bread or one or two cigarettes. Cigarettes were more important to some men than food. They were to become the currency of the prisoner-of-war camp, and the subsequent flourishing black market, I tried, unsuccessfully, to trade my stolen Italian pocket watch in the Cherry Blossom boot polish tin, but because the glass was broken nobody was interested.

The brutality of the Berliners in Salonika Camp was demonstrated to us forcefully shortly after we arrived. All hell was let loose in the early hours one dark moonless night, when our attempted slumbers were interrupted by rifle fire and bursts of machine gun fire. The firing seemed to come from all directions and Lance and I beat a hasty retreat, crawling on hands and knees, bullets whining over our heads, to the doubtful protection of the overcrowded barrack. Even there, we had to keep our heads down below the level of the windows as the indiscriminate fire came through the openings to splatter the plaster on the opposite wall.

At first light we discovered the cause of the mayhem.

Six corpses were scattered around the parade ground, and two more entangled grotesquely in the barbed wire of the perimeter fence. One of the bodies was straddled across the top of the double coils of the fence. The other was caught half way up the inner wall of wire, his torso almost cut in two by the machine-gun fire. The Germans would not let us move or touch the bodies. One of the unfortunate dead men lay spreadeagled at my feet, as I stood over him in the oven-like heat of the dusty parade ground, without food or water, for the rest of that day. They checked and double checked, over and over again, the hundreds of men in the camp, leaving the corpses where they had fallen, and did not dismiss the parade until late afternoon after they were satisfied with their count. It transpired that the escapees were all Palestinians who were attempting to get back home via Turkey, before being transferred to Germany. Rumour had it that six men had managed to get over the fence.

***

Thankfully, I don't remember very much of the four weeks I spent in that stinking prison. Like everyone I grew weaker and weaker and more despondent. Sergeant George Lunt, still the accepted leader of our little group, made valiant efforts to keep our spirits up. The one-time St. Teresa's School teacher, four or five years older than the rest of us, encouraged, or bullied, or persuaded us to shave and wash every morning, soap and razor blades being shared with those who had none. He even goaded us into trying some gentle P.T., and to take a walk around the parade ground. This exercise was carried out in our bare feet, our boots tied by the laces around our necks, bouncing up and down on our chests, George had convinced us back in our early days on Crete that it was necessary to preserve our already worn out boots for as long as possible. Nobody knew when, or if, we would ever get another pair.

Eventually, even George gave up his persistent cajoling, when it became an effort for most of us to even get on our feet without a bout of violent dizzyness and nausea. We grew more lethargic, spending most of the time sitting in the shade with our backs to the wall of the shabby barracks, desultorily trying to rid ourselves of the repulsive nits and lice in our clothes. Smokers were fortunate in this respect – it was remarkable that some men could still produce the odd cigarette end. They used the glowing end of the fag to run down the seam of their trousers, scorching, with a distinct snap, crackle and pop, the unwelcome visitors.

Jack Mooney still had his pack of playing cards used by four of us to play solo, breaking off from time to time to talk of the succulent meals Mother used to make. Sometimes dreaming of the fabulous meat pies I used to buy at Harry Petty's Cocoa Rooms on the way to night school.

So, although I had already been forced to leap for my life out of the frying pan of Greece into the smouldering tinderbox of Crete, when the exploding tinderbox blew me into the hell of Salonika Prison Camp, I thought life couldn't get much worse.

I was not sorry when word came that we were on the move to Germany.

Chapter 13

40 Hommes 8 Chevaux

On the day we left Salonika, after the customary hysterical shouting and foaming at the mouth of our German guards as we were counted, checked, cross checked, and counted again, we were sorted into groups of twenty, each group guarded by two of the sour-faced Berliners. One of them, with an ominous curling of his finger and a guttural command which we didn't understand, beckoned to me and Lance Ferguson.

We followed him to a long table outside the "cook-house" or store room. There we collected the rations for the twenty men in our group for what proved to be a week-long mystery tour. Two small, round, unlabelled tins, no bigger than my Cherry Blossom Boot Polish tin, and two hard biscuits for each man.

Lance and I stuffed the tins into our side packs. To carry the grey anaemic-looking biscuits, we made bags of our pullovers, by tying the sleeves in a knot. On the table was a debris of crumbs and bits and pieces of broken biscuits, like the penny-a-bag "brokes" in Blackledges Cake shop in Breck Road. Luck was with me again when the guard, after he had finished counting the biscuits, swept this pile of remnants and crumbs into my makeshift bag. We were also allowed to refill our now somewhat battered aluminium 4 gallon water container.

The tins contained a kind of corned beef, or the German equivlent of corned beef. Not as solid as Fray Bentos, it swam in a black gravy. Nevertheless it was very palatable and acceptable to our starved stomachs. So palatable that some of the men ate the contents en-route to the station, despite the warning that the food was to last four days. The biscuits were unbelievably rock-hard and almost impossible to break with the fingers. Those unfortunates with false teeth, or teeth loosened with the starvation diet we had endured for the past months, had to soak them first. Luckily, my teeth being sound and strong, I was able to chew successfully on the bits of broken biscuits for the whole of the train journey.

***

In complete contrast to the exuberant and rapturous welcome we had received from the Athenians, when we landed at Piraeus a few weeks earlier, we marched in silence through the almost deserted streets of Salonika to the Railway Station. We came to an exhausted halt at a long train of ancient cattle trucks of French rolling stock, World War 1 vintage. The open sliding doors on the wagons bore a small, brief text in fading white paint.

HOMMES 40

CHEVAUX 8

Egged on by the shouting guards and their brutal use of a rifle butt if someone protested too loudly, I threw into the truck the few possessions I carried, including the precious pullover-bag of remnants of broken biscuits. Lance Fergie and I still carried between us the even more precious container of water. After hoisting it up, we clambered into what was to be our mobile prison for the next six days.

The cattle truck had not been cleaned out after its previous cargo. The floor was littered with blobs of horse manure, clumps of wet straw and still carried the stink of the eight horses previously enjoying the hospitality of this antiquated Orient Express. I can't honestly say how many men were crammed into these ancient wooden trucks, which the French in 1914 had considered suitable for forty, but there must have been seventy or eighty men crowded in the truck in which I found myself. Suffice to say that there was not enough leg room for everyone to lie down at the same time. Men were forced to sit or lie with their knees up, or across someone else's legs or body. The five of us in my combine were fortunate to win a space in one of the corners of the wagon. There we were able to doss down with our backs to the wall under a small, barred opening just beneath the

111

roof.

There were four of these openings, one in each corner of the truck, the only source of light or fresh air. Measuring about twelve inches long by nine inches high, they were festooned with barbed wire hammered into the woodwork both on the inside and the outside of the vans.

We barely had time to sort ourselves out on the grimy floor, when the door closed with a grinding slam leaving us in semi-darkness despite the blazing sunshine outside. I heard the locking bar drop with a clang into position across the door. Then the shouts of the guards fading away as they walked down the train closing the doors.

The door was not opened again until more than two days later.

It seemed to be hours before the train eventually started on our long dreadful journey into the unknown. After jolting and jerking along on apparently octagonal wheels, for five minutes, we came to a juddering halt.

The heat of the afternoon sun very quickly turned the airless wagon into a stifling, baking oven. When darkness fell the temperature dropped dramatically and we were glad of the closeness of our neighbour as we huddled together shivering with the cold. Some of the lads were wishing they were back in the hold of the rusty old Hamburg tramper, that had ferried us from Crete.

There were no sanitary facilities of any sort for the eighty or so men squashed like sardines into the van; unlike the cargo boat's crude, home made, fresh air "heads" clinging precariously to the side of the vessel. A couple of enterprising New Zealanders provided an emergency facility for the many "squiffers" – chronic diarrhoea or dystentry sufferers – by going to work with a pig-sticker (the Army-issue jack-knife) on a loose knot in the floorboards near the door. The Kiwis hacked out a reasonably sized outlet for the troubled squatters, and the easier disposal of urine filled cans. For some of the occupants, like our party in the corner, this necessitated a careful clamber over numerous prostrate bodies, to the accompaniment of obscenities heaped on the careless, or the weak, or the unsteady.

I couldn't help comparing the Kiwis' handiwork with the

newly patented Twyfords Silent Syphonic Closet Suite, which I had been diligently selling on the showroom at Baxendales, some eighteen months previously. Fortunately for me, and to the envy of those in my combine, I never used this home-made hole-in-the-floor closet, as I didn't have a bowel movement during the whole of the journey.

The resourceful Colonials also provided the smokers with a means of lighting their ciggies, thin mini-cigarettes made from carefully hoarded dog-ends hand-rolled in a page from an Army Pay-Book or the paper-thin page of a Bible. Using a piece of thick string, they made a taper, or long spill, lighting one end and suspending it from the roof of the wagon. The end of the string was glowing steadily as a firefly when we left the truck six days later.

There seemed to be no order or method in the progress of the train. It would clank along at a snail's pace, halt for a few minutes and then go backwards to wherever we had come from. Sometimes, after picking up speed, the brakes would suddenly be applied, violently, bringing the train to a grinding, juddering halt. The buffers of the trucks crashed into each other with a staccato clapping reminiscent of a finger running down the keyboard of a piano. I was reminded of the shunting engines in the coal depot at Breck Road railway sidings. Sometimes we would remain stationary for five minutes, sometimes for hours on end. In the complete and utter silence of a lost ghost train, we wondered if our captors had completely abandoned us. During the long halts, the silence would be broken occasionally by frustrated inmates, hammering on the sides of the trucks, answered by the thumping of rifle butts and the occasional burst of rifle fire.

In the late afternoon of the third day, during one of the more prolonged halts, the door was suddenly thrown open. To cries of "raus, raus, schieszen, schieszen" the guards indicated we could get out and attend to the calls of nature.

I will never forget the glorious smell of the countryside as I tumbled out of the cattle truck, my eyes blinking at the sudden change from the darkness of the truck to the bright, brilliant sunshine of a lovely Autumn afternoon.

The train had stopped in a cutting flanked by high grass

banks, rising at an angle from the railway line. The guards, rifles unslung, had lined up along the top of the bank, some manning heavy machine guns spaced at intervals along the line, leaving no doubt as to what would happen if any attempt was made to escape. However most of the prisoners on the train were not in any sort of condition to run away. I doubt that most could have made it to the top of the bank, and we had no idea where we were, anyway. At least I didn't, except that we were somewhere in the middle of the Balkans. I only ever heard of one successful escape from any of the trains taking the thousands of prisoners from Greece to Germany. An infantry major, like our enterprising New Zealanders, dug a hole in the floorboards of the truck. It was large enough to squeeze through. Somehow he made his escape after lying doggo between the moving wheels of the wagons.

The doors were opened on only two more occasions during our journey. The second time we found ourselves in another desolate railway cutting in the middle of nowhere. The weather had changed and our fresh air foray and official toilet stop was accompanied by a steady heavy rain. Although more than welcome after the stink of the truck, it added to our miseries when we climbed back soaked to the skin.

The last occasion when the door was opened before my journey's end was in a busy railway station. The lofty, smoke encrusted, glass-domed ceiling of the station recalled nostalgically the sounds of the chuffing, puffing and hissing steam engines of Lime Street Station, Liverpool, with a high pitched whistle heralding the arrival of the 10 pm passenger train from London. But the station was Belgrade, Yugoslavia, and I was in a cattle truck after a five day trip across Europe.

This time we were not allowed out of the trucks. Surprisingly, however, the Germans had permitted a group of nuns on to the platform to dispense a warm drink to the occupants of the foul smelling cattle wagons. The guards formed a line along the length of the platform, watching silently as these Angels of Mercy moved down the length of the train stopping at each door to give the occupants a welcoming ladle of a warm, fragrant mint tea. There was no talking or communication of any sort between us, except for a subdued smile of compassion, and

114

the brief Sign of the Cross I received from the young novice who ladled the welcome herbal drink into my home made tin cup. The nuns were shadowed, carefully, by guards who watched every move they made. When the occupants of each truck had each received a drink, the door was immediately slammed shut. I never found out to what religious order the nuns belonged, nor did I ever see nuns again during my time as a prisoner-of-war.

We spent yet another very cold and frustrating night crammed in the stationary cattle truck. It was dawn before the train re-commenced its stop, go, stop, go, painful progress.

To relieve the boredom of the monotonous journey, it was possible to stand on kit piled up in the corner, to gaze out of the "window" and gulp in fresh air. Always a fresh air fiend I took advantage of this at every opportunity. The landscape had changed since leaving behind the hot, dry, dusty brown hills and mountains of Crete and Greece. As we entered Germany, or rather the then Southern-Austrian annexe to Germany, we passed through green, thickly wooded mountains and grassy valleys reminiscent of North Wales. But there were no sheep grazing in these lush looking pastures as on Moel Fammau, and I saw very few cattle.

Hay-making was in progress, and when the train stopped, yet again for no apparent reason, alongside one of these Alpine meadows, I watched an elderly man cutting the long grass. He stopped his steady, rhythmical swing of the scythe to gaze, quizzically, at the train as he took out a honing stone from a leather pouch on his belt. Upturning the scythe he scraped the sharpener along the blade half a dozen times and then, after hawking and spitting out the contents of his throat, proceeded to pack tobacco into the large bowl of a strange looking twelve inch long pipe, dangling from his lips down onto his chest. His slow, deliberate movements were the first signs of normal behaviour I had seen for months.

Elderly women were working in the pasture with him, turning over swaths of grass drying in the sun, using a wide wooden hayfork with long curved tines. Others were heaping grass on to pyramid-shaped wooden frames spaced at intervals around the field. Two young boys were forking grass on to a long, four-wheeled, vee-shaped hay-wagon to which were harnessed two gigantic bulls with curled horns three or four feet wide projecting from their heads. They had heavy wooden yokes fixed across their massive shoulders and below their necks. I was to work on many occasions with these gentle giants. Light-brown, smooth coated oxen. Beautiful, patient and peaceful bovines, pulling an empty cart with the same effortless, careful steady pace as a heavily loaded wagon. Or dragging without apparent effort a gigantic, four metre long log over the uneven ground of a forest floor.

Resuming our painful progress after the usual frustrating unexplainable delay, the train slowly bumped its way through the delightful countryside. I was surprised and intrigued at the neatness and cleanliness of the little picturesque stations and villages we were now passing through. I was also intrigued by the attire of the few people standing on the platforms. Particularly the men. Mostly elderly or middle-aged, dressed in peculiar short leather trousers held up by decorated braces over brief smartly-cut waistcoats. Some were wearing green and brown leather jackets with little bone buttons shaped like a cow's horn. All of them wore green trilby hats with badges around the brim, sporting a shaving brush on the side of the crown. Most carried a walking stick which appeared to be decorated with little silver medals, and were smoking pipes like the farmer in the field. Apart from the strange looking pipes, and the distinctive dress, they all looked perfectly normal people to me. Reading the morning paper, or chatting away with each other as they waited for the 11.15 to take them into town or wherever.

In the afternoon on the sixth day of our horrendous journey. we came to a halt at one of these countryside stations. From my vantage point in the corner I could see the name **Wolfsburg** pinned to a lamp-post. After the usual long, frustrating wait in the semi-darkness of the stinking truck, the door was suddenly slung open. The guards, with their now familiar shouts of "raus, raus", "gemma, gemma" bullied us on to the platform.

We had arrived at our destination.

Stalag XV111A.

Once again my luck had held. I found out later that the train had been split into two sections at Wolfsburg. One, with me in it, remaining at Wolfsberg, the other enduring another two day journey to a hell-hole of a Stalag, outside Berlin.

Chapter 14

The Delouser of Wolfsburg

I was in no fit condition to walk very far, so it was a good thing that the Stalag was fairly close to the railway station. I was also in no condition to take in the details of the huge prison camp, being more interested in the "wonderful" meal that the English-speaking German Officer, who greeted us at the entrance, said was ready for us.

To my surprise the meal proved to be a generous helping of cabbage with two potatoes boiled in their skins, bits of Mother Earth sticking to them. The feast was not as good as it appeared, however, although very welcome after the famine I had endured for the last two months. I scoffed the lot, (including the bits of soil), except for the black, putrid blobs in the middle of the potato, a standard feature of all Stalag potatoes, or pig potatoes, as the kriegies (kriegsgefangenener, or prisoner-of-war) called them. The cabbage was, of course, the renowned German Sauerkraut or pickled cabbage. To my sensitive nose, even in those circumstances, the bitter, vinegary, slimey sauerkraut had a rancid smell which I could never get used to. Nevertheless it went down well on that occasion. In my case, having not availed myself of the New Zealanders' version of a Twyford's Silent Syphonic Closet for the six days in the cattle truck, it also proved to be a marvellous opening medicine too!!!

After the "meal", I was more than happy to join the long queue for the delouser, which included the forgotten luxury of a shower. The delousing plant was under the supervision of a couple of guards, who made sure, with the aid of a rifle butt that every man went through the proceedure. Surprisingly some men appeared to be reluctant to take a shower. It was operated by Sergeant Charlie McIlroy and Gunner George Martin, both with me in 424 Battery of the 106th. They had been in the Camp some weeks before I got there having been captured in Greece.

They worked the plant on a conveyor-belt system, syphoning 50 naked men at a time through the shower block, after they had put all their lousy, filthy clothes in a huge, noisy revolving drum to be de-loused and steam-cleaned. When it was my turn to go through, George Martin looked after my few personal possessions including the watch in the Cherry Blossom Boot Polish tin and some photographs and letters.

"Five minutes only, lads. Five minutes, and then the Jerry will turn the water off," shouted Charlie, "so make the most of it and get a move on. Sorry, there's no towels or soap."

There was just enough space in the shower for the men packed shoulder to shoulder and backside to backside, with just enough water to share between two or three men, under the glorious tepid spray from each shower rose. Even without soap, that brief encounter with the limited warm water was heavenly.

After, what seemed to me, only a couple of minutes the water was turned off and the doors at the other end opened. Dripping wet and paddling through pools left by the previous bathers, I rescued my clothes from the delousing drum. Still too hot to touch after the high temperature cleaning, they were wrinkled and shrunk. Before I put them on, my body was sprayed in all the private parts, liberally, with clouds of a delousing powder by a white-coated, masked German orderly. A somewhat humiliating experience accepted by me without demur. Thankfully, the delousing treatment was effective. The nits and lice had vanished, and I never experienced them again, until the last few weeks of my time as a prisoner-of-war.

The shocking nightmare of my early days of captivity in Crete, and the hardships, starvation and brutality of the Salonika Prison Camp followed by the terrible week long journey in the cattle truck, was nothing to that experienced by Russian prisoners taken by the Germans when they overran Russia to the gates of Stalingrad.

I was not in Wolfsburg when the first Russian prisoners arrived, but the following extract from the reminiscences of Padre John Ledgerwood, written in the Stalag in 1944, graphically describe their arrival. This account of life in Stalag XV111A was never published. It came to me from New Zealand in 1998 via Ernie McGrae and "Taffy" Smith, both very much involved with John Ledgerwood in theatrical productions in the Camp.

"Reminiscences, or potted history, of Stalag XV111A, Wolfsberg as remembered and recorded by John Ledgerwood in Wolfsberg, Austria, in July 1944."

"First Russian Prisoners of War Arrive!!!

"Winter was closing in on us at Wolfsberg and already the ground was covered by a thin layer of snow when the first batch of Russions stumbled into the Lager. They had been captured many weeks previously and had tasted no solid food during the seventeen days train journey. The Germans had packed these poor creatures into cattle trucks, one hundred to a truck. The sliding doors were sealed, fresh air filtered through two small apertures where the roof joined the walls of the truck and the occupants stood, more tightly packed than sardines in a tin.

"For want of air, for want of food, for want of facilities to perform their natural functions – and they were all sick – these prisoners died in scores. They died where they stood. Where they stood for as many days as it took the train to arrive at Wolfsberg. The German guards told me that when the doors of the trucks were opened at Wolfsberg railway station the stench was so nauseating that they vomited. Those of the prisoners who were still alive, although mere skeletons, were literally whipped along the mile and a half stretch of roadway to the Lager. Exhaustion compelled many to drop at the wayside, but they were beaten to their feet again and lashed with six-thonged whips by their own specially selected countrymen. At the Lager, they were made to strip themselves naked and stand in the snow until their turn came to be showered and deloused. As the day wore on, life for some of them just ebbed out, and they dropped dead in the snow. Others died under the hot showers and their bodies were pitched out and remained uncovered for hours.

"The Germans would not allow us British to feed, clothe or give medical attention to the Russian prisoners of war. We were locked in our compound and surrounded with an armed guard.

"With the Russians came the dreaded typhus. Stalag

120

XV111A came immediately under quarantine regulations, and all nationalities were confined to camp for nearly two months. Fortunately for us, the Germans, scared of entering the various living quarters of the prisoners of war, left the organizing and carrying out of emergency precautions to the British and French medical Staff. During the two months of quarantine, nearly five hundred Russians died, two French prisoners of war, four Germans and no British. The Germans gave us carte blanche in the matter of emergency precautions, and gave little personal assistance in the efforts made to restrict the spreading of the epidemic, but in fairness, I must say that they gave the best medical attention at their disposal to those British and French prisoners of war who had contracted typhus and were isolated from the rest of the camp. The Russians they ignored.

"The quarantine period had one good result for the British. No one could be sent to work. Christmas came, our first in captivity. I am happy to write that the Russians shared our material benefits. Secretly we were collecting and storing tins of food, sweets, cigarettes and clothing for "Joe's" boys. On December, 24th, 1941, cases of good things were smuggled, under cover of darkness, into the Russian compound."

Russian POW arriving Stalag, XVIIIA, 1941.

Exhausted, I spent my first night in Stalag XV111A sleeping in the comparitive luxury of a one time Austrian cavalry stable, under a grey German "ersatz" blanket, on bare wooden boards.

I was too tired to notice the fug given off by the three hundred comatose bodies, nor the pong of the sweaty feet of my burly Australian neighbour, until I woke up next morning.

My first breakfast in Stalag XV111A was a small wedge-shaped piece of dark brown, blackish bread with a smudge of margarine, a tea-spoonful of a thin watery jam and a ladle of a herbal tea similar to the beverage the nuns of Belgrade had dispensed in the cattle trucks. Very tasty, acceptable and almost a return to civilized eating once again. But it only served to stimulate my appetite alarmingly and make me hungrier still.

We then queued up again, for men still garbed in the shorts and shirts of the Middle East, to receive a motley collection of clothes.

All sorts of strange looking uniforms, or parts of uniforms, were given out at random, irrespective of size or quality. The shabby, fourth-hand collection had come from the far corners of Europe. Pantaloons from Italy, cavalry breeches and colourful jackets from Poland, and saucer-like peaked caps with black ear-muffs from Russia, and for the bootless, solid wooden sabots from Holland. Those unfortunates without socks received an uncomfortable substitute, a twelve inch square of ersatz material, like thin felt, to wrap around tender feet before donning the heavy clogs. I was thankful for the kit I had found in the RASC dump in Canea, when Lance and I dodged out of the compound, but was forced to discard my worn-out, odd-sized boots for the awful one-piece clogs.

For the first time since being captured, I was registered, officially, as a prisoner-of-war. Under the direction of an English-speaking Austrian civilian, my nationality, name and home address, Army Number and Rank, were recorded. I was given a rectangular aluminium identity tag with the number 5567 stamped on it. Henceforth I was known as Kriegsgefangenener Arthur, D. No. 5567.

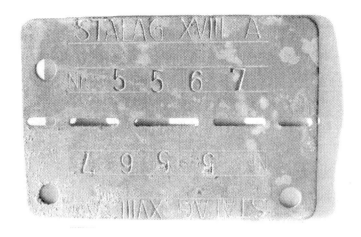

My Identity Disc

I also had to fill in the blanks of a pre-printed post-card, which I addressed to my Mother, telling her that I was safe, sound and being well looked after by my German hosts, in a sort of glorified holiday camp, whether I agreed or not.

The Austrian civilian, promptly christened "The Slave Driver" by the wags of the 106th, was also responsible for allotting us to one of the many arbeitslagers – working camps – attached to Stalag XV111A. We had already discovered that we would be compelled to carry out some kind of work.

When my turn came to stand in front of him, he asked me what work I did in civilian life. When I told him I had been a clerk or salesman, he pointed to one of the smaller groups of men who had already been interviewed and told me to join them.

From that particular moment in time I parted company from the buddies in my Combine. We were five close friends, who from the beginning of the war had been together through thick and thin, hunger and thirst, shot and shell, particularly throughout the Greek and Cretan campaigns.

There was no argument. There was no discussion. There was no time to say "cheerio" or "goodbye". The prisoners went to whichever group the Slave Driver indicated. Mate parting from mate, brother parting from brother, and in one case father parting from son. Little did I realise at the time, that he was doing me a great favour. For all my pals ended up breaking boulders on the side of an iron mountain, the infamous Eisenerz iron mine.

I became one of an assorted group of twenty-four Other Ranks. Three Australians, five New Zealanders, four Liverpool lads, six Welshmen from Swansea, Cardiff and Carmarthen, three Lancashire lads, a Geordie and two Scots. A truly mixed bag, indeed, of mostly volunteer Britons and Colonials who were to become my new close companions and firm friends during the following two years.

Within an hour the group left Stalag XV111A, accompanied by four guards, to board a train at Wolfsburg station. This time, in complete and utter contrast to the horrendous journey across Europe in the stinking cattle truck, I travelled in the comfort and privacy of a luxurious, upholstered railway carriage.

Our destination proved to be Knittelfeld, Carinthia, Lower Austria.

Chapter 15

The Sound of Music in a Gasthaus

On the short march from Knittlefeld Station to the outskirts of the town, we came to the smoking chimneys of a dusty looking brickworks. The German sergeant in charge indicated that this was to be our place of work. We halted at a house, in a road facing the factory, and were ushered up an external staircase to our living, sleeping and eating quarters on the first floor. The ground floor was occupied by the four guards.

The accommodation consisted of one room, the floor space of which was mostly taken up by two sleeping platforms fixed one above the other, from wall to wall. Two trestle tables with forms were squeezed into the remaining space. Each platform had twelve folded blankets, one for each man, indicating his allotted sleeping space. There were no mattresses and no division between each space. I was fortunate enough to collar the space against the wall, at one end of the platform beneath the only window – and source of fresh air – in the room. The few belongings I carried in JM.'s side pack were stored at the head of my sleeping space.

The lavatory was in a tiny, smelly room at the rear of the house on the ground floor. A basic convenience, indeed, comprising a row of rough planks with holes formed in the centre, fastened between the narrow walls, over a frightening stinking cesspit in the ground. There were three or four cold water taps over chipped, enamel bowls on a bench for our washing and bathing facilities. This room was out of bounds after we were locked up at eight o'clock in the evening, a bucket being left for our overnight use. I never made up my mind which was the worst, the cesspit or the night bucket.

After sorting ourselves out as best we could in the limited space available, the Feld-Webel in charge went to great length with his limited English, to explain the conditions and routine we would be expected to follow in the camp.

We were, firstly, to elect an interpreter and/or Man of Confidence or Confidence Man. The Camp Leader, who was to be a willing volunteer, acceptable both by his fellow prisoners and the Sergeant. The onerous job was additional to his work in the Brickworks. He was to act as a go between, or spokesman. All requests, complaints, instructions, orders and arguments to be conveyed solely by the Confidence Man to the Sergeant and vice versa. Picking a Confidence Man was easier said than done. Nobody amongst the motley collection of half-starved strangers thrown together so suddenly, bemused and apprehensive at what lay ahead, wanted to take on such a responsibilty. Nobody spoke German anyway.

Except Dai Davies, one of the Welshmen from the Heavy Ack-Ack Battery on Crete.

Welsh speaking Dai Davies was fluent in French and also had a smattering of German, which he had already tried out on the guards and the Sergeant. So his natural ability with languages coupled with his firm, friendly manner made him the best choice for the job of Confidence Man. After some persuasion, and in the absence of any other volunteer, he reluctantly offered to try his hand. In my later extensive experience of working camps I never met a better 'Vertraunsman' than Dai Davies.

With some difficulty, and now with the aid of Dai, the guard explained to us that we would be starting work the next morning at 7.30, and finish at 5.30 in the afternoon with a break of half an hour at mid-day. We would be employed on all the ancillary work that went with making bricks. Digging clay, filling kilns with uncooked bricks, emptying hot kilns of red hot bricks, loading wagons, brushing up, and generally keeping things tidy.

We were to be paid for our labours in Lagergelt, camp money after a suitable amount had been deducted for our "board and lodging".

It was an almost worthless piece of paper to become known as Monopoly Money by the kriegies. It was a toy-shop imitation of the real Reichmark and could not be passed over shop counters in the normal way. We were not consulted about the amount we were to be paid, nor the amount deducted for our "keep". There was no system of bookkeeping or records that I was aware of. No signatures were requested and no payslips issued. They seemed to pay the wages in varied amounts whenever they felt like it. Some weeks I was paid, but more often than not I wasn't paid at all.

Camp money could only be exchanged at certain shops, for certain limited goods. But only at the convenience of one of the guards to accompany us to the shop, when it was open and when we were not working. We used Lagergelt to buy razor blades (when the shop had them in stock), pencils and childrens' drawing books, Rizla cigarette papers and hand-held cigarette making machines. I bought a cheap cardboard suitcase with the almost worthless notes. Later on Taffy Griffiths and I each bought mandolins. The ancient woman shop-keeper seemed glad to get rid of them.

The 'Lagergelt' was treated with disdain by the prisoner-of-war. It was often used to light cigarettes, as an emergency toilet paper or to start a fire. Those who had the foresight, however, to carefully keep the money in the bottom of their haversack had the last laugh. At the end of the war this despised paper money was exchanged by the British Authorities at a favourable rate.

Saturday afternoon and Sunday was to be our "free time" when we would be expected to bathe, wash our clothes, clean the billet, write letters home, and generally enjoy ourselves in the restrictive confines of the room on the first floor.

The Sergeant also explained that the kitchen facilities on the ground floor had not been completed in time for our arrival. So for two or three weeks we would be taking our meals in the town.

For the first time during the laboured explanations by the Feld Webel on our forthcoming life in a prisoner-of-war working camp, the twenty-four prisoners showed some real interest.

"For Christ's sake, Dai," piped up husky George East, one of the Australians, "tell the fuckin' bastard we're starvin' 'ungry. Ask him when we're goin' to get some bloody tucker."

The German No. 1, although unable to understand "tell the fuckin' bastard we're hungry", nevertheless realised that the flashing eyes and irritableness of the big Australian, was some form of complaint.

"Was ist das fuckin' bastard?" he wanted to know from Dai.

Our newly elected Vertrauensmann – Confidence Man – experiencing for the first time the direction of poisoned arrows fired from the bow of a barrack-room lawyer, poured oil on the troubled waters. As he was to do time and time again.

He learned quickly from experience, however, that awkward decisions and situations were sometimes helped along by the attitude of the Guard Commander and by the guards. They were much older men than us who had been hurriedly mobilised after the outbreak of the war and thrown, most of them unwillingly, into the Army. It soon became obvious that they wanted a quiet life. In particular our Guard Commander, a former head waiter of a restaurant in Vienna. The war in Russia was going particularly well for the Germans at that time, but some comrades from his Unit had already been transferred to the Russian Front. The Feld-Webel didn't relish going to Russia, whether they were winning or not. All he wanted was a smooth-running, trouble-free arbeitslager. We soon found that, often he was more prepared to give, than to take.

So, haltingly, Dai Davis managed to point out that we were all ravenous with hunger, and had not eaten since leaving the Stalag that morning.

Without more ado, the Feldt Webel finished his penny lecture and we formed up again outside, two guards at the head of the squad and two guards at the rear. We marched back to the town centre of Knittlefeld and a Gasthaus on the main road. A sort of restaurant-cum-public house. Civilians were sitting at tables at one side of the spacious dining room. Apart from one or two inquisitive glances at the twenty-four prisoners, attired in the motley collection of multi-coloured uniforms from the four corners of Europe, they ignored us. We, and the guards, sat on the other side of the dining room.

This totally unexpected visit to a civilian pub/restaurant, was just another puzzle in the unaccustomed world of the prisoner-of-war, which I had found myself thrown into. The luxury of the clean, neat Gasthaus was in complete contrast to the privations I had endured since my capture. The tables, seating eight of us on each, were covered by white table cloths and places were set for each man with knives, forks and spoons. There was a large, glass carafe of water in the centre. And, biggest surprise of all, we were waited at the table by an attractive, blonde, buxom young woman wearing a long dirndl or coloured skirt.

Somewhat overawed by our sudden return to the human race, and mouths drooling with the delightful smell emanating from somewhere at the back of the restaurant, we sat in silent anticipation of the gargantuan dinner shortly to be placed before us on the white linen.

The silence was broken when the vision from "The Sound of Music", came hurrying from the kitchen and placed in the middle of the table, not a cauldron of casserole pork or chicken, nor a dishful of the fried German sausage we had heard so much about, but a plate containing eight small wedges of dark brown bread.

To all of us eyeing this offering it presented an obvious problem. A full discussion immediately took place to decide who would get the biggest piece. There were exactly eight pieces of the bread on the plate. One for each man. But they weren't all the same size and they weren't very big wedges at that. So it was agreed that, using an old pack of playing cards someone produced out of his pocket, we draw lots to decide who got the first chance to pick the biggest piece. Or what he thought was the biggest piece. Later this problem was eventually sorted out by the blonde-haired waitress, who guessed the difficulty we were in and solved it herself by placing a piece in front of each man.

The bread was a very dark brown bread – black bread – baked in the form of a flattish, round loaf about eight inches in diameter and an inch and a half thick. We were to learn that it was made with flour containing a goodly proportion of potato "flour" and sawdust "flour", both of which were in plentiful supply in Austria at that time. There was an attractive, crunchy, crusty surface to the loaf, but just underneath the crust there was a repulsive, black slimy deposit, a quarter of an inch thick, the result apparently, of the foreign bodies in the flour. In my state of near starvation this bread was food from the Gods and during the early days of my captivity, particularly, I could never get enough of it. Later, I found the best way to eat it was to toast it. And toast it well.

At that first meal in the Gasthous the bread was accompanied by a portion of a tasty stew. Not exactly the casserole of pork which I had been dreaming about, but tasty because I hadn't eaten anything like it for months. It comprised mostly of potatoes, with a smattering of carrot and turnip floating in a watery, goulash gravy. Lucky was the man who found any scraps of meat in his portion, but just the same the stew was very, very acceptable. But in no way was it satisfying and left me hungrier after I had finished eating than when I started.

We dined in the splendour of the Gasthaus in Knittlefeld for two weeks. The meals were varieties of the potato soup we had on that first day.

Potato soup, potato and turnip soup, cabbage soup, potato, turnip and cabbage soup. Occasionally, hot water soup. This was a clear, sort of consomme soup looking very like dish water and tasting vaguely of chicken. If you were lucky, it came with a few grains of rice or a spoonful of noodles. These soups were sometimes flavoured with herbs like oregano and caraway seeds and the paprika of the goulash. Two days a week they gave us the awful pickled cabbage – sauerkraut – with which they had greeted us on our arrival at Wolfsberg. Not enough of it anyway, but unlike the Stalag variety it was clean and the potatoes free of skins, dirt and rotten centres.

We seemed to be accepted, without comment, by the civilians eating on the other side of the room. We had another pleasant surprise one day when Maria of the 'Sound of Music', placed a mug of beer before each man. On enquiring about our benefactor, Dai was told that the drinks came from one of the civilians. We never found out who had been able to persuade the Sergeant to bend the rules to make this unusual generous gesture to us.

For breakfasts we had another small wedge of bread and, two or three times a week, there was a helping of polienta. A thickish, yellow porridge made of maize – another staple crop of Austria. This was a tasteless, bland dish sometimes enlivened, tantalisingly, by a small spoonful of watery jam, or a dot of hot bacon fat the size of a 10p piece, plonked in the centre of the porridge. A great bacon and egg man in happy days long gone by, I very seldom left home without a bacon and egg breakfast. So I found these tokens or offerings of bacon fat tormenting and frustrating. Some mornings I would carefully scrape every vestige of the yellow porridge off my plate, leaving the bacon fat in the centre to drool over before I mopped it up with my piece of bread. Tormenting myself with memories of "rub-arounds" when my Mother, after finishing cooking bacon and eggs for six of us, would say, "Do you want to rub around the pan, Doug, before I wash it?" Sometimes, unable to hold myself in check, I would hastily eat the warm bacon fat first, then try to barter with one of my comrades for their spoonful, in exchange for my plate of polienta. There were no takers.

We also received at breakfast a mugful of coffee. It was the German version of coffee, a not unpleasant ersatz drink made from ground acorn or beech nuts. There was never any sugar or milk.

Regretfully, after a couple of weeks, our thrice daily trips to the civilised amenities of the Gasthous and the silent ministrations of the pretty waitress, came to an end. Henceforth our meagre meals were prepared by an elderly woman in the kitchen on the ground floor of our lock-up, and eaten on the cramped tables of the overcrowded, smelly room on the first floor.

Chapter 16

A Letter from Home

One night early in November we were sitting down to our evening meal of the usual potato soup, when the excited Feld-Webel came in with his hands full of letters. The first mail to reach us since our capture in June. His obvious excitement and pleasure as the bearer of good news, added to our pleasure in receiving the long awaited letters from home.

There was one for me.

It was from my brother Alf, typed on a standard, folded airmail letter of the kind still available in Post Offices today. Headed in bold letters

PRISONER OF WAR POST
Write very clearly within the lines to avoid delay in censorship

FROM (Sender's full name & address) Mr ALFRED E.
ARTHUR,
3, WOOD LANE,
GREASBY,
WIRRAL, Chesh.
Wednesday, 17th Septr., 1941.

Dear Doug,
It is now a week since we received your first letter and card together and I purposely held up writing to you at once, so that Dad's letter would reach you first.
Well Doug, I do hope the news of Mum's death did not come as too great a shock to you, but frankly Doug, Mother is now far better off and as you know, I am the last fellow in the world to see her go on suffering as she did, knowing

*that there was no real cure, and hoping for her to continue
the struggle. I feel sure that you will feel the same way
about it as I do, so I hope that you are not too upset about it
all. I think it is much harder for you under the
circumstances and goodness only knows, we all felt it at
home at the time, but I am glad to say that everybody has
shown a very brave face and the girls have carried on
wonderfully.*

*I did not like telling you the true position in my previous
letters, but I think you had some idea that Mum's health
was not improving during the last twelve months and when
she took to bed June 19th I felt that the end was in sight
and as a matter of fact she only lay in bed for a month and I
am pleased to say that she passed away quietly in her sleep.
There was only Gran and Rene with her at the time and she
did not say anything at all. I left her at 2.30 to go to the
office and she was quite normal then and spoke to me and
Gran told me that she fell asleep at 3.0 p.m. and passed
away most peacefully at 4.0 p.m.*

*I think Dad has told you that we received the notice
advising us that you were missing about 8 days before Mum
passed away, so naturally we did not let her know, but
Doug, I will never forget that Thursday afternoon, I felt that
our rotten luck would never end.*

*However, on the following Saturday that £10 Draft you sent
Mum arrived and she was so pleased and grateful to
receive it. You see I had told her that I had sent you a cable
to let you know that she was far from well and she thought
you had arranged to send her the money because she was
ill. Of course, she had received an earlier letter from you
stating that you would be sending her a gift of some sorts.*

*I am afraid Mum did a bit of quiet worrying over you and
did not say anything about it to us, so I was very pleased
that she did not know what had happened. She asked me on
several occasions if I thought you were in Crete, but I
always told her I did not think so and this is the truth, so it
came as a terrible shock to me when we received the news
but my word I was pleased when Rene 'phoned me last
Tuesday week to say that your letter and card had arrived.*

It was the best news received at home for weeks.

A further letter has arrived today, just 8 days after the first, so that is not so bad and I think you will be receiving plenty of letters from friends, but I don't know how you will be able to answer them all, as I see that you are rationed for letters and cards. About parcels Doug, we can send them through the Red Cross, once every three months and only next of kin can send them, also we are only allowed to put chocolate in. No other food, but I understand that the R.C. give you a parcel every week. We can send Cigs. through Coopers and Novels through W.H.Smith's, so if you want any let us know, but you did not smoke much before. I have put my home address on this letter, so memorise it in case of need, but you need not reply direct to me as I will follow up your letter at home. If there is anything you require like razor blades or soap let us know and we will see what we can fix up with the Red Cross and will send them with the Woolen things you asked for.

Well Doug, space is getting short, but I will write again in a few days time and I am taking one of these letter-cards home to Dad and will get him to write again.

KEEP SMILING SON & BEST WISHES.

Alf.

I felt the blood drain from my face as I read the unexpected news of my Mother's death. Tears filled my eyes as I got up from the table and made my way, silently, to the barred window of the little balcony at the end of the room. A minute or so later Geoff Hallet, who had been sitting opposite me at the table, joined me.

"Bad news, Doug?" he said.

Without saying anything, I handed him Alf's letter which he quickly read through and then, after putting a sympathetic arm around my shoulders, without comment, he went back into the room and left me on my own. I have never forgotten Geoff's unspoken sympathy and compassion that day.

My thoughts ran riot. I had not received the letter from my Father, mentioned by Alf. I knew my Mother had not been well and that she had been in hospital, but I had no idea that she was seriously ill. There had been no indication in any of the letters I received after my call-up, that in fact her illness was terminal. Nor was the subject mentioned on my week-end leaves and final embarkation leave before the Regiment left Barlborough. I guessed that she had died of cancer, but there was no mention in Alf's letter that she had died of the dreaded disease. Conscience stricken, I wondered whether I had been unthinking and unfeeling when I had refused the opportunity to join the Immatures who left the Regiment at Barlborough because they were under age to go abroad. Should I have taken more notice of my Father's letter when he offered to write to my C.O. for compassionate leave, way back at Barlborough? Should I have done this, or should I have done that?

Like millions of others in those far off dark days, when a man's fate could be decided by the stroke of a clerk's pen in a Battery Office, or by an unknown politician a thousand miles away deciding to honour a long forgotten pledge to a country I had scarcely ever heard of, or the casual wave of the white-gloved hand of a red-hatted Military Policeman to turn right to your death or incarceration for four years, or turn left to Home and Freedom, I never found the answers to life's many disturbing, emotional conundrums. The questions still remain unanswered and unsolved.

But I wasn't the only one to receive bad tidings in those first letters from Home. One of my new companions had lost a young brother, fifteen years old and not long out of school, on a Merchant Ship somewhere in the Atlantic. Two of the South Wales boys heard that their homes in Swansea had been flattened in the bombing of the Battle of Britain, and a "Dear John" letter had been received by another of my comrades saying that his wife had run off with a Polish Airman and taken his eighteen-month old son with her.

However, this was not the time nor place for me to grieve properly. It was four years later that I really had to face the fact of the loss of my Mother. Life in my new environment was hard and uncertain. I never knew what was waiting for me just around the corner. Every day was a day to be lived through without too much thought of the day after.

Living conditions in the arbeitslager were primitive and overcrowded, and food was still the main topic of conversation. I was always hungry.

Chapter 17

The Brickworks

We started work at the siegelfabrick at seven-thirty on the morning after our arrival.

My first job was in the drying sheds where the wet bricks were placed in alternately angled rows, one above the other, a space between each brick, to dry off before baking in the kilns.

A kind, elderly lady, old enough to be my grandmother, was my teacher in the art of handling these wet bricks. Throwing them, two at a time, some seven or eight feet, without damage. An expert, judging from the way she handled the heavy wet clay. She had been brought back to work after her retirement, when the factory was re-opened using the forced labour of the prisoners-of-war. Despite my cack-handed efforts she painstakingly taught me how to throw the bricks, or catch them after being thrown accurately by her from the trolley of bricks pushed by a fellow prisoner from the mixing room.

She also painstakingly taught me my first few halting words of German and was genuinely concerned, when one afternoon, lack of energy forced me to sit down to rest. The next day she gave me two "kuchen", little home-made, shortbread biscuits. A delicious, unexpected surprise.

Unfortunately, I did not stay on that job for very long, for they recruited another civilian worker and I was transferred to the mixing machine where the wet, clay bricks were extruded.

Knittlefeld brick factory was owned and managed by a short, foppish, rotund Austrian-Italian of indeterminate age. He made a tour of inspection of the factory every morning and afternoon. He wore the Austrian "leder-hosen" on the warm days of late summer, the soft leather shorts exposing his pudgy knees and emphasising his barrel-like stomach. With the colder days of autumn he draped a long, kind of theatrical, green cape over his shoulders, reaching down almost to the ground. On his head, was a matching green trilby hat with a feather sticking out of the crown. Prominent on the lapel of his jacket was pinned a round, silver coloured badge embossed with a black swastika, which, we were to learn, indicated he was a leading light in the local branch of the Nazi Party, and Gauleiter of Knittlefeld. He was to become an object of fun and scorn with the kreigefanganers, particularly the ever critical Scousers and the unruly Australians.

From his upper lip there sprouted a stubby, Hitler-like moustache which promptly earned him the nickname "Adolph the Paper Hanger". On his walks around the factory he carried a long ornamental walking stick, like a shepherd's crook, and was accompanied by two small dachshund dogs scampering at his heels, the two low-slung animals forever breaking into a cacophony of yapping whenever they approached a khaki coloured uniform. The result of the kick on the hind-quarters one of them had received from Len Caulfield, when Adolph's back was turned.

It soon became obvious that the reluctant, amateurish endeavours of the kriegies in the brickworks, were not producing enough arbeit, or bricks, for Adolph. One morning he stopped to speak angrily in a babble of German, to Len, who was half-heartedly transferring the wet bricks off the forming machine on to the trolley. Len, unable to keep up with the speed of the chopping cheese-cutter, dropped some with a splurge of mud onto the concrete floor. Adolph's tirade of babbled German became a torrent, which was met with a blank, uncomprehending stare and a muttered "Fook off, why don't thee?" from Len. The confrontation was a signal for the other prisoners within earshot to stop whatever they were supposed to be doing and gather round to try to help.

This only further infuriated the little Austrian.

"Nicht arbeit, nicht essen," he shouted, gesticulating wildly, his cape almost falling away from his shoulders.

"No work, no food," he repeated again and again.

This oft-repeated threat of our captors when they were urging us to put more effort into our work, was met with "stick your fuckin', lousy essen up your backside" and other similar obscenities from Len. These brought on an attack of hysterical anger from Adolph and an attack of hysterical laughter from the onlooking prisoners. The guards on duty weren't too interested in this pantomime, and one of them, not wishing to take any part at all in the drama, quietly slipped away for a smoke in one of the empty brick kilns.

Eventually Dai Davies, our Vertrauansman, was pleased to be summoned from his job of loading a brickwagon to attend an impromptu, unofficial union meeting with Adolph, Hans the factory foreman and the worried Felt Webel, the Head Waiter, the ever anxious to please both his unwelcome employers and the recalcitrant prisoners of war in his charge growing more unruly every day. Dai, with his rapidly increasing knowledge of the German language, charmed them into believing we couldn't work any harder, because we were all permanently hungry and lacking in energy due to the starvation we had endured since being taken prisoner.

So the outcome of the meeting was, that henceforth, the foreman, when he opened up in the morning, threaded 48 potatoes on wires, and baked them by hanging the wires through the inspection plates of the red hot, coke-fired kilns. At 10 o'clock every morning, Tom Hesketh who was working in the kilns, brought two piping-hot, baked potatoes to each prisoner, repeating the ritual every afternoon at 3 o'clock. Unfortunately, there was no butter nor salt to go with them.

It was Hans, the General Foreman, of course, who actually ran the brickworks, albeit under the ever watchful eye of his Boss, Adolph. Hans was a lugubrious, bald-headed old man with a permanent doleful expression on his face. His bloodshot, watery eyes peered accusingly at you over steel-rimmed, pince-nez spectacles perched permanently half way down his nose from which a bead of snot dripped steadily into the filter of his thick, walrus moustache. Hans should really have been at home with his slippers on, in front of the fire, (or the tall, tiled, impersonal room-heater which passed for a fire in Austrian homes), smoking his pipe of ersatz tobacco and drinking his ersatz coffee. Instead, he seemed to be forever in high pitched argument and/or confrontation with Adolph.

The luxury of the extra potatoes baked for us by the rheumy old man was very welcome to our skinny frames and eased the hunger pains somewhat, but did very little to raise our energy and increase production. In fact, the extra potatoes, on top of the potato based soups of our daily main meal, if anything, slowed us down and caused an outbreak of "potato belly", or "pot belly", a condition akin to a six months pregnant housewife or the beer-gut of our new boss Adolph. We all developed them, and the pot bellies didn't recede until we received our first Red Cross food parcels sometime later.

***

Losing my cushy job in the drying shed with Granny Schmitt, I was detailed to help Len Caulfield take the wet bricks off the brick-forming machine. This clumsy apparatus was on a long bench at the base of a huge, antediluvian, vertical concrete mixer something like the revolving, mobile concrete mixer you see on the back of a lorry, but three times bigger and ten times noisier. The materials, like clay, water and lime and whatever else they used to make bricks, was shovelled into the revolving mouth of the machine on the floor above, by Taffy Thomas and "Gash" Hampton, from skips trundled along a narrow-gauge railway line by Arthur Thompson from the clay pit. With an ear-splitting grinding and rumbling of the giant mixer as it slowly revolved, the contents were mixed together and the resultant clay slurry extruded out of the base in the rectangular shape of a house brick, about eight inches long and two and a half inches wide.

As the continuous line of wet clay spewed out of the contrivance, an Auslander, a "volunteer" civilian from Yugo-Slavia, operated a wire-cutter contraption, something like a double wired cheese cutter, cutting with a downward movement two bricks from the end of the extruding clay and sliding them to one side on a moveable platform. The two wet bricks were then lifted off the platform, alternatively by Len and myself and placed on a trolley to be moved to the drying sheds.

This revolving concrete mixer was the Command Post of the Brickworks. The epicentre or fulcrum, on which the whole of the brick-making operation of the brickworks was balanced. If anything went wrong with the contraption, production halted.

The first time this occurred was when small stones in the

140

clay passed through the filter of the machine. When the taut, cheese-cutter wires, slicing through the slowly oozing clay caught one of the stones, the wires snapped with a "zing" which could be plainly heard over the din of the mixer. The extruded clay then spread across the table until our Yugoslav friend pulled an overhead lever, to stop the machine. Then all brick production halted until the wire was replaced, and the overflowing stream of clay was carried back upstairs to the top of the mixer. A slow and laborious procedure not helped by the lethargy of the p.o.w's, or the near hysterics of Hans the Foreman, heaping Austrian obscenities on Boris the Auslander, who meekly took the blame for the mishap.

The second time we experienced this hilarious lash-up was when Len Caulfield and I had an argument, nearly coming to blows. I can't remember what our row was about, but the process of alternately lifting two wet bricks off the sliding plate was suddenly interrupted when Len and I decided to spar up to each other, with fists raised and eyes flashing. The man from Marburg, shouting at us in a mixture of German and Slav which we completely ignored, furiously chopping off two bricks at a time from the end of the line of wet clay, had no option but to slide them on to the floor. Eventually giving up, he pulled the lever above his head to stop the flow, and waited pathetically for the wrath of the Foreman and the hysterics of Adolph. Len and I, our quarrel forgotten, collapsed in a frenzy of laughter.

So it didn't take us very long to realise that with a little judicious planning, we could, figuratively speaking, put a long spoke in the cumbersome wheels of the ancient brick making mixer to relieve the monotony of the endless chop-chopping of the wire cutter, and also have a little fun at the expense of the Yugo-Slav and the Old Man with the Moustache.

It was during one of the temporary lulls when the clay ran out in the filling room above us, that Boris, muttering to himself, "schieszen, sheisen, muss schnell sheisen" and clutching his stomach, made a hurried dash to the cesspit lavatory on the other side of the yard. Len and I decided to "repair" the split pin on the lever controlling the flow of the clay.

Len jumped up on the bench and used an old screwdriver I'd found in a cupboard to loosen the split-pin. Arthur Thompson in the clay pit, primed the day before, sharpened the point of the spoke by adding some suitably sized stones to a skip-load of clay.

Boris, buttoning up the fly of his trousers as he scurried back from the dreaded bog, hurriedly pulled the lever to start the process again.

Ten minutes or so went by during which the slurry flowed freely and smoothly. Len Caulfield and I lifted the wet bricks off the tray in silence, waiting eagerly and hopefully, for the inevitable to happen.

I was beginning to think that our minor sabotage was not going to come off, when the two wires suddenly snapped with a "Zing, Zing", and to muffled oaths, Boris raised his hand to the lever above him and pulled.

To my dismay the mud stopped flowing immediately, as it was supposed to do when the lever was pulled, until without warning, the lever came away from the side of the machine, dropping to the floor with a clatter.

The clay oozed out once more. There were about ten tons of the stuff still churning about in the mixer and now, with nothing to hold it back it was being slowly and relentlessly ejected out of the bottom, like an elephant with chronic diarrhoea, spreading over the cutting bench and spilling on to the floor. Boris' muffled oaths became cries of anguish and panic as Adolph, his two guard dogs at his heel, walked into the room just in time to see his precious brick slurry overflowing from the bench, like molten lava flowing down Mount Vesuvious, spreading across the floor and making its unstoppable progress towards the door.

Adolph lost control of himself.

Rushing across the slippery concrete floor, the two daschunds chasing after him barking their heads off, he slithered on the wet clay, lost his balance and came to a sliding halt on his stomach like a rugby fly-half scoring a muddy try on a pre-war, wet Saturday afternoon at Clubmoor Recreation Ground. The long pea-green cape fell off his shoulders into the mud alongside his feathered hat.

The two hound-dogs went berserk. They had seen Len Caulfield who, like me, by this time was doubled up laughing at this hilarious scenario which couldn't have been bettered by

142

Mack Sennet or The Three Stooges in Hollywood. The two low-slung daschunds flopped their way through the mud to bark and snap ferociously at Len's ankles, Len trying to kick them off and repeatedly shouting, "Fuck off you little bastards, fuck off."

The noise of the still revolving mixer, and the barking of the dogs, and the uncontrolled laughter of Len and I, and the curses of the unfortunate Slav auslander, brought those of the lads in earshot, to join in the fun.

It also brought old Hans the Foreman, who sizing up the situation at a glance squelched his way on gouty legs through the mud and, puffing and grunting with the protest of the aged, he hobbled upstairs to switch off the electric supply to the mixer, bringing to a halt the flow of the slurry.

Also, as it turned out, bringing to a halt brick making at Knittlefeld as far as we were concerned. We moved to another working camp the following day.

For weeks after, Len Caulfield and I swanked that it was the fracas at the sabotaged mixer that caused the move.

Chapter 18

A Kriegie Prayer

We thank thee Lord that we are able,
To shift the grub from off this table.
And when we have eaten this small store
Lord give us grace to scoff some more.
And though we be sinful, give us a skinful,
And make us grateful for every plateful.
Amen.
Company 7, Stalag 383.

Murau, Carinthia, an ancient, sleepy little market town situated on the River Mur midway between Knittlefeld and Spital, was to be my place of work during the winter of 1941 until the early summer of 1942.

Perched on the bank of the Mur, the foundations of the rear wall of the old building washed by the river, the arbeitslager was a one time stable, only recently converted to house its new occupants. The entrance was through double doors directly from the street into a cobbled yard containing a dozen horse stalls. The iron feeding troughs in the stalls were still half full of hay when we arrived, and bits and pieces of leather harness and horse brass were still hanging from hooks on the walls. The strong aroma of horses and horse manure permeated to our living quarters on the floor above for many weeks.

There was an even stronger aroma from the crude lavatory cesspit in one corner, which, to my dismay I realised was for the use of the new residents. But we couldn't use this elementary toilet after we were locked up for the night. We had to make do, at our peril, with the obligatory night bucket. This, full to overflowing, was carried down the stairs each morning to be emptied into the cesspit. An onerous fatigue shared on a rota basis by everyone, any spillages to be cleaned up immediately.

A large brass anti-frost water tap on the wall in the yard provided our only water supply. When the winter temperature dropped below freezing point, a minature valve on the side of the main tap was opened and the trickle of water was left running. This prevented the freezing up of the tap and the only water supply to the building. During the night the trickle of water caused a pyramid of glistening ice to build up from the floor to the tap. This miniature ice-mountain had to be broken up each morning, then barrowed down the side of the building and tipped into the river.

The living quarters at the top of the flight of stairs at the back of the stable were much the same as those in Knittlefeld, except that there were two rooms. The inner room, previously used for the storage of fodder, was almost totally filled with two sleeping "shelves" one above the other. The outer room was our recreation room, dining room, bathroom, kitchen and drying room.

Food came from a small Gasthaus/Flescherie in the town square, a couple of hundred yards from the billet, collected in galvanised buckets twice a day by two men accompanied by a guard. It consisted of the same potato based soups and miniscule wedges of black bread and occasional blob of tasteless white margarine as at the Brickworks. There was never any meat, nor fat and no fruit or vegetables except, occasionally, the awful sauerkraut. There was not very much of that, or the watery soup either.

On my first turn to collect the miserable ration, the landlord of the Gasthaus was standing behind the counter. A tall, thin, elderly man with a full, grey moustache and a shiny bald head, his body was encased from ankle to chin in a long blue and white striped butchers apron, like a character out of a Christmas pantomime. He grinned at me as he reached up, and with a large carving knife cut a snippet of bacon from a black, smoked, ham shank hanging above the counter.

The guard, in animated conversation with a female helper, didn't notice him hand the small offering to me. With a conspiratorial grin on his music-hall face, a finger across his lips as if he was giving a forbidden gift to a naughty child, he said,

"Speck, gut, essen schnell."

I didn't need any second bidding. The little scrap of fatty bacon vanished in an instant. And it was good too. As was the spontaneous kind gesture of the hotel keeper.

***

On the afternoon we arrived at our new camp, we were paraded in the stable-yard, like sheep or cattle in the local market, to be inspected by a delegation of three civilians from the town council. Also present were our guards, the four posten, (privates) and Feld-Webel, (Sergeant) who had accompanied us from Knittlefeld, and their senior officer, Hauptman Schmidt.

This was the first time we had seen the Hauptman. It was not to be the last, for we were paraded in front of him once a week. He was a little man. A bully, who made his loud-mouthed presence felt by striding up and down with his hands behind his back like a characterisation of Hitler, bawling his head off. Sometimes directed at his own men.

He attended these weekly inspections pedalling an ancient sit-up-and-beg ladies bicycle, and no doubt sensed, even if he didn't hear, the muttered, ribald remarks made by the assembled prisoners as he propped the bike up against the wall of the stable. He was to be a thorn in our sides with his haranguing on these weekly parades until, one day, he stood in front of the Manchester lad, 6'3" George Hampton, and slated him at the top of his voice, because he imagined George was grinning at him. As he cycled away down the road, George in a hoarse whisper everyone could hear said, "I hope the little bastard falls off his bike and breaks his neck."

And he did. Fall off his bike that is. He had a heart attack and we never saw him again.

Interpreted by Dai Davies, whose German improved every day we were informed that we were to be employed on council work in the town. Grave digging, street sweeping, snow clearing and odd-jobbing, but mostly digging trenches and general labouring for Italian bricklayers on a building site, a row of new terrace houses on the outskirts of the town. However, one of the inspecting officials caught my eye as he walked past, then said something to the Feld-Webel who tapped me on the shoulder and indicated to me to fall out. He also picked out Elwin Jones and Vic Green.

This was our introduction to Franz Mosshamer, the manager of the Electricitatwerks, a small hydro-electric power station on the River Mur, producing the electric supply for Murau and the surrounding district. The three of us were soon to realise our good fortune in being selected by him, for what turned out to be a soft job in the power station.

***

Thoughts and foreboding about my future in Murau and doubts and interest in the new camp and the work I was to do, were swept to one side when, that same momentous afternoon, we received our first supply of Red Cross food parcels.

It is impossible to describe the relief, the elation, the thrill, the childish excitement, call it what you will, of receiving my first food parcel in the arbeitslager of Murau, after the months of hunger and near starvation I had endured since my capture. Since long before that I had been on short rations from September, 1940, when I first "went up the desert".

There were two British Red Cross parcels and two Canadian Red Cross parcels, per man, in that first consignment. They were issued to us weekly each Saturday afternoon in the run up to my first Christmas as a prisoner-of-war in Austria.

The British parcels contained an assortment of mouth-watering luxuries which I had not tasted or even seen since before my call-up in 1939. Every British parcel was different from the next, and could surprise you with a tin of bacon or beef-steak pudding or fish paste or dried egg or creamed rice or a jam roly-poly suet pudding. In addition they all contained certain basic items. Tea, sugar, jam, chocolate, margarine, water-biscuits and soap.

Very occasionally some homesick young prisoner would find hidden among the contents of the British parcels an illegal note from the female packer of the box. Sometimes these hidden messages were the start of a lengthy "pen-pal" correspondence which, in one case to my knowledge, blossomed into romance and marriage when the war ended.

The contents of the Canadian parcels were all identical and have remained firmly fixed in my memory ever since.

A large tin of KLIM dried milk powder. A carton of twelve, round hard biscuits which were delicious even when eaten dry, and were heavenly covered with one of the luxurious spreads. These biscuits could also be soaked in water or milk to provide the basics for many a gourmet kreigsgefanganer banquet. There was meat loaf – a luncheon meat similar to Spam – salmon or sardines, a packet of butter, a four ounce container of cheese spread, coffee, a packet of dried prunes or raisins, jam, sugar, and, wonder of wonders, a six ounce slab of chocolate, and a tablet of soap, an unheard of luxury for a prisoner-of-war in Austria.

Also with each parcel, came fifty cigarettes, a commodity which was to become the main currency of Austria, and indeed Europe, when the black market eventually flourished.

Even the empty tins in those early days were used by the prisoners-of-war. Particularly the large KLIM tin which doubled as a kettle or saucepan or frying pan, and with a little ingenuity could be converted into a portable cooking stove or oven.

It could be said that the weekly issue of these food parcels, made the British prisoner-of-war one of the best fed communities in the Europe of 1941. Unfortunately, the supply of parcels to the working camps, particularly the smaller or remote camps, was intermittent and deliveries could dry up for weeks at a time. Even so, the Red Cross food parcels were the saviour of the British prisoner-of-war in Germany. Without them, hundreds would have succumbed to starvation or chronic malnutrition, as did the millions of Soviet prisoners who had to survive on the scraps the Germans gave them.

It was interesting to observe the different reactions of my fellow inmates, when we were issued with the first of those long awaited food parcels.

One or two went into hibernation in a corner and gorged on the contents over the weekend, starting with the slab of chocolate which vanished within seconds. Then, unable to stop themselves, opening a tin of that, or a packet of those, followed by a hasty drag on a Players Cork Tip, before delving into another tin. Or surreptitiously, opening the box and taking something out and eating it, as if they didn't want anyone else to see what they were sampling. Then, carefully putting their name on the box before tying it with string or an old boot-lace and stashing it away under their bed blanket.

Five minutes later they took it out again to inspect the contents, as if they couldn't believe their eyes.

Most of us formed ourselves into "combines", the parcels being pooled by two or three friends and the contents shared scrupulously. So was the cooking or heating of the food, and the washing up. I was fortunate to "muck-in" with Dai Davies and George (Gash) Hampton. (Gash, because in his call-up Militia days George would eat every morsel of any sort of food left over – the gash – on anyone's plate). We formed an amicable, close combine and forged friendships, which lasted until Dai and I left the working camp some two years later.

It was about then, also through the International Red Cross, we received much needed new uniforms, shirts, underclothes, boots and socks. A morale booster if ever there was one, for our old uniforms were threadbare and dirty. Boots and socks had long since vanished. Some of the lads still wore the colourful cast-offs or drab hand-me-downs of the defeated armies of Europe. Amazingly, we were all kitted out with new uniforms, which more or less fitted everyone; the tall and the short, the fat and the thin, – not that there were many fatties – in the little working camp.

It was a great tribute to the British administrative staffs at the Wolfsberg Stalag, who organised the distribution to the working camps of the new uniforms, Red Cross parcels and parcels and mail from relatives. And later on, the repair of worn boots, and the issue of books and sports equipment.

Padre Ledgerwood, in his **"Potted History of Stalag XV111A"**, describes the joyous arrival of the first food parcels at the Wolfsburg Camp.

"On July 30th, 1941, the first Red Cross food parcels arrived. Excitement was intense. Who had seen them: what were they like: were they big or small: what was in them? Merciful

heaven, couldn't someone answer a man's question? Poor old Garry, the Chief Man of Confidence, had no peace. Surely he must know all the answers: that was why he was placed in his exalted position. But, as yet, Gary knew no more than Tom, Dick or Harry.

And then came the Official Statement from the German High Command.

Only prisoners of war at working camps could receive the coveted parcel: the sooner the sick and semi-sick got better and went out to work, that much sooner would they receive a Red Cross parcel. Our captors had always enjoyed the reputation of being sadists, and in this instance their reputation suffered no set-back. It was a form of torment which they apparently enjoyed using, and, make no mistake about it, they did use it.

Now, disabuse your minds of hundreds of men rushing to working camps. They were too dumb-struck to be capable of any such rash mobility. Most of them were too under-nourished and many were too sick to summon more physical energy than was necessary to walk around the small compound. The senseless ultimatum had no appreciable effect and on September 11th the first Red Cross parcels were distributed. What a day! All the pent up feelings of weeks of repression overflowed in one memorable torrent of happiness. We became kids again. Even now we chuckle as we recall the madness of those moments.

Imagine, if you please, grown men running from barrack to barrack showing off a tin of jam, a tin of meat or a cake of chocolate. Imagine men carefully reserving the labels of tins and packets and pasting them in a scrap book."

***

So the Homesickness which overtook me on my first Christmas as a Prisoner-of-War, coupled with the news of the death of my Mother in my first letter from home, and the starvation I had endured for many months, was alleviated somewhat by the timely delivery of the Red Cross food parcels and the new clothing.

It has to be said again that many of us would not have survived the Stalags and Arbeitslagers of Nazi Germany without

150

the food parcels. The quality of the food issued to us by the Germans, even those supposedly on "heavy work rations" was abysmal, borne out by the deaths in their thousands of the Russian prisoners-of-war, who received no outside help in their fight against starvation.

***

Sitting at the kitchen table in 26, Vanbrugh Crescent, reading the sports page of last night's Liverpool Echo, my stomach rumbled in time to the unique sound of frizzling bacon, and my nose twitched expectantly at the smell that has no equal.

The kitchen was at long last warming up, for I had lit the coal fire in the adjoining living room, before my Mother came down.

The fire had not been lit at all the day before, until I had returned home from school. Mother had run out of housekeeping money so I had gone to the Post Office, cashed two of my savings stamps and then bought 28 pounds of nutty slack at Worthingtons, the coal-merchant in Brennans' Cottages. I wheeled it home in a battered old toy pram belonging to one of my sisters.

The living room fire, which also heated the domestic hot water in the boiler at the back of the grate, was the only fire in the house. I could now feel the warmth from it coming through the wall against my shoulder. This time-honoured place at the kitchen table, always occupied by my Father when he was having his meal, was a much favoured one with all the family. Particularly when there was heavy snow on the ground, as there was on that dark, bitterly cold winter's morning.

I was also much favoured to be sitting alone at the table, anyway, that morning. An unusual experience in a household of eleven. My brothers and sisters must have been still in bed or gone to work.

Mother was standing in front of her new "Excel" electric cooker, a carving knife in her right hand, turning over strips of bacon frying in a large black, cast iron frying pan. Her left hand held a dish cloth to wipe the bacon fat splattered on the gleaming, grey enamelled iron surface of her pride and joy.

151

"I'll do you some tinned tomatoes, Doug," she said, as she slid the crispy bacon, done to a turn as she knew I liked it, on the plate warming at the side of the cooker.

"There's the twenty-past six," she went on without pausing, looking back over her shoulder through the window. "The snow isn't holding the trains up this morning, anyway."

Through the gaps in the houses at the bottom of the back garden I could see the distant, twinkling lights of the three coaches of the 6.20 passenger train to Lime Street, as it slowed down on its approach to Breck Road Station. Mother could tell the time with the fifteen minute, up and down, regular-as-clockwork service of the passenger trains on the Bootle branch line. Her words were really a warning that it was almost time for me to go out on my paper round.

Mum put the plate of bacon and tomatoes in front of me, and sitting down at the table opposite me picked up the loaf of bread. Holding it to her chest, she cut off a thick slice of the crust. Flicking her head to one side to move a lock of her still jet black hair, which had fallen over her eyes, she said, "Would you like some fried bread, Doug, or should I rub around the pan for you?"

She knew that the "rub-around" was a favourite of mine. The crusty bread, scoured across the pan to collect the remains of the bacon fat and sediments left in the bottom was finger-licking tasty. The practice these days, would promote a candidate for the Heart Hospital, but, in 1934 it was an essential body-warmer and energiser.

"I'll have both, please, Mum," I replied, my mouth watering in anticipation, "if that's all right."

I had just eagerly speared the first forkful of bacon onto a chunk of bread swimming in bacon fat, savouring the taste even before it reached my lips, when I woke with a sudden start from my deep sleep.

My wonderful dream of Home and Food, and Warmth and Comfort, no doubt fuelled by the sliver of bacon given to me by the landlord of the Gasthaus or the recent arrival of the food parcels, was shattered completely when my foot was roughly shaken by Ferdinand.

Ferdy, a youth of about my own age, was one of the guards.

"A penny short of a shilling," as they say in Liverpool, he

152

was the butt of many a practical joke played on him by the inmates of the camp. A tall, thin, pasty-faced lad. Unemployed before he was conscripted into the Army, he missed service in the frozen Russian Steppes because of his shortage of copper. Hence his presence in the sort of Home-Guard Regiment of middle-aged misfits and Grade 4 nondescripts guarding, at that time, the Allied prisoners-of-war taken in Greece and Crete. Ferdy was harmless, and he took it as a great honour and privilege to be guarding British prisoners. Even when they stuffed pellets of wet paper down his rifle barrel, which, slung over his shoulder, was just the right height for those sleeping on the top deck.

"Aufstehen, Artur," he said shaking my foot once more, "est funf eure, los, los." "Get up, Arthur, get up, it's five o'clock, come on."

"Piss off, Ferdy," I muttered sleepily. The standard reply from all of us to Ferdinand on those early mornings. We had already learned which guards to take liberties with.

I turned over in my uncomfortable, but warm blanket-cum-sleeping bag, pulling it closer around my shoulders and automatically drawing my feet up out of harm's way.

But Ferdy wouldn't be put off.

"Nicht schlafen mehr, Artur, bitte," he said, shaking me again. "Raus, raus. Aufstehn, schnell. Herr Gruber kommen."

"No more sleeping, Arthur, please. Get up, quick, Herr Gruber's coming."

My sleeping space – you couldn't call it a bed – was beneath the only window in the room, (a favourite spot of mine if I could get it in those smelly, overcrowded, airless p.o.w. sleeping quarters) at the end of the row of my eleven sleeping comrades on the top shelf.

Reluctantly, bleary eyed and only half awake, my mouth watering and my stomach gurgling in frustration and disappointment at the sudden loss of the fried bacon and tomatoes, I dragged myself out of the blanket and climbed down on to the floor.

On the way I stood on George East's foot sticking out over the edge of the shelf directly beneath me. George, the burly, six foot three Australian from Queensland, whose spidery legs and bony feet overflowed the end of the bed, tucked his foot in hurriedly, saying, "For Christ's sake Doug, watch what yer doin' will yer, yer clumsy little bastard."

George and I were the best of friends.

Ferdy, who had stayed there to make sure I was awake and out of the bunk, said, "Fumptzen minuten, Artur, und entreiten."

His early reveille was to get me down to the Electricitatzverk for the first shift with Gruber, and as he had already crossed swords with this leading light of the local Nazi Party, he didn't want to be late.

Shivering, and still half asleep, I dressed quickly. I had slept in my socks and underpants and shirt, as I had done for two years now, so in two minutes I had pulled on my battledress trousers and tunic. My boots were downstairs in one of the empty stalls of the stable and were probably frozen, for they had been there all night. (Our boots were taken from us when we were locked in at night, the idea being to stop us running off through the snow to Switzerland, three hundred miles away.)

Now five o'clock on a dark, bitterly cold morning in the feotid atmosphere of that overcrowded room, and the prospect of going outside in two foot of snow in frozen boots, without a greatcoat, was no laughing matter.

Particularly after dreaming of bacon breakfasts.

But these early morning reveilles, for some strange, perverse reason, always brought on me a fit of stifled giggles. I was hard put not to break out in gales of laughter at the sight and sound of my twenty-three sleeping comrades, crammed together in two rows on the shelves of that awful room, each rolled up like bundles of khaki cloth on the shelf of a bespoke tailors showroom, emitting sundry noises of the night normally reserved for the privacy of the bedroom.

Some of the bundles were half awake, and like George, were protesting because their sleep had been disturbed and telling me in no uncertain manner to put the so-and-so light out.

Ferdinand was waiting for me in the outer room with my meagre breakfast wedge of black bread. Five minutes later, after a hasty wash in a bowl of freezing cold water, I was trudging, knee deep in a fresh fall of snow, along the bank of the River Mur for my spell at the Electricitatzverk.

Chapter 19

Love in the Power Station

The water generated electric power station was situated a mile or so down river from the town. The power house, with its turbine generating the electric current, was in the basement of a single storey building built on the bank of the river. The turbine, or generator, was turned by water diverted from the river through a system of narrow, deep canals or channels, controlled by manually operated sluice valves and lock gates, somewhat similar to the lock gates on a canal.

Shifting snow at Electricitatzwerk.

Three civilians, Franz Mosshamer, Thomas Gill and Wilhelm Gruber operated the little plant in eight hour shifts from six in the morning. Myself, Elwin Jones and Vic Green were to help them on these shifts, but Hauptman Schmidt vetoed the

155

night shift for the prisoners, so we worked only in the daytime. One of us in the morning and the other two in the afternoon.

Franz Mosshamer was the senior of the trio and Manager of the plant.

Just on retiring age, Franz was a jovial man, with a ready smile unusual with the Austrians. He was sympathetic to our situation and was to prove a good friend. I got on with him particularly well. He made great efforts to teach me the rudiments of German. After I had told him that I had never used skis, he brought his son's skis to let me have a go on the hill at the back of the building. He showed me how to glissade down the hill controlling the slide, haunched on my heels, with a walking stick or a tree branch. Over the Christmas period he loaned the camp an ancient, wind-up gramophone complete with green-painted horn and half a dozen scratchy classical records. On Christmas Day I was on the early morning shift with him. Defying the strict non-fraternisation rules, before returning to the lager, he took me to his home to show me the family Christmas tree and introduce me to his wife and family. My eyes filled with tears of homesickness when his wife gave me a parcel of biscuits from the foot of the decorated tree.

Thomas Gill, a younger, gravel-voiced, taciturn man was also easy to work with. Especially when we learned that he was a communist sympathiser and detested his colleague, Willy Gruber, almost as much as he detested the Nazi Party. Thomas had a permanently stiff leg which had kept him out of the Army. Later on, it was the cause of a near catastrophe for Elwin Jones and me.

Gruber, the third member of the trio, was a prominent member of the local branch of the Nazi Party and always wore the Swastika badge in his lapel to prove it. He was a much younger man than the others and had missed military service because he was blind in one eye. He had a disconcerting way of staring at you, for he had a glass eye in the socket of the missing eye. He also had a permanent chip on his shoulder and a permanent grim face. Conversation with Gruber was strictly business and limited to instructions about the work. Although he was not exactly a slave driver, he always went out of his way to keep us fully occupied.

Our job was to keep the place clean, shift snow from the paths, chop wood for the stoves, and generally help with work connected with the operation of the Electric Works.

One of our first jobs was labouring (for want of a better word) for the town electrician installing an overhead electric supply line to one of the farms near the Station. Zeiber, the foreman in charge of the work, took photographs of us working in the first fall of snow that winter. He took my name and address and promised to send them on to me after the war ended. Although we parted company shortly afterwards, he kept his word and I received the photographs in 1947.

Installing overhead supply.

Geoff Hallett, Len Caulfield, Dai Davies and author
with civilian workers.

Primarily, though, our job was to clear the iron gratings sifting the water as it entered the power station to turn the turbines. The gratings prevented the flotsam and jetsam of rubbish, rotted leaves and broken branches, expired cats and sheep, old boots and discarded newspapers, and essentially, frozen snow and miniature ice-bergs from getting into the turbine tubes and fouling up the system.

If the rubbish or ice blocked the gratings the water couldn't get through to turn the generator, the current failed, and the lights of Murau went out. These slabs of ice and frozen snow, floating down the river one bitterly cold, dark evening in January conspiring with Gill's gammy leg, were to raise my hopes of an early return home.

To break up the ice slabs, we used a long, "boat-hook" like the one used by the boatman on Newsham Park lake, when he was pulling in the rowing boats after their time was up, only bigger and heavier, for the metal point was an iron spear heavy enough to break the ice, combined with a large curved hook to pull the frozen snow, or ice, or dead cats, or whatever, over the top of the grating.

***

I worked in the comfortable confines of the little Electric Power Station for the remainder of the winter of 1941/42. The temperature outside dropped permanently below freezing. The snow lay twelve inches deep on the banks of the river and clung to the fir trees on the surrounding mountains, reminding me of the colourful Christmas Cards of days gone by.

For a reluctant prisoner-of-war, after months of near starvation, only gradually regaining strength through the bounty of the Red Cross food parcels, my spell at the Electricitatzwerk was not without its compensations.

The building was warm with a plentiful supply of wood for the large heating stove. There was always boiling water to make a brew of tea and a hot-plate to fry our Spam. It was unbelievably comfortable, compared with the smelly stable where we were locked up at night

To make life more interesting, old Franz seemed determined to foster a romance between me and his niece, Lore. Very often, when I was on a shift alone with him, she always put in an appearance, seemingly with his full encouragement.

Lore Palm was no sultry Marlene Deitrich or vivacious Lisa Manelli. She was more like a Vicar of Dibley or a shorter version of Hetty Jaques. Shorter than me – I was only five feet four and a bit – and comfortably built. Like her uncle, she had a sense of humour and always had a ready smile on her face. Unusual with the dour, humourless Austrians. She worked in Murau Hospital as a childrens' nurse, so had not been called up for service in the forces.

It soon became obvious to me that Lore was missing her friends. Particularly her boy friends. There were very few youths or boys over the age of fifteen left in Murau. Nor, for that matter very few middle-aged men. They were spread out over Europe. Freezing to death at Stalingrad or careering up and down the Libyan Desert with Rommel in the blinding, searing sandstorms, or digging massive gun-emplacements outside Calais, or avoiding pot-shots from the Partisans in the White Mountains of Crete.

Evidence of this was to be seen in the ever increasing number of fatalities in the Obituary Notices of Franz's newspaper, the "Volkischer Beobactor".

Under the stark heading

THEY GAVE THEIR LIVES FOR FUHRER AND FATHERLAND were sombre photographs, framed in thick black lines of mourning, of the young men and boys lately killed in action. Most of them pictured with an Iron Cross decoration pinned to their tunic.

Having become aware, however, of the perils of fraternisation and the terrible penalties imposed on prisoners-of-war caught with females of the Master Race, and the savage, sadistic sentences of four years hard-labour, with their heads permanently shorn of hair, imposed on young German girls caught in the act, I was cautious and a little nervous of the liaison to say the least.

Nevertheless, I was by no means an unwilling participant.

Towards the end of the winter, with my strength and energy somewhat restored after eating my way through half a dozen Red Cross food parcels, my waking thoughts were no longer permanently on food.

Inevitably, there came an afternoon when Franz, with the usual good natured, knowing grin on his face, and a twinkle in his eye, said to the pair of us, now openly holding hands in front of him, "Why don't you two go into the basement, to be on your own for a while and practice your German and English."

At least that's what I thought he said when Lore linked me by the arm and gently steered me down the staircase to the basement, as if we were taking the floor at the Grafton Ballroom for the last waltz or making our way to the honeymoon-suite at the Adelphi Hotel.

Down in the basement – the noisy, revolving hub of the Electric Works – my hesitant, limited German was muted by the thunder of the rotating generator and the hammering of my heart. For Lore seemed more than anxious to teach another language to an ignoramus like me.

The Language of Love.

The Language of the Young, which has no barrier of the tongue.

It had no barrier in the basement, at any rate, except my chronic shyness. And she was doing her best to overcome that.

Although immature, sadly lacking in amorous experience,

which nearly twelve months in the Western Desert hadn't helped, I was a quick learner. So it wasn't long before romantic and passionate words of endearment and exclamations as old as time itself, passed between us. The ageless words in German, or stuttering German, or English, was softened by the noise of the green painted turbine and the babble of the river, as it passed through the generator and under the building.

On that particular afternoon the physical attractions of this comfortable, lovely, jovial young woman from Murau, determined to have her way with me, were proving incapable for me to resist. Locked in a fierce embrace, she had taken my breath away by forcing her warm, silky, darting tongue between my lips, at the same time taking my hand and inserting it through the loose buttons of her dress and under her chemise. She closed my clammy hand with gentle firmness around a beautiful mound of soft, warm flesh, transporting me into rapturous joy, the first time I had ever experienced such warmth and firm bliss.

I had become completely lost in a state of breathless, heady ecstasy, without thoughts of tomorrow, or the consequences, when I vaguely became aware of Franz Mosshammer's loud, guttural voice and his hurried footsteps clattering down the bare wooden stairs from the control room above.

"Artur, Artur."

He was shouting at the top of his voice to make himself heard above the tumult of the turbine.

"Lore, Lore, gemma, gemma, aufpassen, los. Gruber kommen, scnell, schnell."

And other sundry German words of warning and alarm only half understood by me.

The panic in his voice immediately startled me out of my passionate embrace with Lore and brought me sharply back to the real world. The real world of Courts Martial and firing squads and concentration camps and civilian, hard labour prisons without Red Cross food parcels that I had heard so much about.

Franz had been standing guard at his usual vantage point in front of the panoramic window in the control room overlooking the Mur, keeping watch for slabs of ice drifting down the river threatening to put his power station out of action. The weather had turned bad again and he had seen Wilhelm Gruber looming out of the snow down the path on the bank of the river, heading at a smart pace towards the Electricitatzverks. The miserable Gruber was no friend of Lore, and had already made a couple of surprise visits when he had reason to believe she was at the station.

Lore sized up the situation at once.

She indicated to me to go into the lavatory on the other side of the basement room and then ran back up the stairs fastening the buttons on her dress as she did so. I retired, ungracefully and hastily, red of face and short of breath, to the primitive bog. Where after bolting the door, I sat with my pants down on the draughty lavatory seat cooling my ardour over the rushing waters of the river. The clamour of my heart and my mounting blood pressure slowly returned to normal, as I sat and watched the ice go drifting by.

Eventually, I went back up the stairs to find a heated discussion or argument going on between the three Austrians, most of which went over my head. Although I gathered that Gruber, suspicious of Lore's presence, wanted to know why she wasn't "mit das kinder". "With the children".

Unfortunately – or maybe fortunately – I never got to know, for I did not see Lore again after that heart-stopping afternoon. For a while, though, I could not get the romantic interlude in the cellar out of my mind. In fact I am bound to say that I didn't sleep very well for a fortnight after that afternoon. I can't for the life of me remember whether it was through fright or frustration.

Chapter 20

Angling For Repatriation

It was about six o'clock at the electric works, one freezing cold evening towards the end of the winter, after my unfulfilled affair with Lore, when I was involved in an incident which, for a while, brought me false hope of an early and unexpected repatriation home.

Elwin Jones and I were on the afternoon shift with Thomas Gill, our communist anti-Nazi friendly enemy. The temperature outside, normally well below freezing point, had dropped dramatically. There had been heavy falls of snow, off and on all day and huge slabs of ice had been drifting down the River Mur since we had come on the shift at two o'clock. We had been kept busy breaking the slabs and raking the pieces over the top of the gratings.

Elwin and I were missing the normal easy afternoon spells of bludging and playing cards, keeping the stove well supplied with wood to brew the tea, and speculating on how we could get away with a spot of sabotage by "gumming up the works" of one of the sluices, to overload the gratings and stop the turbine.

Gill was on edge with the sudden drop in the temperature, obviously worried that the lights were going to go out. Muttering under his breath the strange religious (or anti-religious) blasphemies passing for curses in Austria, he kept inspecting the outside thermometer. The blue line of the alcohol had almost vanished into the little bowl at the bottom of the chart. Nervously, he kept trudging through the knee-deep snow blanketing the footpath, to check the ice flowing into the canal from the river.

As darkness fell, it became colder then ever for me and Elwin standing under the dim flickering light of a 40 watt bulb on the metal grid over the grating, only inches above the tumbling water of the river. My wet boots froze and turned into solid blocks of leather, and I lost all feeling in my feet. The homemade, makeshift mitts on my hands crackled with frost as they slid up and down the pole of the heavy rake, now glistening with a thin film of ice. The ends of my fingers had turned white and numb. To add to my misery, I had lost all feeling in my ears and I could sense the hairs in my nose freezing, as clouds of condensation from my breath solidified into a frosty rime down the front of my tunic.

Elwin and I decided enough was enough. It was time to go inside to brew some tea and thaw out.

But Thomas Gill, usually not slow himself to accept a mug of the life saving liquid, coming back from his reconnaissance of the state of the river, took a dim view of this idea saying, in effect, "Never mind the bloody tea, keep outside and make sure the ice doesn't clog the works up."

The words were hardly out of his mouth when the telephone in the control room rang. An unusual occurrence in itself.

The call was from a colleague of Gill's at the Knittlefeld electric works further up the river, warning him that a massive slab of ice was making its way down the Mur towards Murau. Thomas came rushing out calling for us to go with him to make some adjustment to the sluice gates.

It had started to snow heavily, again, as we reluctantly followed him to the two lock-gates on the bridge at the end of the canal where it intercepted the river. He directed us to the sluice on the right telling us to close it down. He went to the other one.

Elwin and I stood facing each other grasping the handle of the control wheel and half-heartedly turned it, the cogs screeching and squawking in protest at our dilatory efforts to force the wooden gate down into the water against the flow of the river.

"I hope the bloody ice chokes the sodden gratings up," I said to Elwin, "and the lights go out."

"Yes," he replied, "then maybe we'll get a bit of peace and a warm. I'm fuckin' freezin' and I'm dyin' for a pee and a cup of tea."

Expecting to hear Gill bawling his head off at our unenthusiastic handling of the wheel, I looked across to the other side of the platform. Just in time to glimpse him, momentarily silhouetted against the background of snow, suddenly disappear over the edge into the canal.

"Christ, El," I shouted, "Gill's fallen in. He's in the bloody water. We'll have to get him out quick or he'll freeze to bloody death."

We left the cumbersome wheel on the sluice to its own devices, the wooden gate only a quarter of the way down to the bottom of the lock, the ice already swirling and spinning on the surface of the water flowing towards the power house. Chance had stepped in to carry out the minor sabotage we had been plotting on and off for the last few days. We slithered our way through the now deep snow to find him clinging with his bare hands to the coping stone of the wall of the canal, his head and shoulders sticking up above the slabs of broken ice on the surface of the water.

I could see right away, that if we tried to get down the steep, snow covered grassy bank of the canal to lift him out, bodily, we would probably join him in the water.

"We can't go down to him, Elly," I shouted, "we'll slide in ourselves. I'll get the boat hook. We'll fish him out with that."

I ran back to the grating and dragged the long, heavy, iron-pointed boat-hook to the top of the bank. Thomas, somehow, was still hanging on like grim death to the ice-covered coping of the wall, Elwin shouting words of encouragement to him in a strange, excited mixture of English, Welsh and pidgin German.

Awkwardly, we manoeuvered the slippery pole down the bank to Gill, who promptly released his perilous grip of the wall and grabbed the hook with both hands. His legs trailed in the flow of the water and rose through the debris of broken ice to the surface. We hauled him out on his stomach, sliding him over the top of the coping on to the snow of the steep bank, up to the safety of the snow-covered footpath.

He turned over on his back, wheezing his thanks, his chest going up and down as if he had just finished a long distance marathon. "Danke, danke," he panted over and over again, "gut, gut" amid a volume of excited German completely lost on us. As he sat up I could see his saturated clothes already beginning to freeze and icicles forming on the peak of his water-logged cap. His moustache, in seconds, became frost encrusted like the front of my tunic. His coat and trousers stiffened like shirts left out on a clothes line on a windless, cold and frosty, wash-day morning.

"Get him up, quick, El," I shouted, "before he fuckin' freezes to death, let's get him inside quick."

We pulled him to his feet and made for the warmth and safety of the power station. But the Electricitatzverk was now in complete darkness for the gratings were packed solidly with ice, the water couldn't get through and the hum of the generator was strangely stilled.

Murau was without electric and all the lights had gone out.

But to my dismay, Gill didn't go in the building. He staggered past it telling us to go on to a cottage along the footpath further up the river. We knew this was where a woman friend of his lived.

Known to us as the "Merry Widow" she had occasionally made clandestine visits to Gill in the basement where I had had my abortive affair with Lore, to give him the latest news of her husband who was somewhere on the Russian Front. That's what he told us anyway. Romantic Elwin Jones had already tried, without success, to make her acquaintance when he had walked down the path for water after the supply in the station had frozen up.

We carried on along the footpath in single file, Elwin leading the way and me pushing and prodding the visibly freezing Thomas Gill to keep him moving. But not long after we had left the safety and welcoming warmth of the blacked-out power station, struggling against what had now become an Arctic snowstorm, Gill suddenly collapsed in the snow, drawing his knees up to his chin and holding his head in his hands.

"Resten must," he said, "resten must, Ich mus schlafen gehen."

"Christ El," I said, "the silly bugger wants to sleep. We'll have to keep him moving or he'll freeze to death. Get him on his bloody feet."

Encouraging him with our limited German and obscene English we lifted him up and, with his arms around our shoulders and his feet dragging in the snow, carried on again, crashing our way through the snow-laden bushes each side of the narrow path. Despite the cold, I started to sweat with fear when I realised that, in the blinding snow, the three of us could stumble into the River Mur flowing alongside in full spate, hidden by the snow-laden bushes.

I don't really know how we managed to get him to the shelter of the little riverside cottage, but I'll never forget the relief when the door was opened promptly in answer to our urgent thumpings.

I'll never forget, either, the wonderful scene which met my eyes when we went inside.

The door opened directly on to a warm, cosy kitchen-cum-living room, brightly lit by an oil lamp under a large, colourful glass shade hanging over a table in the middle of the room. A welcoming ruddy glow came from a wood stove in the corner which had just been stoked with fresh logs for sparks were spitting out from the open door on to a polished red-tiled floor. On the hob of the stove stood a large, shiny, aluminium saucepan, bubbling away with some sort of soup or stew, the source of the delightful smell which set my mouth watering and my stomach rumbling immediately we entered the room.

On the wall facing us, over an ornately carved, wood sideboard, hung an enlarged photograph of a Feld-Webel, immaculately turned out in the uniform of the Waffen SS, the skull and crossbones insignia on his cap and the inevitable Iron Cross award pinned to his chest. Without doubt the husband of our hostess, now lost in the wilderness of the Russian Steppes. To one side of him was a stuffed bird in a glass case, and on the other a three foot long pink and white stuffed salmon. He must have been a sporty individual, the husband of Gil's friend, and I found myself wondering if he was having any success in Russia. On the sideboard, between two large porcelain figurines was an oval metal tray, or salver, glinting in the glow from the stove. On it stood two glass decanters of what looked like red and white wine.

But what my eyes really feasted on after my first hasty glance around the room, was the table in the middle. It was set with a single placing of a knife, fork and spoon and in the centre of the starched table cloth, reposing in all its glory, was a huge, round, double tiered, farm-house loaf of crusty, white bread. Standing on a round wooden board, a breadknife at its side, the bread reminded me of a tiered wedding cake on the bride and groom's table waiting for the ceremonial slicing.

I had completely forgotten such scenes of domestic bliss, and warmth, and comfort, and homeliness, existed anymore. My eyes flooded with tears of self-pity, homesickness, envy, and anger at what I had been missing during the past two years. My thoughts, involuntarily, flashed back to the sparse but homely kitchen of 26, Vanbrugh Crescent and to my Mother, and to a grey enamelled electric stove and to the smell of the delicious, pea soup which she produced so expertly with a sixpenny ham shank from Listers the Pork Butchers, and two pennyworth of pot-herbs from Ashtons the greengrocers.

Gill said to us, "Wait there," and then disappeared into another room with his lady friend, after she had taken a towel and some clothes from a cupboard near the stove.

Elwin and I remained standing just inside the threshold of the front door, like two schoolboys after a snowball contest, water dripping from the melting snow and ice on our clothes and boots forming pools of water on the spotless, tiled floor. At first, we were completely mesmerised by the homely, domestic scene laid out before us.

Elwin was the first to get his breath back.

"Look at that beautiful bread, Doug," he said in a whisper, his Adam's Apple bobbing up and down as he swallowed, compulsively. "I've never seen anything like that since I've been in Austria, have you? I didn't even know they had white bread."

His hoarse whisper brought me back from my daydreams of home. "Nor did I," I replied, "and it's a long time since I've smelt scouse like that, too. I'll bet that tastes a lot better than that lousy spud soup we collect from the Gasthaus."

I nodded my head in the direction of the bubbling, aromatic, aluminium stewpot. "We should be all right for a basinful of that, after what we've just been through with Gill."

But it was not to be.

The miserable woman returned and, unlike the Florence Nightingale of Chania in Crete, who had risked her very life to

168

give me a handful of raisins and rice which she could ill afford, she completely ignored our stamping of freezing feet, our dry, hacking coughs, our rubbing of cold hands and our appreciative sniffs of the gorgeous, aromatic scouse. She put more wood in the stove and hung Thomas Gill's wet clothes on a clothes airer in front of it saying, "Herr Gill will be out in a minute."

We were still standing there ten minutes later, clouds of steam rising from Gill's saturated trousers, when he reappeared wearing the hand-me-downs of his friend's husband, now suffering with frost bite on the Russian Front. He was grinning and apparently none the worse for his ducking in the ice and the exhausting trek through the blizzard. We expected him to ask us to join him in a basinful of the stew. Or, at the very least, a cup of ersatz coffee. But neither he, nor the Merry Widow, took the hint and we were outside in the snow again making our way back to the Power Station.

By the time we got to the Electricitatverk, Franz Mosshammer and Wilhelm Gruber had cleared the grating. The lights of Murau were shining once more.

After Gill's lengthy explanation to his Boss of how he had slipped and fallen in the river, and our bravery and initiative in pulling him out, we trudged back to Murau. Before we reached our billet he stopped at the Gasthaus where we drew our food and bought us a tot of schnapps. Personally, I would have preferred a big basinful of The Merry Widow's stew. He told us that he was going to see about getting us repatriated home as a reward.

There were many such instances of life-saving rescue of civilians by prisoners-of-war, in working camps scattered throughout Germany and Austria. Les Dean, another 106th man, received the everlasting gratitude of a farming family after he pulled a toddler out of a river and saved her life. The gratitude lasted a lifetime, for Les visited the family regularly until he died in the early nineties.

French prisoners carrying out these acts of humanity were usually rewarded by being sent home. Gill, believing we would get the same treatment, approached the Commandant of Stalag XV111A through the Feld Webel in charge of our working camp. He was so confident, he gave me the address of a relation of his in London, a Mrs Hedie Vasialiadon of 45, New Compton Street, Charing Cross Road and asked me to call on her.

But we were not repratiated. Elwin Jones and I were each rewarded the princely sum of 50 Marks in the almost useless "Camp Money", Lagergeld.

The incident was published in "The Camp", a newspaper issued by the Germans to Prisoner-of-War camps.

"The Camp" was a propaganda rag, describing at great length the German successes in Russia and the Western Desert and endeavouring to promote so-called good relations between the prisoners-of-war and the Germans. It regularly featured articles asking for volunteers from the British prisoners, for the British Division of the German Army, with promises of high pay, untold luxuries, and conditions of service away from the fighting fronts, and highly-paid post-war employment in the victorious Reich when the war was over.. This propaganda sheet contained bits of news and details of sports and theatre activities from the various camps. It also reported accounts of rescues by prisoners of civilians. "The Camp" was in great demand to ease the chronic shortage of toilet paper.

When we eventually got back to the stable that night our account of the rescue of Thomas Gill was met with a mixed reception from our comrades. And for that matter many years later from men who had seen the write-up in "The Camp".

"Why didn't you let the bastard drown?"

"You should have hit him over the head with the boat hook. The only good fuckin' German is a dead fuckin' German."

And other sundry derogatory, obscene remarks.

But most of our companions took the commonsense viewpoint that we couldn't have done much else under the circumstances, and that we had acted instinctively and naturally to pull Gill out of the icy water.

I believe there were, also, many unreported instances of rescue of Allied prisoners by Germans like the rescue of Dick Rimmer at the end of the war. Dick and Mick Bulger, two 106th men, instead of waiting patiently for the Americans to release them, went off to dig up some "buried treasure" at a monastery where Mick had once worked. Dick fell down the steep bank of a fast flowing river, his back-pack falling over his head and pulling him under the water. In danger of drowning, he was hauled out by a party of Germans who were fleeing as fast as they could from the advancing Russians. More of this story later.

Chapter 21

Tea Kuchen

There was another occasion towards the end of my first winter in Murau, when the scents of romance floated in the spring air and filled the hay-barns on the slopes above the Electricitatsverk.

Vic Green and Elwin Jones were on an afternoon shift with Franz Mosshamer when, for some reason or other, the water supply in the basement dried up. Franz, the sparkle in his eyes shining brightly, suggested that they could get water for their afternoon brew of tea from a nearby farm. Franz, of course, knew something that they didn't.

Elwin, the tall, handsome, pale-faced Welshman from Cardiff volunteered to go for the water.

He set off up the lane to the farm, nonchalantly swinging a Klim-tin kettle on the end of a piece of string, in time to his tuneless whistling of "Land of our Fathers". A lock of long blonde hair curled out from under his newly aquired forage cap, and there was a knife-edged crease in his new battledress trousers.

It was well over an hour later before he returned, flushed of face, wisps of hay clinging to his crumpled new uniform, and his forage cap skewwhiff on the top of his head. The Klim tin was only half full of water.

"Where the hell have you been, Elwin?" asked Vic Green, a rising note of complaint in his usually good-natured voice. He was missing his afternoon tea. "I was beginning to think you'd done a runner on your own."

I should explain that strength and stamina slowly returning with the contents of the Red Cross parcels, talk amongst the inmates of the Camp had turned for the first time to serious plans of escaping. "Making a break for it" or "doing a runner" was the jargon usually used.

Franz Mosshamer didn't seem a bit perturbed by Elwin's delay in returning, and stood in the background with a sly grin on his face as if he was fully aware of the reason and understood the conversation.

"I got held up a bit," said Elwin, "that's all." And went on to explain to Dai the reason for his delay.

Finding nobody at home in the farmhouse he had wandered through the untidy, deserted farmyard looking for a pump or water tap, picking his way through puddles of dirty water and half a dozen hens busily scratching away in the mud. Hearing activity in the barn he strolled through the open door to see an attractive, "youngish" woman in the hay-loft forking hay from the top of the hay-stack into a cart by the door. According to Elwin's star-struck eyes she was an older and bigger edition of Jean Harlow of Hollywood fame. In full Technicolor.

Mitzi, (Elwin said that was her name) slightly dishevelled, her face glistening with sweat from her exertions with the hay-fork, was at first taken aback by the unexpected appearance of the good-looking stranger. This tall, handsome, blond Aryan in a smart khaki uniform, strolling into her barn whistling his National Anthem and swinging an empty can on the end of a piece of string was a facsimile, if ever there was one, of a member of the Glorious Master Race lauded by Hitler and his Henchmen.

Elwin was the first to recover from the unexpected meeting.

"Guten tag, Fraulein," he said, in his best Welsh-accentated German. "Kann Ich wasser haben bitte, fur tea kuchen?"

"Can I have some water to make a cup of tea, please?"

One of the first German phrases most British prisoners-of-war learned when they arrived in German working camps.

Mitzi, slaving away from dawn to dusk on the never ending, thousand-and-one jobs of the family farm, who hadn't seen her husband for the past two years, was glad of the diversion and seemed more than anxious to show Elwin the water supply. She lost no time in climbing down from the loft and walked towards him with a smile of welcome on her face, brushing hay from her drab clothes and vainly trying to straighten her disordered hair.

"Ya voll, mein Herr, comst du mit mir," she replied,

without any hesitation. And she took him by the hand and led him back to the farmhouse.

That night after lock-up, Elwin related the story of his "tea kuchen" with Mitzi, to an open-mouthed, captive audience lined up, expectantly, on the two sleeping shelves. But, when he drew an erotic veil over the proceedings after explaining how she had led him back to the farmhouse and told him how much she was missing her husband, somebody said, "You're a fuckin' liar Elly, pull the other bloody one. You're a bleedin' romancer who saw too many films before you was called up."

A couple of days later Vic Green, again with the encouragement of Franz Mosshamer, went up to the farm for water. And to console Mitzi about her husband's prolonged absence. That evening, Vic, with his tongue in his cheek, said to me that he had told Mitzi the little lad from Liverpool was on the afternoon shift next week and that she was to look after him and see that he got plenty of water.

But as usual, luck or fate or destiny, again stepped in as far as my "tea kuchen" was concerned. That weekend our cushy job at the Power Station came to an end. The warm spring sunshine had thawed the snow on the mountain tops and melted the ice on the River Mur.

To our regret the gratings on the Electricitatzverk no longer required our services.

***

I spent the remainder of that spring and early summer working on the building site with the rest of the inmates of the arbeitslager. General labouring for Italian bricklayers building a row of terraced cottages.

It was there I completed my apprenticeship in the art of bludging, or dodging the column, which I had commenced at the brickworks some months previously. Goon-baiting and laughing up our sleeves at our captors, carrying out minor works of sabotage on building equipment and competing with each other to see how much work we could not do.

It was there, also, that the handsome, blonde Elwin Jones

174

consummated another unique courtship.

Elwin's illegal romance this time was with a heavily built, middle-aged haus-frau. It was a silent, unusual affair developed over a distance of some hundred yards or so.

Silent, because their courtship was carried out with a secret sign language. Finger and hand and arm and facial gesticulations, like the tic-tac signals between two bookies on the course on Grand National day setting up the odds for the big race. Or a watered down version of the flag-wagging semaphore signalling we had tried to learn in our early days in the Army.

Unusual, for the long distance courtship started, really, because the sensitive Welshman was a bit of a loner. Elwin was unable at times, like most of us, to accept the permanent proximity of his twenty-three fellow inmates. And in the warm, sunny days early that summer, when we were locked up for the weekend in the claustrophobic, overcrowded, smelly stable, Elwin developed a habit of standing in front of a small, barred, open-window in the "recreation" room, his back turned on the rest of his mates, pretending they were not there. Smoking a cigarette, leaning on the window sill with his chin in his hands, his eyes staring into space, filling with unshed tears of homesickness brought on by the emotional, haunting music of Handel's Largo or Cavalera Rusticana. We still had Franz Mosshamer's gramophone and six records, although the points on the needles had long since worn away, Elwin never tired of listening to the scratchy recordings.

Standing at the little window one quiet, sunny Sunday afternoon when most of the lads had taken to their beds or were trying to master Cuthbertson's intricate conventions of rubber-bridge, he was suddenly startled out of his nostalgic, self-inflicted bout of homesickness. As he looked across the little gardens of the houses on the bank of the river alongside our jail, his day-dreaming eye suddenly lit on the comely shape of a female sunbathing on a coloured blanket laid over a green patch of grass in the middle of a tiny, flower-filled garden.

She was lying on her stomach, stark naked except for a pair of blue sunglasses and a white sombrero hat. She could have fallen right out of the middle pages of "The Naturist" the pre-war Health and Fitness magazine.

Remarkably, Elwin, kept this apparition to himself, knowing what would happen if the rest of the bored men in the background became aware of the sun-tanned, overweight Venus in the garden. As he watched, spellbound, guiltily assuming the role of a Peeping Tom, she turned over and sat up exposing to Elwin's now popping eyes two well formed, sun-kissed breasts.

At the same time she pulled her sun-glasses away from her eyes, she in turn noticed the handsome Elwin standing at the window nervously blowing out clouds of Craven A tobacco smoke. Her face broke into wreaths of smiles, prompting the mesmerised Elwin to smile back.

Without more ado, as if playing to an audience, the lady in the garden put down the book she had been reading, took off the wide brimmed hat with a flourish and, arching her back, raised her sun-tanned arms to comb her long, grey/blond, shoulder-length tresses. In the process accentuating her ample bosoms to the now completely spellbound Elwin.

So started a remarkable courtship, carried out in a sign language made up by the courting couple as they went along. A brief, silent courtship eventually consummated, silently, (well, almost silently) in the woods on the bank of the River Mur some two weeks later.

Chapter 22

Topping Out

The fulfilment of Elwin's dumbstruck romance, carried out with the technique of a performing mime artist, happened early one sultry, warm afternoon at the building site.

We had just gone back to work after our usual mid-day, miserly ration of tasteless potato soup, when the Italian bricklayers held a ceremony, or ritual, to mark the completion of the first stage of the building work. Rather like the traditional "topping out" ceremony carried out at British building sites when the highest point of the project has been reached.

The Italians' ceremony took the form of preserving for posterity the names of all the operatives on the site, including the prisoners. Names and addresses, army numbers, prisoner-of-war numbers, messages, sometimes rude and sarcastic sometimes crude and pornographic, were enthusiastically written by the prisoners on the backs of Cadbury's Fruit and Nut Chocolate wrappers or on unwanted letters from Swansea or Liverpool or Sydney, or on pages torn from army pay books. These scribbled artefacts were then securely corked in empty beer bottles and buried by the Italians in the wet shale and cement mix forming a concrete lintel over a door opening. Sundry mementos like pennies and a flattened out Klim tin also went into the mix.

The ever-exuberant Scousers, not to be outdone, followed this ancient Italian tradition with their own "topping out" ceremony as performed on the high-rise apartment blocks of Toxteth.

"Fitzy" Fitzpatrick, a one-time bricklayer's hod-carrier in Liverpool, who knew all about these things, clutching a page from the "Volkischer Beobactor", the propaganda rag, climbed to the top of the scaffold, crawled like an alley cat up the tiled roof to the chimney and fixed a makeshift Union Flag to the brickwork. He then lowered his trousers and, his bare backside exposed to the elements, squatted on the chimney pot and opened his bowels. The prisoners all stopped work to cheer him on and to encourage him. "Fitzy" had already carried out a minor act of sabotage by blocking up the chimney with the judicious placing of bricks in the flue.

The site foreman completely unable to see the funny side of the mad Englander's antics, went hysterical when he saw the grinning Fitzy perched with his pants down on the top of the chimney pot. He literally foamed at the mouth as he spewed out a string of irreligious oaths. One of the guards, normally wandering around the site aimlessly filling in his time, also became quite excited and pulled his rifle off his shoulder, pointedly "put one up the spout", and aimed it skywards in the direction of the crouching Fitzy, ordering him to come down, or else.

Completely ignoring the posten's threat Fitzy got to his feet off the lofty, fresh-air w.c., pulled up his trousers and yelled at the top of his voice to his cheering mates below.

"Tell Jonesy 'is Judy is cummin' down the road. She's on a bike and I think she's lookin' for 'im and she's got sumptin in the basket to give 'im."

Now on this particular day it so happened that I had been delegated to go with Old George for the afternoon load of shingle. One of the easier, much sought after jobs on the building site, labouring for an old man transporting loads of grey shingle from the bank of the nearby River Mur. One load in the morning and one in the afternoon. The pebbles formed the hardcore for the concrete foundations and floors of the houses.

Old George was another civilian reluctantly dragged back from retirement at the outbreak of the war. He was responsible for the only means of transport on the site. A team of two patient, dun-coloured, smooth coated oxen, pulling a four-wheeled flat-topped cart.

He was an easy-going, moustachioed, pipe-smoking character and was nearly as good at dodging the column as most of the prisoners. And he was ably assisted in this respect by his pair of slow-moving beasts of burden with their measured, careful, almost dainty tread as they pulled the cart. So it was a cushy afternoon for anyone detailed to accompany him to collect the shingle from the riverside.

The old man was dressed in the typical Austrian fashion of the day. A battered, green trilby hat with the shaving brush adornment on the brim, a denim-like jacket and, comically to us kriegies when we saw it for the first time, short summer lederhosen worn over dirty-white, "long-john" underpants. The long-johns covered his bony knees as if he was shy of exposing them or if he was reluctant to leave off his winter underclothing and chance the summer sunshine. A long-stemmed, cherry-wood meerschaum pipe, smoked by most elderly Austrian males at that time, dangled permanently from his lips, leaving a dark brown stain on his full, grey moustache. The pipe never left his mouth except when he ate his mid-day break. Usually this was a little piece of fatty, smoked speck from which he cut off snippets with his pocket-knife and chewed with a chunk of black bread. On occasions Old George could be persuaded to swap a piece of this delicious bacon for a tin of sardines or a few cigarettes.

Half the lads on the site stopped work to tell Elwin about his silent lady friend and give him a rally of encouragement. Particularly when she turned around and went riding back towards the river.

She was pedalling an old fashioned ladies bicycle with high, sit-up-and-beg handlebars, her summer frock billowing in the slipstream. Despite her half-hearted, one-handed attempts to keep her dress in order, she provocatively exposed her bare, brown, muscular thighs and momentary glimpses of red drawers. Her long hair was tied up in a pigtail with a silk bandanna, like an overgrown schoolgirl. A coloured cloth hid the contents of a wickerwork basket hooked over the high handlebars of the cycle.

By this time, of course, we were all aware of Elwin's assignations and saucy signalling at the little window. His theatrical mime had developed realistically and became a source of amusement and interest to everyone, relieving the boredom of the confined Sunday afternoons. Despite his protests most of us had tried, unsuccessfully, to get a little piece of the action, so to speak, even if it was only to take in a passing glimpse of the sombrero hat. But, I'm bound to say, she remained faithful to Elwin and would not have anything to do with intruders, quickly covering her nakedness with a robe, or disappearing into the house if someone other than Jonesy stood at the window.

When the cry went up that Elwin's Judy was looking for him, I was just about to depart with Old George to fetch the afternoon's load of shale. Someone said to me, "Eh, Doug, switch with Elwin and see if she follows him on the cart. He might get lucky."

Although reluctant to forfeit my easy afternoon spell with Old George, Elwin was a good friend of mine and we hastily made the switch.

Two minutes later as the cart started its journey to the river, she came back again, to circle it like a cowboy outrider scouting for a wagon train, or a wasp worrying an empty jam jar on a rubbish tip. We watched as the cart trundled along the bumpy lane to the river, until it vanished among the trees, Elwin happily sitting on the plank seat alongside Old George. His "Judy", her frock flying in the wind, following at a safe distance.

***

After lock-up that night, Elwin filled us in with the erotic, romantic details of his spontaneous rendezvous with the lady from the inner pages of "The Naturist".

At the river bank, he had started to load the shingle pebbles on to the cart, when his silent lady-friend caught up with him. She cycled past with a flash of red knickers and vanished into the seclusion of a thick copse of half-grown Douglas Fir conifer trees nearby.

Old George, busily refilling the large pottery bowl of his meerschaum with about half-an-ounce of shag tobacco, didn't see her as she went past, and Elwin took the bull by the horns, so to speak.

"Ich mus scheisen gehen, George. Zen minuten," Elwin said to the old man. "I must go and have a crap George, I'll be back in ten minutes"

So saying, he delved into the large pocket of his battledress trousers and fished out a tin of Princes sardines-in-tomato-sauce, carried there for black market opportunities and emergencies such as this. Elwin handed it to the old man and taking the shovel with him in confirmation of his errand, vanished into the trees.

Two minutes later he caught up with his silent seductress who had already prepared herself for a quick, sun-bathing session in the buff on a grassy bank hidden by a circle of thick bramble bushes. It was a natural, secluded arbour in the middle of the stand of young, fragrant pines. But this time she had the physical pleasure of the company of the gallant Elwin who, without demur and eager to carry out his own personal "topping out" ceremony, applied with trembling hands the sun-lotion which she produced from the basket on the handlebars of the bicycle.

Half an hour later, Old George had finished his sardines, and after wiping splashes of tell-tale tomato sauce from his luxuriant mustache and the front of his jacket, was in the process of looking for the shovel to bury the empty sardine can, when Elwin returned, a blissful smile on his flushed face.

Elwin, afterwards, with his tongue in his cheek, always insisted that throughout the whole proceedings in the love-nest amongst the trees, not a single word passed between them and not a sound was made except for the unintelligible sounds of endearment, of passion and of love-making.

He never learned the lady's name, nor she, his.

***

Notwithstanding the dire penalties meted out to both parties if they were discovered, there were many such brief, opportunist, one-night-stands (or afternoon trysts) by prisoners-of-war. There were also, a few genuine, lasting romances ending in marriage after the war.

Incredibly, there were some prisoners, aided and abetted by a haus-frau, or her teenage daughter, or sometimes both, who completely disregarded the penalties for fraternisation and made themselves completely at home in some small dairy farm tucked away in the mountains. They became one of the family, more than willing to spend the rest of the war living on the fat of the land, with or without Red Cross parcels, taking over the duties in the fields, (and in the bed), of the Man of the House, long gone to Russia.

And it was after the war that I learned that a British prisoner in a remote working camp in Austria courted a local girl and secretly married her in the village church with the full co-operation of her family, the wedding ceremony being carried out with the blessing of the Roman Catholic priest.

CHAPTER 23

Tossing the Doctor

It was in the Murau working camp that I had a simple accident, which was to have a marked effect on the rest of my life.

Just before the end of the winter of 1941/1942, I was taking my turn at breaking up and clearing away the pyramid of ice formed by the dripping anti-frost tap in the yard, when I slipped on the ice and broke a bone in my left wrist. Although causing me quite a lot of pain, there was no swelling or apparent damage and the Feld-Webel in charge refused to let me go on the kranken liste – sick parade – to see a doctor. The Sergeant had become more and more suspicious of the wiles of malingering prisoners trying to "toss the doctor" with minor ailments.

It was two years before I successfully tossed the doctor, and was sent back to Wolfsberg for medical treatment. From there I went to Graz hospital for X-Rays and plaster cast treatment, but by then it was too late to repair the damaged bone.

Tossing the Doctor became a sort of game with many prisoners-of-war. A battle of wits between the work-shy prisoner versus the Arbeitslager Kommandant, and the doctor in the local village. A battle of wits to avoid work and spend the day sleeping, eating, reading, or simply doing nothing.

Sometimes, tossing the doctor was the first stage of an escape plan, to consult the Escape Committee at Wolfsberg for advice and help. Sometimes it was simply to get away from a dreary, uncomfortable working camp to savour the so-called luxuries of the amenities of the Stalag or to try to seek the solace of some lonely farmer's haus-frau on a farm.

Some men went to extraordinary lengths to deceive the doctor with horrible, self-inflicted wounds and feigned illnesses. A young Kiwi, at one of the camps with me, successfully persuaded the Kamp Kommandant that he had a terrible chest pain and it was a matter of life and death that he see a doctor without delay. Waiting his turn to go into the surgery, the hopeful malingerer took out his precious store of cigarettes and shredded butt-ends and after giving a "tailor made" Players Cork Tip to the accompanying guard, lit a "roll up" and cheekily had a smoke to calm his nerves.

The home-made cigarette had previously been prepared with half of a crushed aspirin tablet mixed in with the tobacco. I can't speak from personal experience but I believe that inhaling two or three puffs of a cigarette laced with aspirin, shortly before being examined, caused a thumping of the heart and, hopefully, a hasty trip back to Wolfsberg.

The success of any such deception, of course, depended on the acting ability of the man and the skill, or gullibility, of the village doctor. The subterfuge helped if the doctor was elderly and overworked, or better still if it was a woman doctor, sympathetic and English speaking.

Many other dodges were tried out. From the age-old, "I've got a back-ache, Herr Doctor, and I can't straighten my back, I can't lift anything", to the painful and dangerous trick of wrapping a wet cloth, tightly, around a knee and then tapping the knee-cap, firmly, with a spoon until the knee swelled alarmingly. The wet cloth treatment could also be applied to the sensitive Achilles tendon on the heel.

At one working camp I met a young South African quite determined not to work for the Germans. Before going sick he sprinkled salt into his eyes, causing them to water copiously and making them sore and bloodshot. He and I were put on a charge for "refusing to work", when an uncooperative doctor said we were "nicht krank" and to go back to work. That tale is told later.

In 1944, Jimmy Miller, a tough, athletic soccer player and amateur boxer from Birkenhead, went to even greater lengths to avoid work on a military airfield. At that time the Germans losing the war, completely ignored the Articles of the Geneva Convention, and under gun point forced some fifty men into the daily task of filling bomb craters on the airstrip. Jimmy protested in vain and his attempts to toss the doctor were met with threats of three days in the bunker, without food, and a going-over with the butt of a rifle. So one afternoon after he had finished his stint loading a lorry with earth to fill the bomb holes, he put his left arm under the tailboard of the vehicle, slammed the metal framed tailboard down on his forearm, breaking the bone in two places. He never again worked for the Germans. Nor, sadly, did he ever box again.

My sojourn at the Murau working camp was brought to an end by a spate of unsuccessful attempts to toss the doctor by half the inmates, which culminated in an abortive strike and the eventual closing of the camp.

One welcome rainy morning, (the heavy rain, bringing the prospect that we would be laid off and spend the day playing cards or reading or sleeping), three of the Liverpool Scousers and one of the Australians refused to go out on a grave-digging job. They insisted on seeing the doctor. There were two civilian burials that day and the Feld-Webel was adamant that the graves had to be prepared whatever the weather. He told them that they would have to wait until the next day to see the doctor.

After much argument and raised voices – Dai Davies unsuccessful this time in smoothing things over – the four men still refused to go out in the rain. There was a debate among the rest of the lads, already happily ensconsed on their beds for a day of leisure, on whether we should all strike, in support, the next day. I had a row with one of the Australians when I refused to be bullied by him and said that I would make my own mind up. But the matter was resolved that same afternoon by the swift removal of the four "nicht arbeiters" by three armed guards. We didn't see them again.

Years later I learned from Alf Parker that they had been tried by a military court-martial and were sentenced to four years hard labour, the charges being, refusing to work "in accordance with the Geneva Convention", inciting their fellow prisoners to mutiny, and threatening physical action against one of the guards with a boot. They served their sentence in a "strafe lager". A special punishment camp for prisoners found guilty of refusing to work, or stealing, or striking a civilian or a guard, or other so-called serious misdemeanours. Tom Hesketh got away with it, however, when he discovered that, as a non-commissioned officer, he did not have to work. He finished up in Stalag 383, a non-working Stalag in Bavaria.

Alf Parker also told me that "Fitz" Fitzpatrick, one of the three Liverpool men, (not, however in the 106th) met a tragic end in the strafe lager. He was in a detail of four men carrying betweem them on their shoulders a long, heavy baulk of timber to load on to a lorry. Apparently he was carrying the log on his right shoulder and the other three had it on their left. When the three men simultaneously threw the log from their shoulders on to the vehicle, his neck received the full weight of the log and was broken.

Supposedly, strikes by prisoners-of-war, or anyone else for that matter, were not allowed in Nazi Germany. But there were hundreds of instances of one day strikes, "go slows" and arguments and protests against bad food or bad conditions, inclement weather or shortage of Red Cross parcels. Most differences were resolved there and then, in the camp, by a good Confidence Man and the attitude of the Sergeant in charge. A lot depended on the size of the camp, the number of prisoners it held`and how far the Feld Webel was prepared to go for a quiet life away from the Russian Front. It could also depend to a great extent on the feelings of the prisoners and what sort of work they were doing. Many men accepted their lot philosophically, and resigned themselves to see the rest of the war out in comparative safety, happy to let others take care of the fighting, particularly if the working conditions were easy, the camp relatively comfortable and Red Cross food parcels arrived regularly.

Conditions of employment of prisoners-of-war were supposed to be in accordance with the Articles of the Geneva Convention. Strikes were "verboten". All grievances were supposed to be settled by the camp Confidence Man or, as a last resort, the Chief Man of Confidence of Stalag XV111A, Wolfsberg.

Not that we knew anything at all, at that time, about Geneva Conventions or conditions of employment. Nobody had ever informed us about our rights as a prisoner-of-war or for that matter how to find our way across the desert in Africa if we lost our way. I suppose it was taken for granted that we would never get lost in the desert or taken prisoner, until maybe, it was decided it was better to lose thousands of men in the evacuation of Crete, than dozens of naval vessels.

Chapter 24

Three No Trumps in St. Lambrecht

Nowhere was the game of work-dodging better carried out than at St.Lambrecht, where we found ourselves when the Murau camp was closed a few days after the four "nicht arbeiters" had been forcibly removed.

St.Lambrecht, the home of an ancient and venerated Abbey and Church, is a sleepy little village in the Upper Mur Valley. In those far off days it was an hour's train journey on the miniature mountain railway from Murau and the River Mur. Today the Abbey is a busy tourist attraction with a car park, a bus station, and half-day closing on a Wednesday.

But in July, 1941, when I arrived there as a prisoner-of-war, the four hundred year old Abbey was no longer an Abbey. It had been commandeered by the Nazis and converted into a civilian gaol. So there was no abbot, no monks or novices, nor any other members of the clergy in residence.

The accommodation for the twenty men in the working camp was on the ground floor of what had been a lodge in the lofty, arched entrance to the abbey grounds from the main street of the village. Today, this room is the gift shop and ticket office for entrance into the ancient building, now fully restored to all its former glory.

Our thoughts were filled with foreboding, when we realised this gem of history was a civilian prison. Still comparatively new to the fickle ways of our captors, we assumed that as a punishment for our threatened strike at Murau, we were going to receive the same treatment as the convicts. However, we found that they were completely segregated from us in a gaol in the inner confines of the extensive buildings, at the far end of a paved quadrangle. We didn't see much of them.

At six o'clock in the morning, every day, Sundays included,

we were awakened by the sound of the marching feet of a hundred or so convicts on their way to work, the rythmical tramping on the cobbles of the courtyard echoing in the domed archway, as they marched past our quarters.

The archway echoed the tramping feet of the convicts.

Just before the column entered the main street, there was a barked command. As if to make sure we and the local citizens would be roused from our sleep, the marching convicts would break into the chorus of *"Venn wir Fahren Gegen* England", like a backing male voice choir in a scene from the Student Prince.

"When we march against England."

This German Army propaganda marching song was to become familiar to us whenever we encountered a squad of German Military on the move. A barked order to sing, was given by the N.C.O. in charge, whether or not the squad wanted to sing. Totally different from the singing of a detachment of marching British soldiers, relieving the boredom of a route march, by breaking out spontaneously, into "It's a long way to Tipperary". Half of them usually singing the Music Hall version, "It's the wrong way to tickle Mary".

Occasionally, when we were on our way to the building site where we "worked" we would see the convicts labouring in a field, turning the soil over with the long-handled Austrian shovel-cum-spade. They were working in unison. In straight, orderly, disciplined lines, like automatons, closely supervised by a line of armed warders standing behind them. The warders, in addition to a rifle slung over the shoulder, wielded a cudgel, as long and as thick as the helve of a pick-axe or baseball bat, which I saw being used, unmercifully, on the convicts.

The scene put me in mind of an old Hollywood film. "The Fugitive" with Paul Muni. Even the drab overall uniforms and forage caps, heavily marked with the broad, white arrows of the convict, were the same as in the film. Our guards seemed to have little communication with their opposite numbers, and told us that the convicts were communists, anti-Hitler political prisoners or hardened criminals.

Strangely, in contrast to the obviously strict regime in the civilian prison on our doorstep, the conditions and discipline in our camp proved to be just the opposite. Supervision was almost non-existent. Two guards accompanied us to a building site on the outskirts of the village, where we more or less pleased ourselves what work we carried out. The estate of semi-detached houses had been started just before the war, and building had virtually ground to a halt. Our employment on the site made very little difference.

The poor supervision manifested itself in another way, however, for the quality of the food issued to us at St. Lembrecht was atrocious and meagre, even by the poor standards of our previous lagers in Knittlefeld and Murau. The thin, tasteless potato soup was the unvarying meal each night, and the wedge of black bread each morning became smaller and smaller.

To make matters worse, food-wise, the camp's stock of Red Cross parcels had finished weeks ago, and even the well managed combines were feeling the pinch.

The situation hadn't been helped by a directive to our Kamp Kommandant. All parcels had to be opened by the German guards as they were issued each week. The tins of meat, fish, condensed milk and so on were pierced with a bayonet, and paper wrappings taken off the biscuits and other dry goods. The boxes had to be left in a store room, and the contents given out each night by a guard. Apparently this was a direct order from the German High Command to all British prisoner-of-war camps, to discourage the hoarding of food for escape attempts. The wildly, impractical order, which contravened the Geneva Convention anyway, died a natural death, of course. Even our humourless guards saw the funny side of the instruction, and said it was too stupid to work.

So what had become necessities for living, like Klim milk powder and hard-tack biscuits had disappeared, and we were fast running out of the life-sustaining tea and cigarettes. We re-used the Brook Bond tea leaves, time and time again, until they couldn't produce anymore of the amber liquid. Then the heavy smokers dried the spent tea leaves, and mixed the dusty remains with the remnants of tobacco dog-ends in their tobbaco tin.

The protests of our Confidence Man, Dai Davies, to the Kamp Kommandant had little effect, except promises, which never materialised, that more Red Cross food parcels were on the way to us.

There was also an attempt at St. Lambrecht to impose another crazy directive, which quickly collapsed under the combined hilarity of both the prisoners and, unusually, the guards. Every night after we returned from work, we were "handcuffed" for the evening. Each man, queuing to get at the contents of his box of food, was given an aluminium metal manacle, like the handcuffs in a child's Magician's Box, to handcuff his hands together. Carrying two spoonsful of condensed milk in a tin mug in one hand, and a slice of luncheon meat between two biscuits in the other, he would make his way back to his bunk and promptly unlock the 'cuffs, leaving them on his bed until he returned them, when we were locked up for the night. This was an order which was supposed to have come from Hitler, personally, in retaliation for an incident in a British p.o.w. camp, where German prisoners had been handcuffed to their beds for certain periods of the day.

It was at St. Lambrecht that I became an enthusiastic devotee of rubber bridge. Eight of us, (two teaching the rudiments of the game to the other six) formed a bridge school. "The Three No-Trumpers". We bought the only playing cards

190

left in the village shop of St. Lambrecht with the Lagergelt paid to us as wages.

We were still locked up each night and our boots taken away until morning, but unlike our two previous camps where the electricity was switched off at eight o'clock, the lights were left on all night. The bridge players made good use of this unexpected amenity, by playing bridge sometimes until two or three in the morning.

Play was always interrupted, however, at about ten o'clock each evening, when we were treated to a sort of strip-tease by a buxom, young woman in a room on the ground floor of the building opposite. Every night she undressed in front of her window, seemingly disregarding the audience of twenty young men crowding at the two windows opposite. Ignoring the obscene shouts of encouragement, which she couldn't hear anyway, she stripped to her shapely waist. After carrying out bending and stretching exercises she donned a nightgown and, to groans of dismay from the ogling prisoners, pulled the curtains across the window.

We only ever saw the girl at night-time. I never found out if she was some sort of teasing exhibitionist carrying out the display out of devilment, or if she was just blissfully ignorant of our presence at the windows opposite.

To make up for the missing sleep of the late night bridge sessions, before leaving for work at the building site next day, the "Three No-trumpers" smuggled out blankets concealed underneath trousers and jacket to doss down for a couple of hours of unofficial sleep in the loft of one of the houses.

These antics were just another way of relieving the boredom and monotony of life in the camp. Particularly in the early days before personal parcels of books or board games reached us from home and before the first library books arrived from Wolfsberg.

The lending library covering the working camps was organised and administered by the British Staff in the Stalag. Distribution of the books operated reasonably well from early in 1942 when the Germans were cock-a-hoop with their European victories, but became more and more spasmodic when the tables were slowly turned against them in 1943/44. So did the other

Geneva Conventions such as the safe and regular delivery of food parcels and mail. But even in the comparitively easy, early years, the library books, like the Red Cross food parcels would often fail to reach the camps or would be limited in number.

At St. Lambrecht, writing home became a sort of hobby for me. We were issued with four blank postcards and two letter forms every month. The two letter-forms were similar to the flimsy, Post Office airmail letters which are still available today.

I kept a careful account of these homeward bound letters and cards and also an account of the letters and parcels I received.

I still have the record today.

Copy of list of letters and cards posted in 1943.

So I made sure all my many relatives and friends received a post card or letter from time to time in reply to their most welcome letters. Because, of course, the correspondence was my life-line to sanity, and home; and how things used to be, how things would be again. Unfortunately none of my Stalag letters or cards sent home, survived the passage of time.

However, I still have an interesting letter from Frank Storey, my pre-war collegue and friend at Baxendales.

It was dated March 4th, 1942 and I received it on the 17th May, 1942.

12, Blisworth St.
Litherland,
Liverpool, 21.
March 4th, 1942.

Dear Doug,

You can imagine how surprised I was when I read your card and realised that you were a P.O.W. As a matter of fact I was lucky to get it because as you can see I am not now living at my old address due to the fortunes of war, but fortunately my brother met the Postman and in due course it came to me.

I am awfully sorry about your present position but I realise that you don't want to read a letter from me filled only with expressions of sympathy so as far as circumstances permit I shall endeavour to give you all the news.

I cannot recall just when it was since I saw you last, or had a word from you, so I wonder if you know that I got married on Aug. 3rd, 1940. Believe me Doug it's a great life or at least it will be when the war is over. This next will surprise you most of all, some months ago or 31st Jan.'41 to be exact, we had a lovely baby girl!!! What do you think of that, and how do you fancy me as a "Daddy"? She is coming on splendidly Doug and we have christened her Margaret.

I left the Firm in June '40 along with Larry Osborne and Jimmy Ellis but I have not heard anything of them since.

Actually nearly all the old faces have gone and I don't know where they are, but Alf Henwood is still going strong. I was in (heavily blacked out) for about ten months and I understand Billy Arnold was also there but I did not meet him at any time. I am in quite a good place now and it is only about 10 miles from where they (heavily blacked out) Going on leave on one occasion I made an effort to locate it for some time, if you know what I mean, but I eventually found it in Argyle St. It certainly gave me quite a shock and you will be amazed at the changes in the old town when you get back.

As I myself am away all the time it is really difficult for me to give you very much news because I am to a certain extent out of it myself but I wonder if you know just how the war is going on. Due to the sudden attack on Pearl Harbour, Japan is getting things all her own way in the Far East, but I feel sure she is beginning to lose the initiative. Russia is keeping Germany fully occupied (half of a full page cut out and missing) sustain it to make it worth while. In Libya the battle goes back and forth all the time and we are now roughly in the positions from which General Wavell started. To sum up I think that as soon as America gets into full stride regarding production etc. the war will soon end and I won't be at all surprised if that isn't in 15 months time. Do you think you can stick it that long?

Well Doug I am sure you must have had some very exciting experiences and seen some of the better sights of the world so you will have a lot to tell me when we meet again. It will be a wonderful thing when we can both get together on the old showroom again and renew the old partnership won't it? And I hope for both our sakes that it won't be long now.

I am afraid I must close now Doug, but please send me another card if you can, and let me know how you have received this letter so that I shall know just what I can say in them. So long Doug, and Good Luck,
Yours sincerely,
Frank.

***

It was at St. Lambrecht also, that, slowly and excruciatingly, I learned to "play" the mandoline.

To the good-tempered jibes of my fellow inmates, I picked out the melodies of a few nostalgic tunes. Accompanied by Taffy Griffiths, who proved to be a natural with the instrument, harmonising my laborious melody with great effect, our comrades came to appreciate our feeble efforts to enliven the boring week ends.

Leaving St. Lambrecht came early one afternoon, with the inevitable bust up when a German three striper paid an unexpected visit to the building site and discovered the "Three No Trumpers" wrapped up in blankets, asleep in the loft of one of the houses. There was hell to pay, for the guards more than the prisoners.

Two of them were on their way to the Russian Front later that afternoon. The following day the Englanders were on their way to yet another working camp.

Chapter 25

"Timber, Timber"

I was working with Bill Curtis on the top of a long, two metre high stack of logs piled by the track at the bottom of the valley when I heard the distant, bellowed warning.

"Timb-eeer, timb-eeer!"

Bill and I were hauling logs slid down the steep slope of the mountain above us by our mates. We were dragging them up on to the top of the stack and rolling them into position. It had been raining and the trunks, stripped of their bark, were slippy and awkward to handle with the sapine, the strange logging tool Franz, the civvy boss, had given us. A sort of single bladed pick-axe, with a hook on the end of the pick to bite into the log and haul it into position.

The shouts of alarm were taken up by more of my comrades on the mountainside above, as I turned quickly to see a huge twenty-four inch diameter log, twelve feet long, bouncing and cart-wheeling down the forty-five degree slope like a spent matchstick tossed out of a car. It was heading directly towards us.

"Timber, timber!"

The shouts were now panic stricken screams as our friends above tried to warn us of the danger. They could see the massive tree-trunk was going to hit the stack directly where we were working. For a fleeting moment I was transfixed at the sight of the huge, runaway log, cartwheeling down the side of the mountain. It was the rumbling, smashing noise that brought me to my senses as it crashed into tree stumps, uprooting them with a spider's web of roots and muddy earth.

"Jump, Bill, quick, for Christ's sake," I shouted to my companion.

We turned to the opposite side of the stack and leapt off the top of the stack of logs into the stream running alongside, six feet below. Stumbling and tripping on the boulders, we splashed across the shallow water to the black scree at the foot of the slope on the other side of the water.

As in one of the terrifying nightmares I experienced as a five-year-old, being chased by some frightening, unknown monster, my legs running nineteen to the dozen but my body refusing to move, I scrabbled desperately with my hands and feet to gain a foothold in the deep scree. My feet refused to grip the shale at the foot of the slope. I was taking a short step upwards, and a long slip downwards into the stream. But Lady Luck proved to be on my side once again, when I was able to grab a bush and pull myself clear.

I had just made it to the safety of firmer ground on the slope above when the runaway log exploded, end on, into the stack of logs behind me, like the runaway steam engine I had once seen at the coal depot at Breck Road Station crashing into the buffers at the end of the line. The missile entered the side of the stack midway between the ground and the top, just below the spot where we had been working. The neatly piled logs scattered like confetti, spread-eagled, higgledy-piggledy over the stream, many of them broken, splintered and left standing on end.

My hair's-breadth escape occurred during the first few days at our new arbeitskommando where our German hosts, without warning and without consulting me, promoted me to a fully-fledged forester in a timber camp.

The stacking of the logs on the rough track, ready for transport, was supposed to be an easy introduction to the work. Or so Franz had said. The trees had been felled two or three years before, and the logs left to "weather" on a section of the mountainside above the stream, one log being staked, horizontally across the slope, to hold a dozen or so placed vertically against it facing down the mountainside.

***

Paarl timber camp was part of a tiny hamlet of foresters' cottages high up in the Murauer Mountains, completely off the beaten track. An hour or more walk from Stadl, the nearest village and railway station, or a two-hour trek in the back of a farm cart pulled by a pair of oxen, which I was to experience later.

The area, these days, is a hikers' paradise. And indeed even in those dark days, the mountains and hills of Austria were dotted with walkers' chalets. Wooden refuge huts with emergency food, water, bedding and fuel for a fire. Shelter for the hiker or skier, herdsman or forester, caught in the open by sudden bad weather. I believe the idea of the Youth Hostels Association, originated with these mountain huts in mind.

I arrived at Paarl in the late summer of 1942 with about eighteen of the party which left Wolfsberg so abruptly twelve months previously. By now they were all staunch friends of mine, and it was remarkable how the comradeship and camaraderie between us all had developed in that twelve months.

New Zealanders Vin. Clausen from Wellington, Jim Waller from Geraldine, South Island, Tom Bennett from Taranaki, Arthur Nuttall from Blackball, West Coast and Joe Sainty from Auckland.

Australian George East from Victoria.

Welshmen Stan Thomas from Llanelly, Geoff Hallett from Llandaff, Bill Harris, George Harris and "Taffy" Griffiths from Swansea, Dai Davies from Carmarthen.

Northerners George "Gash" Hampton from Manchester, Charlie Sharp and Len Caulfield from Clitheroe, Frank Clay from Wirkworth, Albert Henderson from Durham, George Hastwell from Preston and Arthur Thompson from Coventry.

Southerners Jack King from Grantham, Eddie Faux from Middlesex, Bill Curtis from Dorset and Ken Bulbeck from London.

Our camp, this time, was a typical, single-storey Austrian, country farmhouse. A large, timber built bungalow, or chalet, somewhat rundown and in dire need of renovation. The timber, clap-board facing of the house was loose and the expansive shingle roof was spotted with white fungi and overgrown with patches of moss. In the Austrian fashion the roof's wide eaves extended over the walls, and the windows had neatly lined flower boxes under the sills. The boxes were empty of geraniums now except for the annexe, where the female former owner (and resident cook) lived.

Like most Austrian country dwellings, chopped billets of wood were stacked along the length of the house from the ground to the overhanging eaves of the roof. Firewood for the winter months. One of the chores in our free time at the week-end was to split logs to re-stock the pile.

Originally, the dwelling had been a farmhouse, the cattle and horses wintering in a byre or stable, cheek by jowl to the living quarters. The sturdy building had been converted into a hostel for civilian forestry workers before the war, so there were a few very welcome amenities which we hadn't had in our previous working camps.

The sleeping arrangements, for instance, were almost luxurious. Each man had his own separate bunk, or cot, complete with a palliasse and fresh straw, spaced two feet from his snoring neighbour. I won my usual place under a window at the end of the room – which nobody else wanted, anyway – so I had only one snoring neighbour. There were nine beds against each wall separated by two rough, plank tables with benches each side.

The room was well heated – sometimes to the point of suffocation – by a flat-topped, wood-burning, black iron stove, which doubled up as a cooker when Red Cross food was available. Thankfully, there was never any shortage of fuel when the freezing weather set in. It was a source of wonder to me that the old wooden building never caught fire, when the sheet metal stovepipe carrying the fumes through the wooden walls became red-hot. There were no fire precautions, except the two night buckets which were brought in each evening when we were locked in at eight-o-clock.

I detested these stinking latrine buckets even though my bed was at the opposite end of the room and under an open window. The buckets were filled to overflowing long before the door was opened next morning until we realised our waterworks flow had been over stimulated by saccharine sweetening tablets. We were able to buy the tablets with the Lagergelt, imitation money paid for our labours, and used them to sweeten the unpalatable tasteless, polienta gruel we sometimes had for breakfast. I stopped using saccharine and only used the buckets in a dire emergency.

Two or three days after we arrived at Paarl, for the first time since becoming a prisoner-of-war, I had a medical inspection by a doctor. It was a cursory, "short arm inspection" as it was called in our Army. We queued in single file to stand before him and drop our trousers. His "inspection" was a brief glance and perhaps a muttered "waschen, waschen" or "gut, gut. Nexte" and the whole proceeding only took a few minutes. Of course, it wasn't a medical inspection in the ordinary sense of the word.

Dr Jew Searcher – as we came to call him – was looking for Jews. He was out of luck this time.

***

There was no electric supply to the farmhouse, or for that matter to the few houses in the little village either. Illumination in the room, after dark, was limited on week days to two carbide lamps dangling from the timber rafters. On Saturdays and Sundays there was the strictly rationed luxury of a smelly oil lamp.

A carbide lamp, for those never hearing of one before, was a miners' safety, lighting lamp fuelled by carbon powder and water. The carbon or carbide powder was held in a covered bowl with a nipple outlet. When water was added to the powder in the container the mixture gave off a form of acetelyne gas through the nipple, which, when a match was put to it, produced a flickering, smoking light. We discovered, with experience, that for some reason or other the lamps gave off a better light if urine was used instead of plain water. This helped to control the overflowing night buckets, too!!!

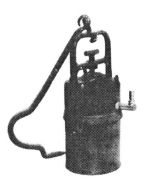

The Carbide lamp.

The temperamental light, blown out by any sudden draught from my open window – to the annoyance of my comrades – reminded me of an occasion when I was a small boy in 1933.

As I passed a policeman one early morning on my way to my newspaper round, I could see that the feeble light of the spluttering carbide lamp on the axle of his Hercules bicycle had blown out.

To muffled curses he was trying, unsuccessfully, to re-light it and when he saw me, he turned and said, "Do you happen to have a match in your pocket, son?"

"I'm sorry Sir," I replied, "but I don't smoke."

It was the same bobby who shouted at us for lighting a fire in the brickfield on Breck Road before peeing on it to put it out.

***

We were unable to read or write, or even play cards, by the light of these antedeluvian lamps, so the Three No Trumpers had to limit their bridge rubbers to weekends. However, Taffy Griffiths and I were in constant demand with our limited repertoire on the mandolines, when sing-songs were the order of the evening, by the flickering light of the carbide lamps and the red-hot glow of the wood stove.

An area at the back of the house had been cordoned off with a few strands of barbed wire to prevent us from running away. This was our so-called recreation area.

For "fussball spielen" they told us.

We never played football there, however, for half of the limited space was taken up by a wooden store-shed doubling up as our bath house and laundry room. The other half, in the long winter months, was permanently under two feet of snow and a sheet of ice from the waste water of our ablutions. We hadn't got a football, anyway.

The shed housed a square, wood-burning brick stove containing a round copper boiler with a roughly fashioned wooden lid. It was similar to the wash-boiler my mother slaved over, with the dolly-peg, in the steam-filled scullery of the little two-bedroomed terrace house in Liverpool, where she spent every Monday washing clothes for our family of ten.

Alongside the boiler, standing against the wall on its end to dry off, was a huge, tapered, wooden tub, or bath. It must have been eight feet long by two feet deep and two feet wide.

This was put to good use every Saturday afternoon when we all treated ourselves to the forgotten luxury of a bath in piping hot water, followed by a hasty scrub of the shirt and underclothes we had been wearing for the past week. The bath was the highlight of my week, albeit there were two of us in the bath and there was a noisy, impatient queue telling us to hurry up for Christ's sake.

Choice of partner, and position in the queue for this coffin-like, ancient jacuzzi, was decided by lots, drawn with a pack of cards in the now time honoured way of the prisoner-of-war.

My buddy in the bath was old Len Caulfield, my ex-belligerent opponent from the brickworks, now one of my best friends. Bigger and bulkier then me, he sat in the wide end of the bath and I wallowed in the narrower, but deeper end, the water up to my arm-pits.

Bald-headed, gummy, pale-faced Len was a dour, unsmiling ex-miner from Lancashire, who took a lot to get to know. He was quite a bit older than the rest of us and looked it because he was completely toothless. He had lost his false teeth in a Stuka raid back in Greece and never tired of telling the

Kommandant he needed new ones.

During the winter Len was never without his blue woollen balaclava, a "comfort" in his first parcel from home. He wore the thick, home-knitted ear-warmer whenever he went outside, even if it was a warm day. And he always had a "roll-up", a wispy, hand-made cigarette, dangling from the corner of his mouth. The first time he got into the old wooden tub of a bath he still had his balaclava on, and a fag-end dangling from his lips.

Len Caulfield was a character. He sang more than he conversed and had a remarkable repertoire of songs, parodies and poetry etched in his memory. Old, sentimental music-hall songs, dirty, army ditties and rugby-union bath-house ballads. But he was well read and could quote long passages from Shakespeare, and recite, from beginning to end, poems like *"If"*, or *"Hiawatha"* or *"The Owl and the Pussycat"* and *"There's a breathless hush in the Close tonight"*.

And, a particular favourite of his, a story in rhyme. *"Dangerous Dan McGrew"* or *"The Green Eye of the Little Yellow God"*.

I still recall the story of Dangerous Dan but could never recite it as Len Caulfield did.

Dangerous Dan McGrew

"There's a one-eyed yellow idol to the North of Katmandu,
There's a little marble cross below the town;
There's a broken-hearted woman tends the grave of Mad Carew,
And the Yellow God forever gazes down.

He was known as "Mad Carew" by the subs at Katmandu,
He was hotter than they felt inclined to tell;
But for all his foolish pranks, he was worshipped in the ranks,
And the Colonel's daughter smiled on him as well.

He had loved her all along, with a passion of the strong,
The fact that she loved him was plain to all.
She was nearly twenty-one and arrangements had begun

204

To celebrate her birthday with a ball.

*He wrote to ask what present she would like from Mad
Carew;*
They met next day as he dismissed a squad;
And jestingly she told him that nothing else would do
But the green eye of the little Yellow God.

*On the night before the dance, Mad Carew seemed in a
trance,*
And they chaffed him as they puffed at their cigars;
But for once he failed to smile, and he sat alone awhile,
Then went out into the night beneath the stars.

He returned before the dawn, with his shirt and tunic torn,
And a gash across his temple dripping red;
*He was patched up right away, and he slept through all the
day*

And the Colonel's daughter watched beside his bed.
*He spoke at last and asked if they could send his tunic
through;*
She brought it, and he thanked her with a nod;
*He bade her search the pocket saying "That's from Mad
Carew".*

And she found the little green eye of the god.
She upbraided poor Carew in the way that women do,
Though both her eyes were strangely hot and wet;
*But she wouldn't take the stone and Mad Carew was left
alone*

With the jewel that he'd chanced his life to get.
*When the ball was at its height, on that still and tropic
night,*
She thought of him and hurried to his room;
*As she crossed the barrack square she could hear the
dreamy air*

Of a waltz tune softly stealing thro' the gloom.
His door was open wide, with silver moonlight shining
through
The place was wet and slipp'ry where she trod;
An ugly knife lay buried in the heart of Mad Carew,
'Twas the "Vengeance of the Little Yellow God"

There's a one-eyed yellow idol to the north of Katmandu,
There's a little marble cross below the town;
There's a broken-hearted woman tends the grave of Mad
Carew,
And the Yellow God forever gazes down,"

John Milton Hayes (1884 – 1940)

It was hilarious when Len and I were the last in the queue for the tub and in no hurry to get out. Talk about "singing in the bath". Len would lie back soaking in the hot water, reciting "Dangerous Dan" or singing nostalgic sentimental songs, one after the other, until the water got cold. I joined in with the few words I knew and most of the lads listened outside the door, standing in the snow.

The long, wooden tub, apt to be a bit slimy if you were at the end of the queue, could be filled to the brim with as much water as you and your partner could carry from the stream and heat on the boiler. Inevitably, some of the queue, too lazy to carry fresh water the fifty yards from the river, would tell the previous occupants to leave the dirty water in the bath.

Surprisingly, there were one or two reluctant, or too lazy, to take a bath and there was even one young English lad who wouldn't have had one at all until, despite his protests, he was forcibly undressed and dunked in the water. He was the black sheep of our little community, slovenly in appearance and dirty in his personal habits even to the extent, at first, of soiling his bed. He was soon cured of this habit though, when he was scrubbed down with a scrubbing brush in the cold water of the big tub.

At the back of the shed, – in the summer within smelling distance of the house – was the usual primitive, stinking,

206

Austrian cesspit privy. Basically a four feet deep square excavation in the ground and, nailed to a framework across the top, the lavatory seat – two planks with a round hole shaped in them. In the winter months, when the temperature dropped to fifteen degress below zero, the contents froze, solid. Opening your bowels over this pit of horrors could sometimes present an unusual hazard in the form of a pyramid of glistening, frozen stools, in varied hues of amber and brown and of indeterminate sizes, the point of the pinnacle of frozen solids reaching up to the so-called lavatory seat like an inverted Walls chocolate ice-cream cornet. To avoid damage to himself the early riser had to break down the cone of frozen turds with a stout cudgel (known as the "shit stirrer") kept in the privy for that purpose.

There was no running water laid on to the lager. Every drop of water for cooking and washing clothes and bathing had to be carried from a tumbling mountain stream on the other side of the road in front of the house. A chore not welcomed by some, particularly when winter came and the river froze over. Then, each morning, the ice had to be broken to form a hole, like an eskimo fishing hole, to get at the water.

Walking past the hut in 1942.

207

The same hut revisited in 1999.

***

Shortly after we arrived at Paarl, much to our relief, the Red Cross parcels caught up with us again. We had been without the food parcels for some weeks and our bellies were beginning to feel the pinch. I was detailed with Dai Davies, "Gash" Hampton and Geoff Hallett to collect them from the stores of the Headquarters of the unit guarding us. Four weeks supply for each man, we were told.

Thrilled with our unexpected day-out from the daily grind and routine of the camp, and excited at the prospect of getting more food parcels, we trekked the five miles down the mountain road from Paarl to the railway station at Stadl-am-dem-Mur. Accompanied by two guards, resplendent in full kit and fixed bayonets, who I think were equally pleased with the prospect of their day out, we caught the little narrow-gauge, mountain steam-train to a station some way down the line towards Murau.

I, like most of the kriegies, always accepted these

unexpected train journeys with enthusiam. Collecting Red Cross parcels or being transferred from camp to camp, or even being hauled before the Commanding Officer on a charge, was a "day out". A picnic and a sight-seeing tour of the countryside. A welcome break from the boredom of the close confines of the working camp and the daily grind of work.

At that time the train services on smaller, local branch lines in Austria was efficient. Passenger trains were always on time but limited to one or two trains a day, up and down the line. So consequently we spent a great deal of the journey sitting around in little country railway stations, waiting for trains or connections.

On these excursions, I travelled well prepared, carrying tea and KLIM dried milk, a billy to boil water, a biscuit or two, and if I had them, a few cigarettes. During the winters of 1941/42 and 1942/3 the waiting rooms in the little picturesque mountain railway stations of Austria always had cheery little wood stoves burning away, where tea could always be brewed. In the summertime I would give the guard a cigarette and then walk down to the chuffing, miniature steam-engine and ask the driver to brew the tea with a jet of steam from his safety valve. He, too, was usually pleased to get the cigarette that went with the request.

At the village of St. Georgen we dismounted from the train at the same time as three other parties from working camps in the Murau area. Our immediate reaction, despite the protests of the guards, was to mingle with the other parties to get "all the latest griff". Any news at all of the outside world, or the progress of the war or the latest happenings at Stalag XV111A, Wolfsberg.

I walked the short distance up the road to the German barracks exchanging the latest news, and reminiscing about Liverpool with a Scouser in one of the other parties. In the ten or fifteen minutes we walked up the hill together we swopped life stories, and learned that we had lived only a quarter of a mile from each other in Anfield. We both supported Liverpool F.C. in happier days and both had gone to Campbell's Dancing Academy on Friday nights. He was limping badly, the result of a lump of concrete falling on his leg during an air raid in Greece.

I didn't learn his name.

Digressing from my story again, as is my wont, I have to

say that all my life I have had an aptitude for remembering faces and although I was only in his company for a quarter of an hour, some fifty years later I recognized him immediately one day in Liverpool, just before I retired in 1983. I was driving down Muirhead Avenue, when I stopped at a crossing to let a pedestrian go across. I recognised him as the man from St. Georgen. He was walking badly, rolling to one side and leaning heavily on a walking stick. I pulled in and ran across to stop him and recall the incident so long ago in Austria. Astonished at my feat of memory he couldn't remember my face but could clearly recall walking up the road to the village of St. Georgen with "the young lad from Liverpool" to collect the Red Cross parcels.

He remembered the incident well because when we arrived at the German barracks our excitement at the prospect of getting a second supply of food parcels faded, when to our dismay we found that we were in fact collecting Medical Parcels intended for the British Hospital in Stalag XV111A. They had been sent to the Arbeitslagers by mistake. The Germans were adamant that we would have to take them. No way could they be returned to the Stalag and clearly their attitude was, "like it or lump it".

Disappointed and crestfallen, for food was still the most important feature of our life, we loaded the parcels on to a cart, dragged them down to the station and got back to Stadl late in the afternoon.

There was a team of oxen harnessed to a hay-cart – the only taxi service from Paarl – waiting at the station and, still subdued, we loaded the parcels and with heavy hearts made our ponderous way back up the mountain to the camp.

We arrived there just as it was getting dark and were greeted with a rousing cheer as we turned in at the gate of the compound. Some of the lads had foregone the usual evening repast of grotty potato soup, and their mouths were watering in anticipation of the meal of fried luncheon meat followed by a helping of Del Monte tinned pineapples, or some other exotic dinner which they were expecting to make, after our return.

Nobody was as disappointed as I, when eventually, that evening, by the light of the flickering carbide lamps, I opened parcel No.1.

There was no actual food in it at all, except for a small tin of Bournville cocoa and a packet of a glucose sugar. To my dismay, instead of the well remembered contents of a Canadian Red Cross parcel, there were four large tins of a syrup-like concoction called Malt and Cod Liver Oil, a toilet roll, (yes, a toilet roll, travelling to us half way across the world via Switzerland to the top of a remote mountain in Austria where we didn't even have a toilet). There was a packet of Vitamin E tablets, a bottle of Aspirin tablets, a roll of sticking plaster, a flat metal box containing a hundred halibut-liver-oil capsules, and a tablet of Sunlight soap. There were no cigarettes and, the saddest blow of all, no chocolate.

Despite my more or less permanent hunger, no way could I get down the malt and cod liver oil. Most of the lads mixed it with the paltry, potato soup, spread it on the thin wedge of black bread or the polienta porridge we had for breakfast, or simply spooned it down, three times a day, straight from the tin. Hungry as I was, I gagged even at the smell of the stuff. No doubt recalling the bottle of Scotts' Emulsion and its picture of the fisherman with a sou'wester hat and a huge fish dangling over his left shoulder, that mother used to cajole and bribe me into swallowing when I was a weakling child.

Big George East solved the problem for me, although it did little to alleviate my hunger pangs.

"I'll swop my tin of halibut oil capsules for a tin of your cod liver oil," he said, "then you'll get some sort of nourishment in that puny frame of yours."

George loved the cod liver oil and by the time he had consumed the contents of his four parcels, plus the oil he had traded with me, to my distaste, I could actually smell fish oil oozing out of his skin every time he broke out into a light sweat.

For my part, I did a roaring trade, swopping my malt and cod for the flat, easily stored, easily swallowed tins of tasteless, halibut liver oil capsules. I used them carefully, augmenting my fluctuating diet for the rest of my time as a prisoner-of-war. I still had some left when I was eventually released in 1945.

But the medical parcels were only a blip and shortly afterwards, normal service was resumed. For the rest of that winter and the following summer the camp received a fairly regular supply of parcels and cigarettes.

***

In February, 1943 I received a letter from the father of Arthur Taylor, my friend from our Territorial and call-up days in 1939.

Written on a standard PRISONER OF WAR POST, or KRIEGSGEFANGENENPOST, air-mail folding letter, it was from:

> *Mr Stanley Taylor,*
> *9, Eric Street,*
> *Widnes,*
> *Lancs.*

> *DATE 4-1-43*

Dear Douglas: We received your P.C. dated October 11th about ten days before Christmas, and were glad to hear you are keeping well. Groups of photos often appear in the Echo, of men in the prison camps, and they always look happy and content, but we never see Arthur among them. Things must be a bit monotonous at times for you but the fact that you are out of the fighting and know you will be returned home when it is over, helps you to stick it.

We received your letter, telling us how you and Arthur parted, and what you thought of his chances. I wonder if you have heard anything since, which gives you hope to think he is still alive.

We have had no more news since he was posted as missing, and that was 20 months since, and this long wait for news makes the strain hard to bear especially for his mother. I have not heard of any of your battery coming home. I have written to Sgt.Major Basford's sister in Liverpool but nothing has been heard of him since Greece. She says that a man named Colbeck came home, but he was suffering from loss of memory, so they couldn't learn much from him.

*Mrs. Taylor and I send you our best regards and hope you
will keep in good health to the end, and we are hoping you
will pay us a visit on your return.*

Cheerio,
Yours sincerely,
S. Taylor.

I replied to the letter on the 11th April, 1943 but I have to
confess that I did not contact the Taylors on my return home in
1945. I thought that meeting them would only revive their grief. In
the letters I wrote to them from Germany I had given them all the
information I could about Arthur, who was killed on the SLAMAT
in the evacuation of Greece in 1941. His name, and that of Sergeant-
Major Basford mentioned in the letter, is on the Memorial Tablet in
the British War Cemetery, Phaleron, Greece. Two of one hundred
and sixty-three names of men of the 106th Lancashire Yeomanry
who died in the evacuation from Greece in 1941.

Chapter 26

Nicht Arbeiten, Nicht Essen

Life in the timber camp at Paarl, during the winter of 1942 and the summer of 1943, developed into an easy, boring routine, more or less acceptable so long as Red Cross food parcels arrived regularly.

From early spring-time, after the snows melted, our job was to fell trees in a clearing of the mountain half-an-hour's steep walk uphill from the camp.

We were not overworked. Franz, the civilian overseer directing our labours, seemed happy enough if we even made some token pretence at getting on with the work he set us.

We set off each morning at about seven o'clock. Franz leading the way, a short-barrelled sports rifle slung over his shoulder making him a sort of co-opted guard. I copied his long, steady, rhythmical pace as he took the steep mountain path with the slow, swinging stride of a man accustomed to the terrain. The lads, most of them city dwellers, huffing and puffing complaints about the incline, were strung out behind him, crocodile fashion. Bringing up the rear, like a shepherd herding his sheep, was Ferdinand, the young guard "a penny short of a shilling". Also with a rifle over his shoulder, to make sure we wouldn't run off to Switzerland.

It was a breathtaking landscape.

As we toiled up the track in the valley, surrounded by rolling, tree-clad hills and mountains, on clear days we could see the morning sun glistening on the icy, pointed peak of the Gross-Glockner mountain, one of the highest in Austria.

Some mornings in the early spring, when we arrived at the site, we surprised wild, red deer feeding on the fresh bark stripped from logs felled the previous day. Or licking at blocks of salt, and munching hay, left for the animals by the foresters

214

on the lower slopes of the mountain during the snowbound, winter months. Quick, at first, to scatter in a minor stampede when they saw us, these lovely, timid animals grew used to our approach and we could get quite close to them before they dispersed higher up the mountain.

The deer had found its way into the local food chain, for at the Paarl timber camp, I tasted roast venison for the first time in my life. We were treated to snippetts of this unexpected delicacy on two or three occasions that summer. However, we had to educate the lady-cook, for the first time she served it she spoilt the delicious meat by smothering it with caraway seeds.

I think this was black-market venison given to us as an unofficial extra, as meat of any sort was almost non-existent in the normal meals we received. The same lady-cook, on one occasion made us a sort of sugarless, crumble-pie from bilberries we had gathered from bushes on the site.

After a five minute break to get our breath back, and to have the obligatory smoke, Franz would direct us to our various jobs for the day.

We were split into groups or pairs, some felling trees and, after lopping off the branches, cutting them into four metre lengths. Others stripped the thick bark from the logs in one piece, making a cut through the bark down the length of the log with a broad, chisel-like tool. The logs were then stacked in groups against the slope and left to weather, or season, for, so we were told, two years.

My working partner in the clearing on the steep slopes of the mountainside was Joe Sainty, from Auckland, New Zealand, a one-time upholsterer turned infantry-man, now a reluctant lumberjack.

Our job was to fell trees. Douglas Fir conifers selected by Franz. They could be any size from saplings six inches thick and twenty feet high, to giants three feet in diameter, their sparse, green foliage at the top soaring two hundred feet or more, vanishing into the early morning mist. Franz marked the tree to be felled with his axe, showing us the position to make the cut, to drop it safely without snagging other trees.

For an ex-shop assistant and ex-upholsterer, coerced against our wishes to take up a new profession, Joe and I became quite

215

adept at felling trees. Although I can't say we were the quickest lumberjacks in Austria.

Joe Sainty did most of the axe work, for my left wrist was giving me trouble after breaking it at the working camp in Murau. In between his yarns of life in New Zealand, and how he was going to start a reupholstering business when he got home, and how he would like me to go out there to help him, he used the broad, heavy woodsman's axe to cut a deep vee-shaped indentation, or notch, in the tree in the direction in which it was to fall. Then with a six-foot long, double-handled, lumberjack's cross-cut saw, we made a saw-cut across from the opposite side of the vee until we were about two inches from the indentation of the axe cut.

After our loud, shouted warnings of "timber, timber", to alert our comrades on the slope below, we drove two eight inch steel, tapered wedges in the saw-cut at the back of the vee. The strip of uncut wood keeping the tree upright finally parted under the strain of the weight of the massive tree being forced over by the wedges driven into the saw-cuts.

Slowly at first, the narrow strip groaning and creaking loudly in protest as the wood fibres cracked and splintered, the majestic tree would crash to the ground with a cloud of dust, pine-needles and broken branches, dislodging from the top a shower of conical seed-cones as big as coconuts, to bounce down the mountain-side.

Joe and I just about managed to fell and strip one of these giants each day. Franz gave up grumbling about the output and stopped telling us that his lumberjacks, recently called up by the Army, cut down as many as fifteen trees each day. Franz of course was a true woodsman, so it was interesting to watch him, after he had handed over his rifle to one of the lads for safekeeping, make two cross-facing notches in a tree to bring it down the opposite way to which it was leaning, to avoid a fence or another tree.

In better circumstances I could have enjoyed the work on the mountainside. I liked the satisfaction of cutting down the huge conifers and dropping them in the correct spot. The fresh air and the glorious scenery suited me. Apart from the damage to my wrist I was fit and in good health. The more regular supply

216

of food parcels was having its effect.

Looking back, after a lifetime of pen-pushing, sitting at a desk, I think that working at the timber camp was the most satisfying physical labour I ever performed. After I returned home I made enquiries about starting a life in forestry work but had to abandon the idea when it was discovered that the bone in my wrist had become diseased.

***

With the more regular supply of food parcels during the spring and early summer of 1943 and the consequent slow return to better health, our thoughts were no longer confined solely to the quality and quantity of our next meal. Some of us began to get bored and discontented with the routine we had fallen into.

We were completely out of touch with news from the outside world, except for the few letters from home. In these, any war news or place names or mention of theatres of war, was heavily blacked out by either the British or the German censors. Some correspondents tried to develop simple codes with words of double meaning, or using the first letter in every word of a sentence to spell out the name of a town. Most of these were also blacked out by the censors.

So talk in the camp turned to escaping. "Doing a runner." Or "a moonlight flit". Trying to get to Switzerland some hundreds of miles away. Or simply dodging work and getting back to the amenities of the main camp at Wolfsberg.

Escaping from the camp would have been easy. For the first to attempt it, anyway. A simple matter of packing some hoarded chocolate and tinned food in a home-made haversack, hiding it in the undergrowth, forgetting to come back from a call of nature and losing oneself in the dense forests. But it was really a bit of a pipe dream because nobody in the camp had very much idea where we actually were and where we would make for if we did escape. The only map we had, was a map of Europe showing the victories of the German Reich, on the back of a children's exercise book I had pinched during a visit to the doctor at Stadl.

A visit which is worthy of a mention at this stage.

I had woken one freezing cold morning under my open

window, to find that I was completely immobile from the neck down. Stiff as a ramrod. I couldn't move an inch. I couldn't even get out of bed.

After urgent consultation with the Kommandant it was decided I should make the perilous journey over the ice-bound mountain road to the doctor in Stadl, in the back of the only taxi in Paarl, a farm-cart pulled by a pair of oxen. Dai Davies and Geoff Hallett, with great difficulty and howls of complaint by me to "watch it, for Christ's sake," pulled on my trousers and shirt and carried me outside to the patiently waiting oxen transport and deposited me, flat on my back, on wispy straw in the bottom of the cart. We set off down the track to Stadl, the guard, rifle between his knees with bayonet fixed, sitting up on the platform in front with the taxi driver.

For the first few miles it was purgatory for me with every jolt and slide of the cart's steel-rimmed wheels on the unmade ice-bound track. But as we skidded down the hill, I found to my relief, that the stiffness of my body seemed to be easing. In fact by the time we got down the mountain to Stadl I was beginning to think that the stiffness was preferable to being thrown about in the cart.

When we arrived at the doctors, I was regretting I had had no breakfast that morning, a sure sign that I was feeling somewhat better. But I didn't tell the guard that and he and the ancient taxi-driver had to help me get down from the cart, half-dragging, half-carrying me to the waiting-room. It was when the guard was giving my details to the elderly receptionist I spotted a child's homework book with the map on the back, and a "Volkischer Beobactor" newspaper, on a chair alongside me. With great difficulty, I promptly stuffed them down the inside of my long-johns.

The doctor wasn't too interested in my predicament and didn't even examine me. However, he gave me a bottle of a greenish looking mixture and told me to rub it on the affected parts night and morning and, muttering "nicht arbeit nicht essen," – no work, no food – told me to get back to work right away. The repulsive-looking concoction smelled like the horse liniment the quack doctor at the back of St. Johns market in Liverpool, sold as a cure-for-all, on a Saturday night.

Unfortunately, the tiny propaganda map above the multiplication tables on the back of Willie Schmidt's homework book, did very little to enlighten us on our exact whereabouts. And the German newspaper with shots of German troops storming unknown villages in Russia, and blurry, indecipherable aeriel photographs of bombs dropping on London, taken by German bombers at 30,000 feet, was printed in an unintelligible Gothic script and gave no indication of the true progress of the war.

In fact, the first reliable British news of the momentous happenings in the outside world during the past two years, came from Len Caulfield when he was sent back to Wolfsberg for a new set of false teeth. On his return, his mouth gleaming with shiny, white top and bottom molars, he was full of the latest war news which he had heard before he left Wolfsberg that morning.

"An actual BBC news bulletin," he said. "They read them out every day, in each British barrack in Wolfsburg."

That night, after lock-up, he enlarged on his visit, and held spellbound the captive audience in the smelly room with his account of prisoner-of-war life in the confines of Stalag XV111A.

He told us about the regular food parcels, the marvellous variety shows in the camp theatre with a full orchestra and chorus "girls" who looked like the real thing, and the George Bernard Shaw play he'd seen the night before he came away. He went on about the Sunday church services, the football matches, the sports days, the educational classes with courses in accountancy, or law or foreign languages, or whatever.

He told us about the two British doctors in the hospital, and the New Zealand dentist who had fixed him up with his false teeth. (Unfortunately they didn't do much for his appearance and not much, either, for the rock-hard biscuits in the parcels). He told us of the Escape Committee helping would-be escapees with maps, compasses, clothes, food, even able to arrange a transfer to a suitable working camp as a jumping off place.

He told us, also, of the bunker in the Stalag. A jail where they put the re-captured escapees, serving twenty-one days bread and water punishment for escaping from dreadful arbeitslagers. He told us that some of these working camps were really slave camps of a hundred, or two hundred men, working on unbroken shifts down coal mines. Or in stifling, dangerous munition factories, or on bomb-damaged airfields or the towering iron mountains in Lower Austria, extracting iron ore from the frozen, rock-strewn mountainside.

So after endless debate, a few of us, on that first night of discussion, decided to have a go at escaping. Or, anyway, at least to sample the delights of Stalag.

Others arguing, "don't be such bloody fools, better the devil you know than the devil on the other side of the mountain, particularly if it's an iron mountain." "Anyway this wasn't a bad sort of camp and Franz wasn't a slave driver, and where else would we get roast venison occasionally, so it's best to stick it out here." And so on. Two or three said nothing and lit another cigarette.

After much discussion over many days, Dai Davies, Len Caulfield and myself decided to try our luck and have a go at "doing a runner". The first stage of which, would be to toss the doctor and return to Wolfsberg to consult the so-called Escape Committee.

***

I was the first of the three of us to 'toss the doctor'.

On my third attempt, when I arrived at the doctor's surgery at Stadl I found that the ill-tempered, old, Jew-Searcher of a doctor, who had examined my private parts so casually when I first arrived at Paarl and who had prescribed the awful horse liniment for my stiff back, had been replaced by a pleasant, middle-aged woman. On the two previous occasions when I had gone sick, Dr Jew-Searcher had simply dismissed me with a wave of his hand and said "Sie sind nicht krank, must arbeiten gehen. Nicht arbeiten, nicht essen". In effect, "You're not sick, go back to work. If you don't work you won't get anything to eat."

The pleasant, lady doctor was another kettle of fish. I explained in halting German, that I was unable to use the heavy woodsman's axe to knock down the trees, because of the accident to my wrist. With a broad smile she replied in perfect

220

English, "You speak good German, did you learn at school?"

Swelling with pride I told her I had "learned the language!" during my time as a prisoner-of-war.

Luckily for me we carried out the rest of our brief conversation in English. She said I looked very young, asked my age, where I came from in England, what did I think of Austria and hadn't the weather been kind.

I was glad she seemed anxious to practice her English instead of my German.

I said yes, I liked the mountains and the countryside, but I had been in a state of near starvation ever since I had arrived in Austria and was looking forward to going home after the Allies had won the war.

She grinned again at my last remark and to my delight, finished her little talk by saying she was going to send me back to Wolfsberg for an X-ray and treatment to my wrist.

I had tossed the doctor.

* * *

Two days later, although I had been told by the Kamp Kommandant that I would be returning to the arbeitslager after treatment, I packed all my belongings in the cheap cardboard suitcase I had bought back in Murau. I wasn't going to lose all my precious kit, as I had done twice before in my short army career.

Into the case, with my share of the contents of the combine's food parcels and the hoarded chocolate and cigarettes, went the fruits of "comfort" parcels sent to me from home with much loving care and great cost. Spare socks and shirts and winter long-johns, woollen balaclavas and gloves, pyjamas and handkerchiefs.

A book by Cuthbertson on Contract Bridge went in with two packs of playing cards and a cribbage board. I had kept all the letters I had received and had revived the old soldier's habit of collecting souvenirs. So, with the letters, I gathered my collection of Austrian pot-bellied, tasselled, meerschaum pipes, an assortment of patent cigarette-making machines, the mandolin, and the wooden sabots the Germans had given me when I first arrived at Wolfsberg. I was determined to get those clogs home.

I hadn't yet considered what I was going to do with it all when I made my escape. But, the memory of my previous losses, in particular those of the 1st June, 1941, made me reluctant to part with my hard won possessions.

So in the early summer of 1943, with mixed feelings – a little trepidation and a lot of regret – I said my good-byes to the twenty comrades who had been my close companions and friends for over two years.

***

Ferdinand, the young guard, accompanied me to Wolfsberg. He was obviously pleased with the idea because he knew he'd get the odd cigarette and slice of corned beef wrapped up in a biscuit. In return he was happy to help me lug my heavy suitcase when I tired on the walk from Wolfsberg railway station to the camp.

When we halted at the massive, barbed wire, double entrance gates of the Stalag at Wolfsberg, I was disheartened and fell to wondering what I had let myself in for. I couldn't help comparing this wired, impregnable fortress, with the compound of the remote and quiet logging camp on the top of the mountain.

For the wire fence, surrounding the camp on all sides, was huge and forbidding. It was two fences, really, each of thick barbed wire strung six inches apart on twelve feet high concrete posts. Filling the space in between were concertinaed coils of barbed wire piled one on top of the other to the height of the posts. Inside the compound, in front of the inner fence, was an electrified cable on which was hooked at intervals an ominous, black and red, skull and crossbones warning sign.

High, wooden watchtowers, manned day and night, were spaced fifty yards apart around the heavily wired compound. So every inch of the perimeter fence was overlooked by a guard, armed with a rifle or machine gun. After dark a powerful, probing searchlight ceaselessly swept the enclosure and fence. I don't think a cat could have found its way through that wire wall but I was to discover, anyway, that there were far easier ways to get out of the camp than crawling through the barbed wire.

An armed sentry opened a wicket gate set in the massive double doors and let us through into the prison proper, instructing Ferdinand to report at a reception office inside. My arrival in Wolfsberg in 1943 was somewhat different from that of two years previously when I had staggered through the gates with hundreds of others after the horrendous journey from Salonika in the cattle trucks. For then, in their haste to make room for the next consignment from Greece, I was "processed" and sent out to a working camp the next day.

Ferdinand, wiping the crumbs of a corned beef sandwich from his mouth, now all spit and polish, standing to attention and Heiling Hitler for all he was worth, handed me over to a wooden-faced, smartly uniformed officer. Ferdy received a signature for me as if I was a lost sheep and, without even a glance in my direction, seemingly glad to get rid of me, or scared stiff of being kept inside himself, vanished from sight.

A short, bandy-legged guard dumped the contents of my paper suitcase, without ceremony, on the floor of the office in front of the highly polished knee-length boots of an Officer. SS Major Karl Schafer. Resplendent in well-cut riding breeches, a heavy revolver stuck in a holster in his belt and the usual Iron Cross decoration pinned to his chest, the Major didn't move an inch except to push to one side with the toe of his shiny boot, my cherished letters from home. He said something to bandy-legs who picked up the bundle of letters and handed it to him. He checked to see if they had passed the censor and were marked with the "Geprust" stamp and then let them fall to the floor.

Another elderly guard searched me, roughly, frisking my clothes from ankles to shoulders and made me turn out my pockets. They also checked every pocket in the spare clothes on the floor, turned the socks inside out, shook the mandolin and carefully felt around the lining on the cheap suitcase.

The Major riffed through Cutherbertson's "The Art of Bridge" and, in perfect English, asked what the cribbage board was for. Without waiting for a reply he said, curtly, "Barrack 3."

Stuffing my belongings back into the case, I made my way to the British compound escorted by the bandy-legged guard.

223

Chapter 27

Kriegsgefangenen-Mannschaftsstammlager XV111A

Stalag XV111A, Wolfsburg, was one of the biggest prisoner-of-war camps in Austria. From 1939, until the end of the war, nearly 50,000 prisoners-of-war of various nationalities were incarcerated there or in one of the hundreds of Arbeitskommandos under its orbit. The working camps provided labour throughout Southern Austria for factories, coal and iron mines, farms and forestry camps and road and railway refurbishment.

The prisoners interned there were from Great Britain, Ireland, Canada, Australia, New Zealand, Holland, Belgium, France, Italy, Serbia, Yugoslavia, the U.S.A. and uncounted Ukranians from the Soviet Union.

Upwards of 12,000 British and Colonial prisoners registered in the Stalag, had been captured in Greece and Crete in 1941.

The day-to-day administration of the British Compound in the Stalag, and the attached working camps, was under the control of a "Chief Man of Confidence". Generally known as the "Confidence Man", he was a Senior Warrant Officer, a volunteer, elected by his fellow Warrant Officers and approved by the Germans. An official Camp Interpreter was also appointed and, as in the working camps, all requests and orders to or from the Germans came through the Camp Interpreter and the Chief Man of Confidence.

Prisoners were employed as clerks and storemen in the "Kommandatur", the office of the Chief Man of Confidence. He and his staff were responsible, ultimately, for the welfare of the twelve or thirteen hundred men in the Stalag and also for the thousands of British prisoners-of-war in the working camps. For two-and-a-half years they had, more or less, complete control of the distribution of Red Cross food parcels, library books, outgoing and incoming mail, new clothing and boots. A daunting task, successfully carried out despite the never-ending red-tape, the arguments and the verbal fights with the controlling Germans.

Stalag XV111A was the only P.O.W. camp in Germany where the occupants controlled the issue and distribution of these essential and life-saving supplies to the working camps.

John Ledgerwood, in his 1944 "**Potted History of Stalag XV111A**", pays due tribute to the Chief Man of Confidence.

"The Chief Man of Confidence... had grasped the full importance of his post and was doing a "super" job in controlling the welfare of the working detachments. For him, it was one long fight. Armed with the Geneva Convention, Gary Cooper was abroad redressing human wrongs and establishing a reputation for hard work and plenty of it. More and more objectionable German guards were withdrawn from the British Compound and the British administered their own affairs."

***

When I arrived there in the summer of 1943, Wolfsburg Camp, basically, was divided into French, British and Russian compounds, each strictly segregated from the other.

The English, Welsh, Scottish, Irish, Australian and New Zealand prisoners were in the British compound. Roman Catholics, Protestants, Presbyterians, Baptists, Plymouth Brethren, Believers and Non-Believers (and one or two hidden Jews), all living amicably together in perfect harmony, (except when International football matches were being played).

The camp at Wolfsberg had originally been the headquarters of an Austrian cavalry regiment. Barrack 3 was one of the converted stables in the top corner of the British compound.

It was a long, clapboard timber building divided into two sections. The larger section housed about two hundred prisoners;

the smaller about a hundred. Separating the two grossly overcrowded rooms, was a small washing area with a line of cracked concrete horse troughs, relics of the old stables, on each side. Over the battered troughs dripped a dozen brass taps screwed into iron water pipes apt to freeze in the winter and run out of water in the high summer. These were the ablutions; the only washing facilities for some three hundred men.

I was given a space – I hesitate to call it a bed – by the Barrack Commander, an Australian Infantry Sergeant-Major. It was in the middle of three on the top shelf of nine, fixed back-to-back to another block of nine. I had to find room for all my worldly belongings on the bare boards – two of which were missing, having been used as fuel by a previous occupant – including the cardboard suitcase and the mandolin and a dirty ersatz blanket and, at night, my precious boots. I could take my pick whether to doss down, head against head, with the bloke on the top of the adjoining tier of nine, or top-and-tail with my head on the outer end next to a six-foot-six Digger, his sweaty feet sticking out of his bed-space not twelve inches from my nose.

There were six blocks of these tiered shelves, each containing eighteen sleeping spaces, down both sides of the barrack. In the aisle down the centre were three or four rough deal tables and forms, and a brick-built cooking stove. The six blocks were situated so close to the outer wall there was barely enough room for two men to pass each other.

The bleak, overcrowded living and sleeping quarters were in a state of permanent semi-gloom, for daylight was limited to a few tiny, square windows level with the top tiers of the beds. Lucky was the man whose space was near one of these windows, the only source of fresh air. After lights out, the atmosphere in the hut grew more and more foetid and unbearable, as the night wore on.

The British compound comprised three of these converted stables together with four smaller barracks, the former sleeping quarters of the Austrian cavalrymen, now occupied by the permanent staff of the administration offices and stores of the Kommandanteur.

The "parade ground" (for want of a better name), which also doubled as the football pitch, was in the space between barrack 2 and 3. The smaller section of barrack 1 had been converted into a theatre and was also used every day as a Lecture or Schoolroom, and on Sundays for Church Services.

Separated by a barbed wire fence, but still within the compound, were the British hospital, the Officers' Mess and the living quarters of the resident British Commissioned Officers in the Camp. Two medical officers, Major Kinmont and Captain Woods R.A.M.C., Father Juneau a French/Canadian Roman Catholic Priest, Captain Hobling an Anglican chaplain, and John Ledgerwood, a New Zealand Army padre. All these officers had volunteered to remain in Stalag XV111A instead of going to a far more comfortable Oflag for Commissioned Officers.

The "delouser" and showers were outside the British Compound in the centre of the camp, adjoining a bigger parade ground which later on was used by the British as a football pitch.

In a corner of the compound was the Dreaded Bog.

This foul-smelling, draughty, communal privy was a rectangular, doorless, wooden shed, eighteen feet long by twelve feet wide, erected over a frightening cesspit, six feet deep. It was freezing cold in winter and "stinking" hot in summer. The two lavatory "seats" were tree trunks, like telegraph poles, fixed over the pit on each side of the shed from wall to wall. Each pole, now polished smooth by bums from the length and breadth of the United Kingdom and the far flung corners of the British Empire, accommodated about twelve men. (Thirteen, if they were little fellows like me). Squatting alongside each other, knee to knee, minding their own business, gossiping away like women in the public wash-house of Netherfield Road.

After the mid-day ration of potato soup the Germans gave us every day, there was always an impatient queue of griping men waiting their turn to occupy the poles, stamping their feet in exasperation in the freezing snow or trying to shelter from the driving rain.

Periodically, when the cess-pit of sludge appeared to be in danger of overflowing on to the parade-ground-cum-football pitch, a local farmer would appear with a team of oxen pulling a farm cart loaded with a long cylindrical tank. In the absence of the prisoner-of-war "schieszen-hausen" detail, who had vanished to the four points of the compass when they spotted the cart

227

coming through the gates, he would empty the cesspit by hand using a bucket on the end of a long pole, perilously transferring the muck from the pit to a manhole on the top of the mobile tank.

We could smell the stuff for days on end after it had been spread on the surrounding farm land.

The communal toilet.

Chapter 28

The Cobblers

With my usual good fortune, after a couple of days I was rescued from the overcrowded larger section of Barrack 3, through the influence of three 106th men, Ernie McGrae, Jack Ward and Dick Rimmer, and transferred to the overcrowded, but very much smaller section. The Schusters Barrack.

I was to find that the 106th Regiment was well represented by some dozen or so men working in the Stalag.

Charlie McIlroy and George Martin operated the showers and delouser. Ernie Mack was the "hot Water engineer" and, with Ernie Carroll, looked after a hot water boiler in the library. Danny Nolan, Jack Ward and Max Mouna were hospital orderlies, Billy Brougham, Johnny Jones and Mick Bolger scrounged in the clothing stores and Dick Rimmer bludged successfully in the Schusters, a cobblers' shop employing about thirty men repairing boots sent in from the working camps.

As respected members of the Wolfsburg hierarchy, pulling long thin strings, they "worked" me a job in the Schusters alongside Dick Rimmer. I didn't know anything about boot repairing. But that made little difference as none of the others did either.

There was a vacant bed-space for me, too, in the centre of the top shelf next to Dick. A coveted space really, for it was up against a wall at the end of the room and alongside a window, which from spring onwards, actually flooded with sunshine. In the space on the other side of me was an elderly Cockney, old enough to be my father, who was to leave Wolfsberg a few weeks later to join his son in another Stalag after the International Red Cross had issued a directive that related prisoners could be incarcerated together. This space was eventually taken by Ted McShea, another 106th man who was to become a particularly good friend of mine.

I was also invited by Dick to "muck-in" with him. A two-man combine which I was to find had its faults.

The Schusters barrack was comfortable in comparison with the larger section of Barrack 3. There were fewer men in it for a start. There was no floating population, for most of the occupants worked in the cobblers' shop. The worn leather soles stripped from the old boots, and the off cuts of the replacements, provided extra fuel for the Schusters' cooking stove. A boon in XV111A, for fuel was in extremely short supply, despite Wolfsberg being surrounded on all sides by extensive, rolling conifer forests.

The brick stove, used only to heat food and water, was lit an hour before the mid-day and evening meals. Or for as long as the allotted fuel lasted. Hot water for the breakfast cup of tea was obtained from The Two Ernies in their "heises wasser" engineering shop at the end of Barrack 2. And you had to be up early to get that.

Cooking or heating of the Red Cross food on the stove was the subject of judicious planning and became something of an art. For by the time the tiny grate, built into the end of the stove, was lit before mealtime, the top of the brick stove was covered with a variety of strange cooking utensils.

Aluminium pots and pans of varied shapes and sizes, battered British Army mess-tins and Italian Army dinged, oval water bottles. Most of the makeshift cooking appliances were discarded Malt-and-Cod-Liver-Oil tins or KLIM powdered milk tins, cunningly cut and shaped into drinking mugs, frying pans or saucepans. Miniature, self-contained ovens fuelled by scraps of paper and splinters of wood, or anything that would burn, were fashioned out of Klim tins.

Strange varieties of kriegie dinners were cooked or warmed up on the top of the brick stoves. Exotic recipes from the bounty of the Red Cross parcels. Sardines, flecked with tomato sauce, in a ready-to-cook McDougall's pancake mixture congealing around the edge of a KLIM-tin fry pan, as its chief cook jostled for a warmer spot on the stove. Outlandish mixtures of cheese-spread and Hartley's raspberry jam and pilchards in olive oil, hard biscuits soaked in sugared water, a sure sign that somebody had gone through his parcel and only had biscuits left. Or was having trouble with his teeth.

It was a case of first come, first served – or first come, first cooked. And you had to stand guard over your dinner, for if your back was turned too long you would lose your place on the stove top after someone had decided his Spam was cooked enough and removed his frypan. For then everyone standing around the stove, would move his home-made appliance a little bit nearer the hot plate over the fire at the end.

The whole business was like a solemn game of musical chairs, without the music; or a game of draughts or chess, patiently played with unusually shaped pawns or bishops. Checkmate was to get your frying pan to the centre of the hot-plate over the paltry fire before the allotted fuel was burnt up. The unfortunates at the back of the queue were sometimes being forced to burn anything they could lay their hands on; pages from their Army Paybook or precious letters from home, or in dire emergencies, slats of wood from their bed-space. And sometimes might be forced to consume the aforesaid McDougall's ready mixed pancake mixture, cold or only half done.

I have to record, though, that there were very few arguments in the daily jostling for the hot spots on the cooking stoves of Stalag XV111A. But many a fine tale was told and many barbed wire rumours sprang up in the patient queues of budding chefs.

***

Soon forgetting the mixed feelings I had on the day I arrived at the forbidding, barbed wire gates of Stalag XV111A. I very soon adapted to the conditions of life there, which I found more agreeable than those I had experienced in the working camps of the Mur Valley.

At that period, Red Cross food parcels and cigarettes were issued regularly to Stalag residents, even small stocks being built up by well managed combines to be kept in reserve or used for trading on the black market.

The Germans never missed our daily issue of rations; a

small wedge of black bread every morning accompanied, two or three times a week, by a spoonful of watery jam and once a week by a spoonful of a white, tasteless margarine. And at mid-day the main and only other meal of the day; a cupful of watery potato soup, the potatoes still in their jackets and very often only half cooked and rotten (Pig potatoes to the British prisoner), or a small portion of the smelly, rancid sauerkraut. Very occasionally a thin slice of spicy German sausage would be issued – the only meat of any kind we received from our hosts.

Many of the British prisoners scorned these rations when Red Cross parcels were being received weekly, but I always stood in the queue to draw my issue if only to rescue the sound parts of the potatoes in the soup, or to try to give them to some starving Ukrainian prisoner standing in his queue the other side of the fence. This wasn't always possible, for the compounds were strictly segregated and a Russian took his life in his hands if he was caught taking food from the British or French, the only other residents at that time.

Russian POWs queuing for soup, a comrade carrying a dead Russian in order to receive his ration.

The work in the cobblers' shop was easy and I soon learned how to carry out the simple repairs to the boots sent in from the arbeitslagers. The N.C.O in charge of the Schusters, under the direction of a German Feldwebel, was another Liverpool man, Harry Jones, a Sergeant in the Service Corps and a one-time manager of a shoe-repairs and leatherwork factory in Liverpool.

I was quick to take advantage of the many amenities and the organised entertainment which I had so sorely missed in the working camps, although, apparently, these had become restricted shortly before I had arrived because of the transfer of 250 non-commissioned officers to an Oflag. Many of these N.C.Os had been responsible for the organisation of the entertainment and sporting activities of the Camp. They had successfully established "schools" with regular lectures and lessons in a variety of subjects ranging from law and accountancy to building construction and civil engineering. For the most part these educational classes ceased after they left.

106 NCOs leaving Wolfsberg.

Nevertheless, I took advantage of the many, to me, luxurious facilities and wonderful entertainments still available in Wolfsberg.

For instance, I found it a delight to be able to exchange a book in the library whenever I wanted to. And as the months

233

went by the library grew bigger.

Starved of world and war news for over two years I never missed the News Bulletins read out each day by a New Zealand Sergeant Major, standing on the brick stove in the centre of each barrack. It was news received the previous evening. (It wasn't till many years after the war that I found out that the camp radio was hidden in the Two Ernies' "heises wasser" engineering shop.)

I never missed Eric Fearnside's "Searchlight" lectures on the progress of the war, which he graphically presented each week in the camp theatre after the Sunday Church Service.

Corporal Eric Fearnside of the Royal Engineers – "General Fearnside", or "Fearless Fanny Fearnside" – as he affectionately became known, was the Richard Dimbleby or Jon Snow of XV111A.

At his weekly "Searchlight" lectures, editing and condensing the previous week's news summaries from the hidden radio and highlighted by his own colourfully illustrated and accurate maps, he kept flagging spirits up, and hope in our hearts, with his vivid descriptions of the progress of the war on the various fronts. Names of cities and rivers in Soviet Russia became familiar to me through Eric Fearnside's lectures. Stalingrad and Smolensk, the Dniepr and the Don.

Eric's predictions of the progress of the war were uncannily accurate although he was to admit, later, that his forecast of Turkey entering the war, on our side, proved to be wrong.

I never missed my turn at the strictly rationed visits to the showers in the Delouser, and even made a few unofficial visits when I got the nod from George Martin or Sergeant Charlie McIlroy, fellow gunners in my Battery of the 106th, who operated the Delouser.

And for the first time in my life I had a full dental examination.

A dental surgery, with enough basic equipment to extract a tooth or fill a minor cavity, had been squeezed in a room at the end of one of the barracks. The dentist was a New Zealander and after congratulating me on the state of my teeth, he pulled out the root of a tooth left in by a Barlborough back-parlour dentist, in 1939, which had been troubling me ever since.

I had a thorough check-up by Captain Woods, one of the

two Medical Officers in the British Hospital. He said I was as fit as a fiddle, but like everyone else, "a bit on the thin side". He thought a small bone in my damaged wrist had become diseased and said he would put in a request for an X-ray at a hospital. He had my records in the Kommandantur marked "light work only". (Not that this made much difference with the Germans, as I found to my cost some time later.) He noticed an ugly looking varicose vein in my leg which he moved with an injection. It has never bothered me since.

I became an active member of the Bridge Club (shades of the Three No-Trumpers) and took part in the Camp Bridge Drives and Bridge Tournaments, partnering, very successfully, John (I've forgotten his other name) a Sergeant Major from the Notts Hussars. We met the aforesaid Captain Woods twice in finals, sharing the "honours".

Where I found the energy from, I don't know, but I played football once a week on the pitch between the walls of barracks 2 and 3. Hectic, seven-a-side soccer, in borrowed, colourful strips made from dyed army shirts, home-made white shorts and discarded army boots converted by the Schusters into football togs.

The games were played half an hour each way, with a break of ten minutes at half time. And very often, that was after spending the morning clearing away the snow fallen the previous night. No sliding tackles, for a heavy fall on the cinder pitch could rip your backside open. But plenty of skilful dribbling, using the walls of the barracks as a dumb outside-right, recalling boyhood days of football in the back entries of Townsend Lane with an old tennis ball, or rolled up newspapers tied with string.

Everybody was given the chance to have a game if they wanted to play. Although I was never a particularly robust footballer I played in the second team.

Soccer of course had become the great passion in the British compound at Wolfsberg, like everywhere else where bored, young British males congregated in numbers above twenty-two. By the time I arrived, the games had progressed from scratch sides, kicking about a heavy, water-logged case-ball made in the Schusters from off cuts of filched leather, to highly competitive "International" League matches, with teams representing England, Ireland, Scotland, Wales, Australia and New Zealand, playing with dubbined, leather footballs donated by the Red Cross.

It was shortly after I arrived, too, that our hard worked Confidence Man finally won permission from the German Kamp Kommandant to use the parade ground in the centre of the camp for soccer matches. Outside the British compound, it was about half the size of a regular football pitch. You didn't quite take your life in your hands to play on the grassless, stony surface of this pitch, although it was baked hard in summer and frozen solid in winter.

There was any amount of enthusiastic amateur footballers in the Stalag, and also a goodly number of ex-professionals. mostly part-timers from the pre-war, professional and semi-professional English Third Divisions, who had been drafted into the British Army as physical training instructors.

The British "International" football games in Stalag XV111A, were played with great gusto, and intense rivalry and competitiveness. Cheered on at every game by the football-mad nationals, sporting the colours of their team and remembering Saturday afternoons on the terraces of Glasgow Rangers or the Kop at Anfield.

The barracks of the British Compound emptied completely when these matches were played, particularly for the needle games of the top teams, England v Scotland, or Wales v Ireland. The colonial teams, also, always had a full "gate", their lack of expertise with the round ball made up by the skills and exuberance of their national games with the oval ball, Australian Rules and Rugby League.

Unofficial spectators from the French and Italian compounds mingled with the supporters when these needle games were played. Together with off-duty German guards, their Kommandant among them, turning a blind eye to this infringement of Camp Regulations. I believe there was talk, too, of a game between the British and the German guards. This never materialised as the guards were, mainly, middle-aged or elderly men.

There came the time, however, when every International game turned into a needle match and, believe it or not, arguments, leading sometimes to fist-fights, broke out among the British spectators. Many a mixed combine, the "family" of the British prisoner-of-war, was broken up because of defeat in an International football match.

Inevitably, and sensibly, the Sports Committee, decided to call a halt to the over-enthusiastic games of the "International" League. Particularly after England had twice been successful in finishing top.

So, irrespective of nationality or expertise, teams were drawn out of a hat and given random names like Everton and Sunderland, Auckland and Sidney.

The football matches of Stalag XV111A were never again the same.

A typical Stalag XV111A football team, Danny George's "Yorkshire Terriers". Note the nets made from Red Cross string.

CHAPTER 29

You Wouldn't Bet on it?

The Australians in Wolfsberg regularly played one of their own national games. "Two-up", a gambling game requiring no equipment except two pennies, and it didn't matter whether the coins were English, Australian or Austrian provided they had the head of King George or Franz Joseph on one side.

"Two up" intrigued me, for it took me back to the illegal game of "pitch and toss" I remembered as a small boy in Liverpool during the days of the great depression of the middle twenties. Played by bored gangs of young unemployed, as an alternative to the Liverpool street game of "ollies", pennies and ha'pennies were gambled on the toss of coins. Pitch and toss in Liverpool was strictly against the law, so "dowsers" were stationed at strategic corners of the back entries to watch out for the "scuffer", the policeman on the beat.

The Cobbers from Australia didn't need dowsers to play two-up in Wolfsburg, however. During the summer, it was not unusual to see in a corner of the compound, tucked away behind the Dreaded Bog, a group of twenty or thirty Australians with a sprinkling of Kiwis and Pommies on the fringe, playing their national pastime. A clamouring crowd, would gather in a circle, cheering on a burly Aussie in the centre flipping two coins into the air from a flat sliver of wood held between his thumb and forefinger. Sundry bets had been placed on which way the coins would land on the ground.

Would they come down two heads or two tails or a head and tail?

The amounts staked, the excitement, the noise, the curses, and the cries of encouragement to the man in the middle, increased each time the two coins landed the same side up. The fervour and excitement reaching its pitch when the flipper flipped a sequence of ten double heads.

The "currency" changing hands, was cigarettes. The currency of the prisoner-of-war and the black market. During that period from 1943 to early 1944, when Red Cross parcels and cigarettes were received fairly regularly, there was no shortage. It was not unusual for bets of a couple of hundred cigarettes to be wagered on whether two heads would be thrown six times on the run. At that time ten cigarettes could buy a loaf of bread from the right contact.

Many of the Australians were compulsive gamblers, so the stakes in the games of "two up" were not always limited to cigarettes. Sometimes IOUs would pass between hands in these open air betting rings, to be redeemed after the war. Bets were also placed by the Australians on horses running in the Melbourne Cup, the Australian Grand National, through the military pay-offices in Sydney. Incredibly, small fortunes were lost and won by prisoners-of-war in Stalag XV111A on the toss of two coins, or on race meetings held the other side of the globe.

During the years from early 1942 until about the end of 1943, it was not uncommon for a prisoner-of-war to issue pay instructions to his Regimental Paymaster. I used the service myself after I heard of the death of my Mother. I transferred my weekly allotment, which had been in her name since I had been called up, to my Father.

Although I wasn't in the camp at the time, it is well documented by Eric Fearnside in his "The Joy of Freedom" that, in the summer of 1943, a fund raising event in aid of the Red Cross Society was held in Stalag XV111A. The Regimental Paymasters of the British and Colonial Armies being the go-between, transferring the monies raised.

The occasion took the form of a grand Summer Fair extravaganza staged in the open on the football pitch.

The theme was "A Roman Holiday" and featured a parade of Roman Centurions clad in glittering, lifelike armour and helmets (flattened KLIM milk tins), armed with lances, swords and circular dimpled shields (flattened Malt-and-Cod-Liver-Oil tins). A Roman Guard-of-Honour escorted a sultry, languid Cleopatra, reclining with Mark Anthony, in a gaily decorated

240

two-wheeled chariot pulled around the arena by two white horses. The horses had been "borrowed" from a farmer's field next to the camp. The farmer, a spectator at the show, nervously chain-smoking Craven A cigarettes.

Every man watching the lavishly costumed spectacle on that day was handed a postcard and invited to write to his regimental paymaster authorising him to transfer £5.00 or £10.00, or whatever, from his accumulated pay, to the Red Cross Society.

Even the Camp Commandant, Herr Steiner, was tricked into making an unofficial contribution to the fund when he was charged a Deutchmark for a programme. As Eric Fearnside said, "he was paying for a programme which we shouldn't have had printed, with money that was not allowed."

According to Eric, the total sum raised that day was £32,000 pounds. An enormous sum of money in those days, reflecting the everlasting gratitude and thanks of British Prisoners-of-War to the Red Cross for the food parcels that, without any doubt whatever, saved their lives.

Chapter 30

The Hula Hula and the Bolero

The Wolfsberg Theatre was one of the most popular ways of passing time, and killing the boredom and confinement of kreigsgafanganer life in Stalag XV111A.

Very few of the prisoners, locked up behind the barbed wire for two or three years, missed an opportunity to see the excellent variety shows, revues, orchestral concerts, classical plays and dramas staged in the Wolfsberg Theatre. Many of the musical productions and plays were written and produced by inmates of the Camp.

Important morale boosters, these shows took the men out of themselves for a couple of hours, helping them to forget, for a little while, at least, the barbed wire, the boredom, the sorrows and sordidness, the stink and the shouting of the overcrowded barracks, the lousy food, dirty water, dust and mud.

Well worth the two cigarettes admission, an Ernie Mack variety show recalled nostalgic, pre-war visits to the thousands of cinemas in every village, town and city throughout Great Britain, when, long before the days of the television screen, two or three trips a week to the "pics" was the norm. And reminded them, as the tide of the war turned in our favour, that these happier times would return.

The shows, also, recalled the twice nightly "live" shows in the hundreds of pre-war theatres, when the names of variety artistes and "big band shows" were familiar, and on everybody's lips.

The earliest attempt at organised theatrical entertainment in Stalag XV111A is described by John Ledgerwood in his "**Potted History of Stalag XV111A**" of 1944.

"Organised entertainment had not as yet been very seriously attempted. Occasional impromptu concerts were

given in the barrack rooms, and the quality of entertainment was exceedingly poor. Yet, lacking anything better, those scrappy efforts of 1941 were, in their own way, bright spots in an otherwise drab existence.

Men were in the mood for being amused and what did it matter if the only available source of amusement was the ribaldry of the soldiers' common room? Anyone who could and would entertain mounted the rough planking which was the concert platform and made his contribution to a crazy programme.

From somewhere or other the prisoners of war had brought to light an old piano and upon this Stan Summers kept the pulse of music very much alive.

Away in dark corners two indefatigable N.C.Os were preparing the pantomime "Cinderella", and Lance Corporal "Fritz" Southworth's newly formed camp orchestra was putting in hours of practice. Musical scores were being written from memory and costumes were being made from crepe paper, wrapping from Red Cross parcels, odd assortments of old blankets and glue made from the Yorkshire Pudding mixture in English food parcels. An electrician was stealing wire and fittings from under the Jerries' noses and a Stage Manager was erecting Stalag XVIIIA's first semi-permanent stage consisting of two huge barrack doors set upon blocks of stolen wood.

When "Cinderella" opened in the New Year 1942. it was to the most enthusiastic audience that could possibly come together anywhere. The show ran for ten nights to packed houses.

The "theatre" was a small room separated from the main barrack by two small "bunk" rooms. It accommodated 110 persons seated on long undressed planks set on top of piles of loose bricks. The orchestra was separated from the audience by a low partition made of the three-ply sides of Red Cross packing cases. There were no "wings" to the stage which was fifteen feet deep and eighteen feet wide.

But what did it matter, when somehow or other those undaunted thespians contrived seven changes of scenery, one hundred and nineteen different "pantomime" dresses –

243

all paper – innumerable wigs fashioned from Red Cross
string and a lighting system which had to be seen to be
believed.
"Cinderella" was for Stalag XV111A, an event of most
noteworthy importance."

When I arrived in XV111A, in the late summer of 1943, "Wolfsburg Theatre" had long been established in the smaller section of Barrack 1. Back-breaking work had been carried out by former joiners and carpenters, electricians and plumbers, painters and decorators. Willing volunteers converted the one-time grubby stable into a presentable, workable theatre. In the process, many German fingers had been stained with the distinctive nicotine of Players Medium cigarettes, and an invisible chain had been forged between the camp gates and the Black Marketeers of Wolfsberg.

Padre John Ledgerwood, a vital link in the chain, had been *"personally influential in a nefarious business deal, acquiring the theatre's baby grand piano for 500 cigarettes and ten cakes of Lux toilet soap."*

Wolfsberg Theatre was a theatre in every sense of the word. It had an auditorium seating a culture-starved audience of about three hundred, a separate orchestra pit for a ten-piece orchestra, and beyond the coloured footlights of the roomy stage, dressing rooms, workshops and storage space for stage props. It was, to all intents and purposes, a true theatre, better than many a small theatre or church hall I had attended at home.

Orchestra rehearsing in auditorium of theatre.

"Fritz" Southworth's Stalag Orchestra was the mainstay or backbone of Wolfsberg Theatre. A dedicated, professional musician, "Fritz" had been a member of the B.B.C. Symphony Orchestra until September, 1939. He returned to the B.B.C. after the war.

Prominent among the musicians of XV111A was Ken Willmott, a regular soldier in the 4th Hussars. For three and a half years, at the Royal Military School of Music, Ken had studied the violin and the oboe, harmony, score arranging, music composition and conducting. His musical ambitions and dreams were shattered when the war broke out and he became a stretcher-bearer. Ken, eventually, played with the Liverpool Philharmonic Orchestra and the B.B.C. Northern Orchestra.

There was no shortage of musicians in Stalag XV111A. The orchestra was drawn from talented bandsmen of the Regimental bands of the Guards and Hussars Regiments; ex-miners who had played the cornet or bassoon as a hobby in colliery brass bands; an organist from the Odeon Cinema in Manchester; a drummer who played with Teddy Joyce, a well known broadcasting dance band in 1939/40 and a London busker, Arthur Albrow, a veritable maestro of the banjo who could sing the words of every popular song that was ever written. Arthur returned to busking outside the theatre queues of London after he returned home. The pianist was Max Mouna, a 106th man from Liverpool, a talented, self-taught musician who was one of the most popular inmates of the camp. Our paths didn't cross during our service in the 106th, as we were in different batteries, but I am proud to say that, through the theatre, I was honoured to become a great friend of Max Mouna. Sadly we had to leave Max behind in Austria when he died of cancer in the last months of the war.

Maxie Mouna at piano.

It was in late 1943 that reluctantly, I embarked on my one and only brief stage career, beginning and ending in the Wolfsberg Theatre. I was cajoled, bullied, and persuaded by Ernie McGrae, (Ernie Mack) an impresario and producer of popular shows in the camp, into taking a part as a chorus "girl" in a variety show he was about to produce.

Despite my protests that I was tongue-tied standing in front of an audience of even half a dozen people, that I had never done any acting, and had never been on a stage in my life except the Liverpool Landing Stage, he was very persuasive and his smooth tongue won me over.

"Somebody's got to do it," he said. "We all have to dress up and seriously act the fool and those men out there need entertaining." He had a dozen arguments and to cut a long story short, and in any case, ever ready to hold my hand up and try something new, I became a "Chocolate Soldier" in a chorus line of four, in his next show.

The Chocolate Soldier.

The female impersonators of the Wolfsberg Theatre were typical young British soldiers of the time, mostly Territorials and Militiamen from the length and breadth of the British Isles, caught up in the disastrous calamities of the early days of the war and becoming prisoners-of-war in the spring of 1941. In no way effeminate they were youngsters who were not afraid to have a go. Almost all of them took part in the sports activities of XVlllA and played for one or other of the football teams. Most of them had been outside in arbeitslagers, had had brushes with the Germans and had successfully tossed the doctor to avoid work and return to Wolfsberg.

Some had made repeated unsuccessful attempts to escape, including the natural blonde who let his hair grow and fooled the guards at a working camp by dressing as an Austrian fraulein. He walked away from the site carrying his hoarded chocolate and Fray Bentos corned beef in a home-made handbag, dangling from his shoulder. His disguise was blown by the wolf-whistles he received as he minced past a road-gang of British prisoners from another camp. A dedicated escapee, and wanted by the Germans for transfer to "an escape-proof punishment camp", he was hiding in the Stalag under an assumed name.

No "passes" were made to these good looking young men, converted on the stage into convincing and glamorous young women by the skill of a professional make-up artist and hairdresser. Homosexuality, as far as I was aware was not practised in Stalag XVlllA.

I never saw, or even heard of secret assignations. I never came across any furtive fumblings in dark places nor saw any doubling up in the narrow bed spaces in the eighteen-bunk blocks of the overcrowded barracks. Nor heard of them. In the Dreaded Bog, to answer a call of nature, you were usually accompanied by a dozen other evacuees. I had hardly ever heard the word "homosexual" and wasn't quite sure what it meant. Eyebrows were sometimes raised and the word "queer" muttered, but "gay" was a word meaning bright, or merry or happy and wasn't in great use, except when the "Gay Gordons" dance was announced in a pre-war ballroom.

There was only one occasion when I overheard a sneered reference to a "queer". I was heating a can of McConachies stew in the chess game on the brick stove. In the crowd around the stove, also trying to cook his dinner, was a hefty Yorkshire lad. A Stalag dandy. It should be explained that at this time there

248

were a number of men who had become quite paranoid about their appearance. "Barbed-wire happy" as it became known. Polishing their boots and ironing their shirts, creasing their trousers and greasing their hair. Cultivating pencil-thin, Ronald Colman moustaches and sporting silk cravats or ties around their necks. Even using a scented after-shave lotion, received in a comforts parcel from home.

The bluff Yorkshire man was just such a dandy. Somebody made the mistake of muttering, in his earshot, something about a "bloody queer smelling like a May Horse".

Without more ado, the big man took off his jacket and his silk cravat, and invited his critic outside to show him whether he was a "queer" or not. The fist fight, the only one I saw as a POW, was brought to a halt by a Troop Sergeant Major from the Notts Hussars.

Of course a great deal of horse-play went on in the shared dressing room behind the stage of the theatre. Laughter was never far away. Long before the show started, jokes were played with stuffed homemade bras and items of female stage apparel being "borrowed". Or "someone" would have an acute attack of stage fright and the belly-ache that went with it. Then dressed in the flowing costume and head-dress of a Bedouin girl from the chorus of the Desert Song, a sudden dash would be made in a minor snowstorm, get to the Dreaded Bog and back in time for the opening curtain.

In fact, notwithstanding my natural shyness and chronic stage-fright and self-consciousness of taking the part of a girl, I came to enjoy the amateur dramatics and musical shows of the Wolfsberg Theatre.

I appeared in bit parts as a waitress or a kitchen maid in plays and one act sketches. I even tried my hand at singing and dancing.

In the "Two Ernie's" Production of "Hittin' High", one of the highlights? Of the show was *"THE BOLERO, an adagio by John Harding and Doug Arthur"*.

Dressed in a short black skirt, a red, be-ribboned blouse, mock, black boots reaching to my knees and a vivid, red scarf tied around my head, I attempted to mimic, a girl of easy virtue soliciting a client in a run-down Parisian bistro.

For six hectic performances, I was thrown around the grotty floor of the stage by a Londoner, John Harding, a giant ex-professional wrestler and amateur ballroom dancer. John was also a bit of a Stalag dandy with his jet black, well oiled hair parted down the middle, his pencil moustache, goatee beard and the long mother-of-pearl cigarette holder which he affected both on and off the stage.

The frenzied climax of the "adagio" came when John, gripping me by an ankle and wrist, – my good one – threw me across the stage, from corner to corner, as the hypnotic rhythm of Ravel's Bolero, reached its crescendo.

Every time I see Morecambe and Wise's hilarious version of the Bolero I am reminded of the rough, unplaned boards of the Stalag stage. Our dance was not funny, it was deadly serious. I still have the scratch marks on my backside to prove it.

Encouraged by Ernie Mack, I sang a duet with Ted McShea in a couple of shows and was one of a trio of "Andrews Sisters" look-alikes harmonising "When Johnny Comes Marching Home". Having no natural "ear" for music, I learnt my harmony part the hard way with hours of practice under the patient guidance of Maxie Mouna, picking the notes out for me on the piano. In the same show, I surprised myself by singing solo the popular wartime ballad, "You'll Never Know".

EMPIRE THEATRE

PRESENTS

M U S I C

C O M E D Y

HITTIN'

HIGH

D A N C I N G

S O N G S

A "Two Ernie's" Production

STALAG XVIII A
Wolfsberg - Austria

Commencing
J U N E 19 th 1 9 4 4

Hittin' High programme.

My nervous vocal solo debut should have been "Look What You've Done To My Heart", a catchy refrain composed by Ken Willmott to words by Ernie Mack. But at an early rehearsal, after singing the song through for the first time, I innocently remarked that it "was a bit like so and so," mentioning another popular tune of the day. Without more ado, Ken Willmott insisted on cutting the song out of the show.

251

'Look What You've Done To My Heart'.

Fame very nearly came my way when I had brief walk-on, walk-off parts in two short comedy sketches with Buddy Clive – later Clive Dunne, the television star. (Corporal Jones in Dad's Army).

But I suppose I reached the peak of my short stage career when I played the lead in a musical play, "Hawaiian Paradise", written and produced by Eric Fearnside.

Based on a short story by Somerset Maugham, "Hawaiian Paradise" was set on a South Sea Island. In addition to the full Stalag Orchestra, a feature of the show was a six piece Hawaiian Band with an electric guitar, three genuine Hawaiian ukuleles and a couple of bongo drums.

I played a native girl. Lei Lani.

Many years later, my sentimental, much-loved Mother-in-Law, Lucy, insisted that our first-born, should it be a girl, was to be named Leilani. Fortunately it was a boy.

I suppose my somewhat diminutive size and semi-starved frame, plus my black hair and a natural, dark complexion tanned by the sunshine of the Libyan Desert and twelve months in the open air of a forestry camp on the top of a mountain, made me a suitable candidate for the role.

The props man, Norman Allman, a tailor from Manchester,

produced out of Red Cross parcel string, an authentic-looking grass skirt. He also fabricated a colourful garland of flowers from tissue paper rescued from the food parcels. The garland, fashioned into a lei to go round my neck, partly concealed a pair of imitation, flesh-coloured, budding breasts and taut, tantalising nipples. A realistic white hibiscus flower, fixed in my hair above my ear, just about completed my portrayal of a larger-than-life, dusky, South Sea Island maiden.

A pre-war pupil at the famous Campbell's Academy of Ballroom Dancing in Liverpool, I could dance a light fandango with the best of them, and with a good partner, I could shake a reasonable leg in a Latin American rhumba or tango. So the art of the South Seas hula-hula dance, a feature of my solo part in "Hawaiian Paradise", didn't present me with much of a problem.

I was coached in this bottom-wriggling, arm-waving, hand-gesticulating, eye-raising performance by Alan Rauhini and his friend, Paki Jones, two patient easy-going Maoris, latterly, fierce, front line, bayonet-wielding warriors in a New Zealand Infantry battalion who had put the fear of God into young German paratroopers at Malame on Crete after a fearsome rendering of the haka war chant. Formerly, a solicitor and chartered accountant, from Christchurch.

My *piece de resistance* in the musical, was a solo performance of the grass-skirted, hula-hula dance after singing a romantic South Sea Island love song.

As far as I remember, the words were

Take this, my flowered Lei
And wear it through the day,
My Sweetheart.
Violets and roses too,
They all look well on you,
My Sweetheart.
When you go sailing, far away,
My Lei will bring you
Back to me, someday.
Although we're far apart
You're always in my heart,
Until we meet again someday,

253

My Sweetheart.

On the opening night, I don't know how I managed to conquer my bout of stage fright, in front of the usual packed house of about three hundred and fifty.

But as I gyrated around the stage, swishing my string grass skirt in time to the music, my confidence grew as I became aware that the only sounds I could hear were the lilting twangs of the guitars, accompanied by the strums of the ukuleles and the finger tapping rhythm of the bongo drums. I realised, as I floated about the stage in my bare feet, that the packed theatre audience was absolutely quiet. Where were the catcalls and the derisory raspberries I had been nervously expecting?

There was no one more surprised than I, when I finished the hula dance to an explosion of applause. Eric hissing in a hoarse whisper from the wings, "Take an encore, Doug! Do the dance again. Take an encore!"

Looking back on this experience, I think it must have been a bit of a blow to the theatrical profession after the war when, instead of going on the stage, I decided to go back to Baxendales, the Plumbers' Merchants, selling all white "P" trap closets.

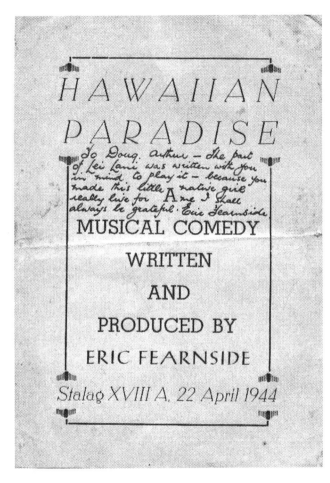

HAWAIIAN
PARADISE

To Doug. Arthur – the part of Lei Lani was written with you in mind, to play it – because you made this little native girl really live for Ame & shall always be grateful. Eric Fearnside

MUSICAL COMEDY

WRITTEN

AND

PRODUCED BY

ERIC FEARNSIDE

Stalag XVIII A, 22 April 1944

Hawaiian Paradise.

Prominent among the many New Zealanders in Wolfsberg was the camp unofficial watch and clock repairer. If your watch wanted repairing, Teddy Smith could, usually, fix it for you for the price of a few cigarettes.

Ted Smith was one of the "Barons" of Stalag XV111A, operating a black market within the black market. When I took my liberated pocket watch to him, to see if he could fix me up with a new glass, I caught a glimpse of the contents of the locked portmantau he kept under his bed, when he delved inside it to find a suitable glass. The case was half full of cigarettes and black-market eggs, tomatoes and onions, a veritable small fortune in prisoner-of-war terms. When I read the novel "King Rat" many years later, I was reminded of Teddy Smith and his suitcase full of cigarettes.

A likeable rogue, if ever there was one, Ted Smith, the "provider" (at great cost) of the electric guitar and the other native instruments for "Hawaiian Paradise", took a keen interest in the show.

Like many New Zealanders, before the war he had been a keen yachtsman and was the owner of a cruising yacht. He was planning, on his return home, to take a year's holiday, sailing the South Sea islands. He had decided to invite a Britisher to accompany him, preferably someone who was thinking about emigrating to New Zealand after the war – as I was. With his interest in "Hawaiian Paradise" he was offering the holiday to the pommy whom he thought took the best part in the show. He asked me.

The general idea was that after the twelve month's holiday was finished he would help me to find work if I wanted to stay in New Zealand, or help me with the cost of returning to England if I decided to go back home.

In the event I did not take up the offer, as circumstances beyond my control and the everlasting finger-of-fate pointing in another direction, dictated otherwise. I never went to New Zealand.

Chapter 31

Aladdin and his Wonderful Plonk

Christmas, 1943, in Stalag XV111A, was my fifth Christmas away from home. Four of them abroad under harsh conditions. The 1943 celebration sticks in my memory for three things.

Firstly, I went to a special Christmas Carol Service. It was the first time I had heard the old familiar carols sung so beautifully by an all-male well-rehearsed choir.

Secondly, I took part in a spectacular Christmas pantomime, "Aladdin and His Wonderful Lamp", written and produced by Bill Merrill, Richard Harpwood and John McGeorge. I played "Petal". One of a cast of thirty, supported by the Stalag Orchestra of ten, aided and abetted by twenty-five technicians and helpers. Stage Manager, House Managers, Electrician, Commissionaire, Scenic Artists, Costume Designers and cigarette "ticket" collectors.

Thirdly, on Boxing Day, after the final performance of the show, I got blinding, paralytic drunk, for the one and only occasion in my life.

This came about because it was the general opinion in the camp that 1943 would be the last Christmas in captivity so it had been decided by most of the inmates to have a special Christmas "nosh-up". Red Cross food parcels had been received fairly regularly during 1943 so there was no drastic shortage of goodies to eat, although there was the usual problem of finding enough fuel to cook them.

The Aladdin programme.

To help with the celebrations half a dozen illicit liquor stills had been set up in the British compound, including one in the Schusters hut. Dick Rimmer had bribed the German Feld-Webel in charge of the boot repair shop to smuggle in a five gallon wooden beer cask and some bits of rubber gas tubing.

A few weeks before Christmas, Dick assembled his

homemade distilling apparatus, finding a hiding place for it in a corner under his bunk. Loading the barrel with prunes and raisins from the food parcels, reinforced with peelings from the rotten potatoes the Germans gave us, the still was soon fermenting and bubbling away, the clear alcohol dripping slowly and steadily into an empty KLIM tin.

The innocent-looking but deadly potent poteen, one hundred per cent alcohol, was ready in time for our last Christmas "celebrations" as prisoners-of-war.

There were six Schusters taking part in "Aladdin" and after the final show the cask of firewater was broached by Hu Flung Dung (Dick Rimmer), assisted by Wishee Washee (Harry Garvey), Wun-Big-Cli, The Town Crier (Lou. Griffin) and Ping Pong (John McGeorge).

Before the tasting of the firewater we had our Christmas supper. I can remember vividly how I had, somehow, contrived to cook this splendid repast on the community brick stove that night.

Sliced luncheon meat dipped in a McDougall's ready-to-cook pancake mixture batter, fried with a spoonful of margarine in an old army dixie. Followed by a delicious, tinned treacle sponge pudding, which I had been saving for months for this occasion. The pudding had been warming up all day on the stove. I washed all of it down with half a bottle of Austrian lager, another unexpected Christmas present. (The lager by courtesy of Dick Rimmer, the Feld-Webel, and the fifty cigarettes Christmas present which Dick had received earlier from his pre-war employers, the Liverpool Co-operative Society).

I can remember, too, taking my first sip of Dick's home-brewed rat poison and wondering whether it was going to burn my tongue or throat, or take my head off. But I don't remember anything else, except waking next morning with a cracking headache and then retching and vomiting all day without leaving my bunk.

I wasn't the only one feeling the effects of "Wolfsberg Plonk", as many of the revellers were violently ill. Ill enough for the British medical staff to impose a ban on all plonk distilleries and order their destruction.

Plonk was never brewed again in Stalag XV111A.

Chapter 32

Research on a SS Farm

In case you're concluding from the foregoing that I was in some kind of Butlin's Holiday Camp, I hasten to remind you that this narrative is an account of my personal experiences and not a history of Stalag XV111A. My stay there, really, reflects my unusual good fortune to be incarcerated in Wolfsberg during an "easy" period – if I could call it that – in the summer of 1943.

Living conditions had not always been easy in the Stalag and I was most fortunate not to be there during the terrible typhus epidemic which hit the camp after the Russians arrived in late 1941. The outbreak of the plague is described vividly by Padre John Ledgerwood in his Reminiscences.

> *"With the Russians came the dreaded typhus.*
> *Shortly after their arrival and their being crowded into inadequate accommodation, with men dying like flies, and sick men being denied the attention which was offered by the British Medical Staff, typhus broke out.*
> *Stalag XV111A came immediately under quarantine regulations, and all nationalities were confined to camp for nearly two months. The medical officers faced a very dangerous situation and tackled it with energy. Fortunately for us, the Germans, scared of entering the various living quarters of the prisoners-of-war, left the organising and carrying out of emergency precautions to the British and French medical staff.*
> *During the two months of quarantine, nearly five hundred Russians died, two French prisoners-of-war, four Germans and no British. It was touch and go with us, and I for one, feel that the British prisoners-of-war do not fully appreciate the debt they owe to our Medical officers and orderlies for*

260

preventing a disaster.

It is true the Germans gave us carte blanche in the matter of emergency precautions, and gave little personal assistance in the efforts made to restrict the spreading of the epidemic, but in fairness, I must say that they gave the best medical attention at their disposal to those British and French prisoners-of-war who had contracted typhus and were isolated from the rest of the camp.

The Russians they ignored.

The quarantine period had one good result for the British. No one could be sent to work. Thus, for two months at least, we were able to consolidate our resources and lay the foundation upon which to build a very good superstructure of camp projects.

Christmas came, our first in captivity, and I can assure you it was a proper festival, conceived and observed in the true tradition.

I am happy to write that the Russians shared our material benefits even though they could not share our physical robustness. Secretly, and with a rare enthusiasm, we were collecting and storing tins of food, sweets, cigarettes and clothing for Joe's boys. On December 24th, 1941, cases of good things were smuggled, under cover of darkness, into the Russian compound, so that on Christmas morning there was a real meaning in the singing of the British across the barbed wire to the Russians, "God and Sinners reconciled".

Padre Ledgerwood's foundation was still holding up the superstructure of camp projects when I got there, although the whole thing was to come crashing down, twofold, later in 1944.

However, I found that no opportunity had been lost to put fleas in the ears of our German guards. "Goon-baiting" was a hobby carried out by most of the work-dodgers in the camp. Every guard in the place was catalogued. We knew who the "good ones" were. The ones who had been hooked into the black market with English cigarettes and Princes tinned salmon – unheard of luxuries in Nazi Germany – and then unscrupulously blackmailed with threat of disclosure.

For a while, the early morning parades were like something

out of a Laurel and Hardy film, only half the men turning out of bed and the other half attending the parade in pyjamas. I can still see in my mind's eye, Maxie Mouna, a look of utter boredom on his face, his trousers pulled over his pyjamas, leaning with his fist under his chin, his elbow on the ground, openly defying the bandy-legged guard and saying he hadn't had his breakfast yet.

In the summer of 1944, the Gestapo put a stop to these shenanigans. It was shortly after Tito's partisans had raided an arbeitslager on the Yugoslav border, killed all the German guards and spirited away the hundred British occupants of the camp. The Germans were convinced that Stalag XV111A was in secret radio contact with England, and Tito in Yugoslavia. They also knew that wanted prisoners were in hiding in the lager or living there under assumed names. Captain Steiner and his henchmen had long been aware that there was a hidden radio receiver in the camp.

Perfunctory searches had been carried out from time to time, without much success, by Hauptman Steiner and his middle-aged guards. A few of them were in cahoots with the prisoners, anyway, and were even able to give warning of impending searches.

There was no warning, however, when the grim-faced leather-coated, pistol-wielding Gestapo, made a surprise inspection of the camp at three o'clock one cold early winter morning. They were reinforced by fifty Storm Troopers and half-a-dozen dog-handlers dragged along by huge, apparently half-wild, German Shepherd dogs.

To the baying of the demented animals and the threatening jabbing and poking of bayonets, we were rousted out of our beds still half asleep and paraded on the football field outside the British compound. Many in their bare feet. Even the sick, confined to their beds in the British hospital, had to turn out, despite the protests of our Medical Officers. Forced to stand in line, with arms and legs spreadeagled to avoid contact with his neighbour, each man was searched by these hardest of hard men. The Gestapo were long wise to the old POW trick of transferring illegal contrabrand from hand to hand down the lines of a crowded parade ground.

Dissension of any sort, even a derisory grin or muttered

protest or a look of dumb insolence, was met with a savage blow from a rifle butt or pistol, and sometimes ended in a hasty trip, escorted by two SS men, to the bunker and a beating.

While the frenzied personal search was being carried out on the football pitch, the huts were being turned inside out as if by maniacs. With ruthless efficiency nothing missed their attention. Suitcases, kit-bags, haversacks, containers of any sort, Red Cross food parcels with half-eaten tins of jam or marmalade or bully beef, KLIM tin kettles on the brick stove, were all thrown on to the floor. Blankets and spare uniforms were strewn all over the place and bed boards loosened and broken.

They didn't find anything. Nothing of very much importance, anyway. They latched on to a few home-made compasses and one or two maps, but the radio receiver remained in its hiding place. It was years later I learned that Wolfsberg's radio was hidden in a special container at the bottom of Ernie Mack's water boiler in the "heiszes wasser engineering shop".

The men in hiding were never discovered. There were six or seven men secreted about the camp and I still don't know to this day how they got away with the deception. It was rumoured around the brick cooking stoves, that one of the runaways hid in a purpose-made concealed shelf in the Dreaded Bog. Six inches away from drowning in the terrifying sludge, and almost dead from asphyxia when he was pulled out. Three men were hidden in the roof space in the Padre's living quarters.

***

I experienced three of these abortive raids by the Gestapo in 1944, and after the last one, early in July, the Germans decided to reduce the number of men in the camp. This had happened before, of course, and I had weathered the storm, but this time my usual good luck deserted me. I lost the job in the Schusters and despite my records being marked "light work only" I received my marching orders.

Accompanied by Ted McShea, I was sent to "a research farm". A working camp on the outskirts of Graz. At least, our friends in the Kommandanteur said it was a research farm. They also said it would be an "easy" job and we should be "all right" there.

Ted and I weren't unduly bothered with being turfed out of the camp. Like a lot of the men in the Stalag we were beginning to feel a little uneasy with the sight of the ever increasing number of bombers flying over the camp, although they were friendly American. Lately, there had been a falling off in the issue of Red Cross food parcels. Food was easier to get hold of if you were working outside the camp.

Anyway, a "research farm" sounded good. We imagined ourselves wearing white dust coats, washing equipment in a laboratory or tending tomatoes and spring onions in greenhouses.

So, as had been our lot since 1939, we accepted the situation with equanimity.

We were jolted out of our resigned acceptance, however, when we arrived at the arbeitslager to find that the research farm was run by a detachment of the infamous SS. They were experimenting with plants and crops and animals commandeered from most of the countries of Europe.

But all Ted and I researched were baby cabbages – fledgling sauerkraut – planted in acres of fields which seemed to stretch forever. Hoeing cabbages in long, endless drills of muddy soil, overgrown with weeds, like the civilian convicts way back in St.Lambrecht. Like the gaol-birds also, we worked bent double in line abreast, chopping at the voracious weeds choking the life out of the cabbages. Supervised by bullying SS guards at our backs.

It was no fun working in those muddy fields after the comparatively easy life we had had in the Stalag. Our guards dragooned us into a back breaking work routine of fifty-five minutes hoeing, and a five minutes break; ignoring pleas for "muss schiezsen gehen" and requests for drinks of water and other tricks of the work-shy prisoner-of-war.

I remember we did get a small break on a couple of occasions when we all stopped, guards as well, to watch a dog fight between American and German fighters overhead. They were very high in the sky, and the first we knew of the aerial battle was when two reserve petrol tanks ejected by the American planes, fell almost on top of us. We had no knowledge of these long, torpedo-shaped cylinders carried under the wings of the American fighters on long distance flights. At first we mistook them for some sort of bomb. They made an unusual, disconcerting noise as they fell to the ground. A loud, swooshing noise as the air caught the empty tanks, swirling them over and over.

***

One day shortly after beginning my apprenticeship on the vast cabbage patch, without warning, I received a vicious blow in the middle of my back with the butt of a rifle. Accompanied by a guttural "Du. Was machen sie mit der kraut?" and a mouthful of untranslateable blasphemy.

"What are you doing with the cabbages for Christ's sake?"

One of the SS men behind had caught me chopping cabbages instead of weeds. Well to be honest, it wasn't exactly a blow. More of a derogatory shove with his rifle. Taking me by surprise, I was sent sprawling on my face into the mud.

I resolved there and then to give the research a bit of a miss and get back to Wolfsberg.

Ted and I went sick next day, me with my gammy wrist and Ted with a bloody, suppurating sore (self-inflicted) on the heel of his foot.

I 'tossed the doctor' on my first visit, but much to my dismay, I was not sent back to Wolfsberg. I was taken by one of the SS men to another arbeits kommando.

Chapter 33

The Glassworks and the Apple Crusher

I discovered, not for the first time in my life, I had jumped right out of the frying pan again. Not into a fire, this time, but into a flaming Dante's Inferno. A hell-hole of a glass factory.

Fifty British prisoners were working in this ancient glassworks when I arrived there, most of them since their arrival from Greece and Crete three years before. It was apparent they were quite content to stay there until the war ended. Even though American bombers were flying over the plant, every day, in ever increasing numbers.

When not at work in the Inferno they were confined in a purpose-built hut in a wired compound, within a bigger compound in the factory grounds. By prisoner-of-war standards the accommodation was 5-Star. Straw-filled palliases on the bunks, electric light, central heating and hot water showers and, never before seen by me in Austria, flushing toilets. They received "heavy industry" food rations which included some sort of meat, three times a week, white bread occasionally, and a weekly issue of an ersatz margarine. And importantly, every Sunday without fail, a Canadian Red Cross food parcel. The Germans made doubly sure the glassworks prisoners received a regular supply of Red Cross food parcels.

They were making glassware of all kinds. Milk bottles, beer bottles, wine bottles, and, as a side line, jam jars and small, glass food jars like fish-paste jars.

A three shift system operated, producing glassware twenty-four hours a day, every day of the week, non-stop. So I found to my horror that I would be expected to work "nights" every third week.

I soon discovered, however, the main reason – apart from the food and luxurious living conditions – for the prisoners' complacency, and acceptance of the dreadful Victorian conditions of labour in the glassworks.

Adjoining the British compound was another separate wired enclosure housing a number of young Ukranian women, also employed at the works. Many of the men had formed liaisons – for want of a better word – with the Ukranian girls, carrying out their unofficial courtship in off-shift periods, aided by a loose window in the shower room specially prepared for the purpose, and tins of salmon and slabs of Cadburys' chocolate.

I'm pretty sure the German Kamp Kommandant knew what was going on and was happy to turn a blind eye. The factory was only able to operate with the combined labour of the prisoners-of-war and the Ukranian women. He was probably worried that if he was to lose his job he would have to go and help stop the Russian Army, which was now making steady progress from the East.

The British prisoners, also, were happy. Never before had they been given the chance of so much free love. (Well almost free). Since working in the glassworks they had never missed a weekly issue of a Red Cross food parcel.

And the Ukranian girls were happy because they had never been so well fed since being abruptly plucked from their homes in the Ukraine. If they became pregnant, they got a week's holiday when the baby was born.

I wasn't there long enough to take advantage of these nocturnal assignations, although I was assured that "I would soon get fixed up" if I wanted to. There was no chance of that, though, for the place frightened the hell out of me and I made my mind up to toss the doctor again as soon as I could.

***

At six o'clock next morning I started my first shift in the glassworks.

To get the shock of my life.

For I had never before even been inside a factory – let alone worked in one – except for brief educational visits, as a schoolboy, to Bootle Gas Works, Clarence Dock Electric Power Station and the Meccano factory.

The glassworks, a hive of bustling activity and a bedlam of noise completely foreign to my ears, was a dusty, oppressive, cavernous steel shed, in which stood a line of huge, glowing furnaces or retorts.

Glass boilers.

The scorching heat took my breath away when I walked in from the fresh air.

I was put to work on the hottest, most difficult, most unpleasant job in the factory. One of a team of four, stripped to the waist, working at the foot of one of the gigantic, red-hot, bulbous-shaped monsters.

The bottle-making boiler.

Compared to which, the brick-making machine I had worked on at Knittlefeld brickworks, was a mere toy.

The iron furnace, its glowing, red sides vanishing into the girders of the roof overhead, cooked or boiled or melted the sand, the salt and whatever other chemicals are required to make glass. The liquified glass was then extruded into bottle moulds on a revolving turntable underneath. The bottles, after they were formed, and still white hot, were automatically released to go skittering down a steel conveyor at intervals of one every two or three seconds.

Three men worked in the intense heat at the bottom of the conveyor, fifteen minutes each on three positions, each one getting closer to the glowing inferno. The other exhausted member of the team recovered and rested on a bench for fifteen minutes after his forty-five minute stint, drinking copious amounts of water or swigging at a sort of lemonade drink, kindly provided by our slave-drivers to replace the sweat streaming from his body.

My introduction to this sweated labour was a fifteen minute spell on the "hot spot", closest to the cauldron of molten glass. It was so hot that, if I had been wearing my Hawaaian Paradise grass skirt, it would have caught fire. Using a pair of sprung, steel tongs, I was required to lift the white hot bottles from the conveyor and place them on a flat, shovel-like iron receptacle, or tray, on the end of a long steel handle. As in the nursery rhyme, I gingerly placed ten glass bottles on the shovel which was then carried by the second and third members of the team, alternately,

268

to another conveyor in a cooling chamber. There they released the bottles by operating a gadget on the end of the handle.

That first morning, after my fifteen minutes exhausting spell on the hot spot, we changed positions and I took over one of the iron "shovels" carrying the ten bottles to the cooling oven. The searing heat was a degree or two easier, for I was now ten feet away from the furnace.

I found the clumsy, cumbersome shovel very awkward to handle. It was some twelve inches longer then me, extremely heavy and unbearably hot in my gloveless hands. At my first attempt, I couldn't operate the key in the handle to release the bottles. This caused some consternation for of course the bottles were still being churned out at the foot of the conveyor.

I was valiantly carrying the second tray of white-hot bottles, my hands dripping and my eyes half closed with sweat, when I made out the factory foreman with the Kamp Kommandant and "Digger" John McGinty the Confidence Man, approaching along the factory floor towards me.

I came to an instant decision, there and then, that this was not the job for me. When they got to within about five yards, I stumbled and dropped the lot. The long iron pole with the tray on the end crashed to the floor, almost at their feet, spilling the ten glass bottles and shattering them into a million sparkling, red-hot shards.

There was a hurried and undignified retreat by the three men from the dazzling fragments scattered in front of them on the concrete floor. There was much shouting, swearing and gnashing of teeth by the Austrian manager. After much argument, I convinced him, and the German Unteroffizer Kommandant, that the tray was too heavy for me and I couldn't do the job. Anyway, I wanted to see a doctor about my wrist.

They removed me from the bottle furnace immediately. Collecting my shirt off the bench, I was put on another smaller machine partnering a young, plump Ukrainian girl. This machine, a miniature version of the bottle boiler, spewed out, at an incredible rate, round glass jars about two inches deep and three inches in diameter. Olga and I sat on low, three-legged wooden stools each side of a smaller conveyor, something like a child's garden slide. We took turn and turn about to lift off the meat-paste jars and put them into an adjacent cooling oven. Olga, I'm afraid, lifting two to my one.

Still sweating blood in the unaccustomed heat, after an hour I was bored stiff with the monotonous, repetitive, but much easier work. The tedium wasn't relieved by the impassive, slant eyes of the Mongolian/Ukrainian girl sitting opposite me, with her skirt hitched up over her knees exposing dirty grey, unwashed baggy bloomers and red-veined legs being slowly roasted by the retort.

Thankfully, at nine o'clock I was relieved by John McGinty, the Aussie Confidence Man, who told me to to go and pack my bag.

I was on my way to another camp.

***

Altogether, I was sent to five different working camps, in a period of seven or eight weeks, before I was able to make it back to Wolfsberg. The names of the towns and villages I have long since forgotten but certain incidents stick out in my memory like the burnt thumb I suffered in the glass factory. Some comical, some strange, some a bit frightening.

I left the glassworks in the company of one of the more elderly guards. He was glad of the opportunity to have a day off, for it took us a full day of travelling on the overcrowded trains before we reached a small camp, lost in the hills somewhere in Steirmark.

There were about fifteen British prisoners in this camp, working on local farms and smallholdings. Most of these lads had been there since their arrival in Austria in 1941.

The Confidence Man, a young Cockney militia lad, showed me the ropes. Where the bog was, and where I could make a cup of tea and so on. As he pointed out my bunk in the living quarters, he remarked, almost apologetically, "I'd better tell you right away that Mitzi is my girl and we've been going out together since I got here three years ago. She might take a bit of a shine to you, but I hope you'll leave her alone. She's my girl."

He was almost apologetic but quite serious, as if he was in the habit of taking his fiancee out to the Grafton Ballroom or the

270

Odeon Cinema, two or three times a week.

Puzzled, I said, "Who's Mitzi?"

"Oh," he said, "she looks after the Jerry guards. Cooks and cleans for them and so on and cooks our spud soup at night. She also does my washing for me on the side, but she's too busy to do anymore, and I have to tell you, she's my girl."

Incredibly, Mitzi turned out to be a frowsy, middle-aged woman who looked as if she was badly in need of a bath. Like Ferdinand, the guard at Murau, she was a "penny short of a shilling". And I began to wonder if my new Confidence Man was, too. Mitzi, did in fact, take a bit of a shine to me and also offered to do my washing, as she had done with every other member of the camp at one time or another. I don't think poor Mitzi wanted the war to end, for she had never been surrounded by so many men in her life.

* * *

We were up before six o'clock next day, and marched to various local farms by a guard. I was left with Hans, the owner of a small dairy farm half way up a mountain.

Gaunt and as thin as a lath, shabby and unshaven, but openly proud of the Swastika badge he wore on his lapel, it was obvious to me that Hans was shortly to become another casualty of the war. He was working himself to death. Cows to milk every morning and night, an old mare and a pair of oxen to be groomed, fed, watered and mucked out every day; half-a-dozen squealing pigs with insatiable appetites, up to their eyes in pig-muck in a filthy pig-sty, and acres of grass paddock waiting to be scythed, dried and carted into the barn for winter feed. He weeded his vegetable patch and made his apple-must in his spare time in the evening. Hans had no sense of humour and I never saw him laugh or his face break into a smile.

Mind you, he had nothing to laugh about.

In fact, the dreary, mud-laden, untidy farmyard itself, was enough to put years on anyone.

Hans was always in a hurry. His high pitched Austrian sing-song voice nagged continuously at his wife and four young children whenever they were in earshot. When his nagging complaints were directed at me, they fell on deaf ears or were met with the standard prisoner-of-war reply. "Nicht verstehen." Or "Ich verstehen nicht." "I don't understand." The only help he got to run the farm was a young schoolboy from the local village and a work-shy prisoner-of-war, such as I. As he was a bit of a slave-driver the turnover of his p.o.w. helpers was high.

I started work about six-thirty and my first job, before I had had anything to eat, was to cut fresh grass in the apple orchard, for the animals. My new boss, with a few deft strokes of the scythe I had carried over my shoulder, like a beardless Father Time, gave me a brief demonstration on how to cut a swathe in the thick, dew-soaked grass. Then he hurried away saying he would be back in half an hour.

Interested, I picked up the funny-shaped grass cutter. It was a lengthy, cumbersome tool with a broad, curved blade at the end of a long, lob-sided handle with two awkward grips. I swished it over the grass two or three times, in the authorative manner of a golfer on the first tee practicing a swing with his driver before driving the ball three hundred yards down the fairway. I then made a few tentative stabs at the wet grass trying to emulate Hans' sweeping, effortless style. But the blade either dug itself into the soil under the roots of the grass and uprooted a clod, or sliced through the air missing the grass altogether, like the authorative golfer's fresh-air golf shot.

It was ten minutes before I got the knack.

Satisfied with my efforts after I had made a couple of clean sweeps, I put the scythe down and turned my attention to the ripe, red apples in the tree above my head. It was years since I had had the pleasure of crunching my teeth on a fresh, crisp apple and in the next ten minutes I did my best to make up for those missing years.

The inviting, ripe, red apples were not the same apples as English Cox's pippins however. They were bland, the texture of cotton wool. The flawless red skin, mouth-watering to look at, was tough and hard to chew. Nevertheless, I had my fill. I don't know how many apples I had munched my way through before the farmer came back pulling a small handcart.

When he saw the few clods of muddy grass I had managed to prise from the paddock, he went berserk.

"Verdampting," "verflucting" and "mein gotting," and raising his eyes heavenwards cursing all "Englander," he snatched the scythe out of my hands. In five minutes he had cut enough grass to fill the cart.

By the time I had trudged after him, pulling the handcart through the morass of mud and manure of the farmyard, he had cooled down somewhat. He told me to give the grass to the horse in the stable, for her breakfast, and come into the house for mine.

The unexpected invitation took me by surprise. It was the first time I had been invited into an Austrian home for a meal.

I tidied myself up, did my best to scrape the mud off my boots and politely doffed my forage cap as I walked into the kitchen. My head was clouded with visions of a couple of boiled eggs and a slice of smoked speck – the delicious bacon which I had traded on a couple of occasions for a can of salmon – or maybe even a slice or two of the awful, spicy German blood sausage and white bread.

Once again, my illusions were shattered.

I joined the family of father, mother and four young children in the dreary, uncomfortable kitchen, sitting with them on two long forms each side of a rough, planked table. I found the experience to be a bit of an ordeal.

Breakfast for us all, children as well, consisted of a wedge of dry, black bread and a spoonful of jam. Some mornings there was a pan of lukewarm polienta, the tasteless, maize porridge so beloved by the Austrians, and a jug of milk. The panful of polienta was placed in the centre of the table with a dirty-looking aluminium ladle, and we helped ourselves. The farmer first, followed by his wife, then the four children and then me. The order never changed. I was pleased to see the milk on the table because the youngsters seemed to be very much in need of it.

At the mid-day meal – if you could call it that – the dry bread was accompanied by a bowl of salad. Well, it wasn't exactly a salad. It was a few leaves of a dark green, bitter lettuce and a scattering of spring onions and slices of tomatoes dowsed in some sort of vinegary oil. As a keen bacon-and-egg man, in those days, it was not exactly to my taste and did little to satisfy my permanent hunger.

There were no plates and, unlike the breakfast meal, there

was no order of precedence. It was a case of every man, woman and child for himself. Slightly embarrassed, I was shy of stretching "the long arm of the Arthurs" – to use an old Arthur saying at Sunday teatime, when Wally reached for the Neopolitan Slice before anyone else could get it – to pick out the tastier bits of tomato as the hungry family leaned over the table to help themselves from the bowl.

I felt sorry for the four youngsters. Quietly sitting there with spoons in their hands like four Oliver Twists, dying to ask for more. Looking at me with a certain expectancy out of the corner of their eyes, for they had all heard of the rich "Englander" with their slabs of chocolate and tins of sardines. I regretted that Red Cross food parcels were now scarce and my stock of chocolate and other goodies had vanished. I would have loved to have given them a treat. On the other hand, I thought it was just as well, because if I started to feed the enemy, in what was a crucial stage of the war, the hostilities might never end!

***

I spent Friday afternoon collecting apples from the orchard and carting them to the barn ready for the traditional, annual must-making ceremony which happended to be held that week-end. Apparently, Hans's sweet-and-sour apple cider was renowned throughout the Region. The trees were stripped of every apple, ripe or not. And the half-rotten, worm-eaten windfalls were raked from under the trees, with sundry other vegetation and loaded into the cart with my botched grass-cutting efforts.

The apple-juice was extracted by a huge, Heath-Robinson contraption which would have won first prize in any Antiques Road Show.

Perilously poised in the rafters of the barn it was a massive baulk of roughly dressed timber, fashioned from a single tree into a square beam, twenty feet long by three feet square. The beam – the apple crusher – was suspended in the air from an axle fixed to the main roof purlin. The device was operated by a rope threaded through a simple pulley, a wooden, grooved wheel. When the rope was pulled, the huge beam, creaking and groaning alarmingly, forced down a circular, wooden press into an open, staved barrel filled to the top with apples.

The yellow juice squashed out of the apples trickled through gaps in the staves of the barrel, and then flowed down the wooden platform, to be funnelled into small storage or fermenting casks at the end.

Everything went in the barrel to be crushed by Heath Robinson. Over-ripe red apples, sour, green apples, rotting windfalls, beetles, ants, spiders as big as half-crowns and the occasional dead bird. Hans wasn't too particular about hygiene. I had to barrow the squashed remains to the squealing pigs in the pig-sty.

Hans got quite excited about his traditional, apple-pressing ceremony, evidently looking at it as a sort of holiday or high-light of the year. He couldn't understand when I wouldn't "volunteer" to work on the press in my time off on the Saturday afternoon and Sunday, for he seemed to consider it an honour for me to help him with his must-making. But I had other things to do on my rest days like washing my clothes, taking a bath, writing a letter, catching up on my sleep and fighting off the attentions of Mitzi.

So I didn't last long with the struggling Hans.

Within days I was transferred to yet another arbeitslager.

Chapter 34

Frau Dreadnaught

This newly established lager of twelve men was under the command of a nervous, middle-aged Felt-Webel, a one-time clerk from an office in Vienna. He was assisted by an elderly private, who really should have been at home looking after his grandchildren. Under their supervision the British prisoners were attempting to repair the banks of a narrow, swift-flowing river, which, in heavy rains, was apt to engulf a nearby village. They were trimming into shape large, granite rocks and hauling them into position on the banks of the river. The work was awkward, heavy, wet, and finger-nipping and I didn't relish it a bit. But again I managed to avoid taking part when I explained to the Feld-Webel, in my limited German, about my wrist.

We were the first to occupy the new camp and the Felt Webel, agreeing that I couldn't work on the river bank, appointed me Confidence Man, Camp Interpreter, head chef to cook the potato soup, floor brusher-upper and general dogsbody. Although the Russians in the East, the Americans in the West and the British in the South were making their slow but steady progress towards us – and everybody knew it – the Feld Webel, steeped in the Red Tape and Officialdom of the German Army and anxious to make an impression to his superiors, asked me to produce a very important looking, painted placard indicating the official name and number of the Arbeitskommando, to display on a post outside the camp.

He provided me with the necessary paper and paints and brushes. It took me a week before I was happy with my first attempt at signwriting, in 2" deep, red and black script.

KREIGSGEFANGENEN-MANSCHAFTSSTAMLAGER
XV111A
ARBEITSKOMMANDO A 413/2
KANEINDORF

However, in the inexplicable, mysterious ways of the movements of troops of those times, particularly prisoners-of-war in working camps, the day after I had dug a hole outside the camp and erected the imposing, illuminating sign – the Feld-Webel, preening himself in front of it and patting me on the back – the camp was closed. We were all moved en bloc to a milk processing plant somewhere near Villach.

***

A newly-built, modern factory, spotlessly clean, it contrasted sharply with the dirty, ancient glassworks I had left only a few weeks before. The dairy processed milk from the farms in the area, turning it into butter and skimmed milk. I could hardly believe it when I was told that, when I was at work in the factory, I could help myself to as much milk as I wanted, from a special churn set aside for the purpose. They knew what they were doing, of course, for I quickly got sick of the taste of watery, skimmed milk. They wouldn't let us work on the butter bashing, however.

The accommodation, in a barbed wire compound in the factory grounds, was reasonably good compared with most I had been in, and the civvy rations were the best I had come across. The camp received a regular supply of Red Cross food parcels. Most of the lads had been working there for some time and seemed happy with their lot. They were a friendly crowd and when they found that I could "play" the mandoline, I was co-opted into their "orchestra".

My first job at the dairy, accompanied by Frank Robinson, a quiet, softly spoken Geordie from Newcastle, was to unload coal wagons in the nearby railway siding. The wagons were full to the brim with a bright, clean, industrial coal. Small, dust-free chippings or nuggets which we found easy to handle with the broad coal shovel which went with the job. We shovelled the coal over the side of the railway wagon into a cart pulled by two oxen, and a somewhat dilapidated civilian lorry.

This battered truck was a charcoal burner, the first time I had seen such an animal. To fire the engine the charcoal was converted into gas in a large horizontal cylinder fixed across the lorry behind the driver. Clouds of black smoke belched into the air above the cab, as the ancient vehicle trundled along at fifteen miles an hour. The driver had to make frequent stops to stoke up the burner with fresh charcoal. The cylinder, or tank, together with the enormous bags of charcoal needed to fuel it, took up half the space in the back of the lorry.

On our first day on the coal job, the boss man said we could work "arcourt". That is, when the wagon was emptied we could have the rest of the day off. This was the first time I had been given "contract" work, when a given stint of work completed earned the rest of the day off.

Frank and I got stuck into the coal and by mid-day the wagon was empty. True to the foreman's word, we were back in the billet at one o'clock.

The next day, of course, was another story. Despite our protests about dirty tricks and going back on his word, and pointing out that an Englishman's word was his bond, and so on, our "arcourt" for the day was two wagons to empty before we could go back to the camp.

Shirts off, and drinking pints of skimmed milk, we emptied the two wagons by about half-past three. Even after manhandling out of the way, the charcoal-burning lorry when it conked out alongside the truck, Geordie and I staggered back to the compound proud of ourselves to have beaten the system.

We were told the next day to empty three wagons!

Accustomed to German Slave Trader tricks, this time we didn't even bother to argue with the manager. But, although working diligently, especially when he put in an appearance, the first wagon was only half empty when we finished at six o'clock.

Sacked from my job on the coal wagons, I spent the remainder of my few days in the dairy working on the milk churn washing machine with my new friend from Newcastle. Me at one end, lifting the empty 20 gallon galvanised milk churns, and placing them upside down on 2" steel rollers on a long conveyor. The conveyor rolling the upturned churns over jets of scalding steam, and hot and cold water, to be lifted off at the other end, cleaned and shining, by Frank.

You can imagine the noise. Cacophony doesn't do it justice. Dozens of empty galvanised steel milk churns, the lids face down alongside, bouncing and rattling as they rolled along, upside down, on 2" steel rollers. The noise was frightening. After a day's shift it took hours for my ears to return to anything like normal.

Needless to say, I went sick with earache, 'tossed the doctor', and was on my way once more.

***

I landed another farm job. For a while I thought I had finally found a niche for myself in the comfort of one of the "Home from Home" farm jobs I had heard so much about. They were in the middle of haymaking when I arrived, gathering in the second crop of hay for the winter feed.

The weather was perfect. The scenery gorgeous. It could have been the setting for "The Sound of Music". There were no sky battles going on over my head; there was no guard with a bayonet stuck on the end of a rifle, breathing down my neck.

It was a refreshing change. I was put to work with six or seven females, helping them to harvest the hay. They were friendly, elderly grannies welcoming me in the morning with a smile and the polite "Gruss Gott" or "Javous" greeting of the area. There were a couple of middle-aged mothers, with their small offspring chasing fieldmice out of the haystacks. They showed me how to turn over the swathes of grass with a wide, curved wooden hayfork. And how to stack the grass on to wooden hay ricks, to dry in the sun. They were very good at it, but despite their shouts of encouragement, I was hard put to keep up with the old dears. I loaded hay into a deep V-shaped hay-cart and rode atop of the load with Lilla, a Ukranian girl, to the farm, where we forked it into the barn.

I appreciated the holiday-like atmosphere of the haymaking, and almost enjoyed working in the grass paddocks in the hot autumn sunshine. I had never before experienced the

279

wonderful fragrance of a newly-mown hayfield at about 11 o'clock in the morning under a hot sun in a cloudless sky. I found it delightful.

Our thirty minute mid-day break was taken under the shade of a hay cart or haystack. We had a sort of picnic and I was given the same food as the women from the village. As much bread as I wanted. It was only black bread and there was no butter or margarine to go with it. But it was fresh with a crunchy crust and accompanied by a slice of garlicky German sausage or a small piece of fatty, smoked bacon, or a nibble of strong cheese and an apple. I washed down these unaccustomed victuals with long drinks from a flagon of sweet apple cider, which had been immersed in water to keep cool, in a ditch at the edge of the field.

I couldn't believe my luck and couldn't wait to sample more of the delicious spek, and become better acquainted with little Lilla.

BUT – and it was a big BUT – the farm and the village shop, restaurant, Gast-Haus, butcher, slaughterhouse and defunct petrol pump, was owned and ruthlessly managed by a war-widow about forty years old. Her husband had been sent to the Russian Front and had never been heard of again.

She was a big woman. Dressed in long black mourning clothes which made her look bigger still. Big bosomed, big limbed, big bottomed. And big headed, to boot. A human battleship, if ever there was one, towering over my five feet four, like a dreadnaught towering over a minesweeper. She seemed to own the whole of the little village and ruled the place with a rod of iron. What Frau Dreadnaught said was law.

I crossed swords with her the day after we finished the haymaking.

The bulk of the work on the farm was carried out by a Polish prisoner-of-war slaving away from dawn to dusk, assisted by a local lad who had not long left school, and the little Ukranian girl. I was the last in a long line of British prisoners detailed to work on the farm. The Pole slept in the hayloft over the stable, and had already been working for an hour when I arrived at seven o'clock in the morning. Lilla, the Ukranian girl slaved away from early morning to late at night in the house and restaurant, and helped the Pole with the farmwork. There was always plenty to do on that farm.

Lilla, who said she was nineteen – but looked about fourteen – unburdened herself to me on one of the trips back to the barn with a load of hay. She broke down weeping, when, lying together on top of the swaying load of hay with my arms around her in the way that young people do, my mind racing away with all sorts of ideas, she told me that in 1941 she had been studying at University. She, with her father and mother and two brothers were press-ganged by the Germans, as were millions of other Russians. Somewhere on the long seventeen day trip to Germany in a cattle truck, she lost her family and had no idea whether or not they were still alive. She considered herself very lucky to be working on the farm, and silently accepted the bullying of the boy from the village and the backbreaking work.

I didn't stay long enough on the farm to really get to know Lilla. There was not a lot I could do to help her, although the young hooligan from the village left her alone when I was about, after I had words with him. Red Cross food parcels had become scarce, but I was able to give her one or two items of winter clothing from a belated comforts parcel I had recently received from home.

My confrontation with Frau Dreadnaught began on the morning after the hay-making finished and, to my regret, left little Lilla, the Ukranian girl, somewhat in the shit, so to speak.

I had fed and watered the horse, mucked-out the stable, barrowed the manure to the steaming heap on the other side of the yard, and then swilled the concrete floor.

Never having been near a horse before – although an erstwhile member of the Royal Horse Artillery – let alone groomed one, I overcame my nervousness and currycombed the animal's broad, brown flanks. I sensed that she seemed to enjoy the experience, as she munched away on the fresh grass I had stacked in the manger to keep her quiet. Although I had to give her a punch in the ribs when she leaned heavily on me, pressing me against the wall.

As I applied the currycomb with one hand and a stiff bristle brush with the other, I day-dreamed about what my life would have been if my father had had his way, and apprenticed me to a Newmarket racing stable when I left school at fourteen. (Fond of a threepence-each-way bet, he had always said I would make a good jockey.)

Just as I was about to pass the winning post in the Grand National, I was startled out of my daydream with a jolt, when Frau Dreadnaught walked into the stable.

"Artur," she said, crooking her raised forefinger at me, imperiously, "comst du mit mir zum der shiesenhausen."

"Arthur," she said, "Come with me to the shit-house."

Frau Dreadnaught was the most plain spoken of the plain spoken Austrians of that time. She had had plenty of practice with the local villagers. A shit-house was a shit-house, was a shit-house. No pretence was made that it was the la' or the w.c. or the toilet or the Ladies Room or the Powder Room or the lavatory. Or even the Bog. The smell made sure of that, anyway.

I followed her to the cess-pit alongside the slaughterhouse.

I had, of course, already become fully aquainted with the primitive toilet facilities of the establishment, used thrice daily, by the Frau, the Gasthaus staff, prisoners-of-war and the many customers. Man, woman and child. Very sensitive in matters personal, I didn't think much of the arrangements.

So it must be quite apparent to any reader of this narrative, that Austrian cess-pits were the bane of my life. And Frau Dreadnaught's inconveniences were just about the worst I had come across. The extraordinary outside w.c. (to give it its posh title) was situated across the yard opposite the back door of the restaurant. It was little more than a shed, erected over a pit about five feet wide and six or seven feet long and of unknown depth. Unknown to me at any rate.

It comprised two separate, waterless compartments. The wooden doors had a twelve inch gap at the top and bottom, and were locked with a simple wooden peg when the compartment was occupied. Muddy boots and concertinaerd trousers of anyone going about their business were plainly visible. On the wall within hand reach of the rough plank seats was a nail from which hung squares of the "VOLKISCHER BEOBACHTER", on a loop of string. (There couldn't have been a better place for the disposal of this German propaganga newspaper.)

I followed Frau Dreadnaught to the back of the shed just as my Polish workmate was in the process of lifting off the wooden cover of the awesome pit. Standing near it was the farm cart and Lilla.

The cart was carrying a long, cylinder-like tank with a round access hole on the top, and a four inch stop cock or gate valve at the rear. The muck-spreader was encrusted with the blackened, congealed excreta of years. I had seen this type of waste disposal unit before in Stalag XV111A, when half the camp went into hiding as it was trundled through the gates.

Frau Dreadnaught indicated that I was to empty, by hand, the contents of the cess pit into the opening on top of the muck spreader. I don't mean by hand, literally. That would have taken too long. I mean with the use of a two gallon bucket, or scoop, fixed on the end of a long, sturdy pole.

She stood there, explaining in mime, as I shook my head in disbelief.

"Nicht verstehen, Ich verstehen nicht," I said.

"I don't understand," I said.

Bowing to my stupidity she gave the long-handled scoop to the Pole and asked him to demonstrate.

Swearing under his breath in Polish, he dipped the bucket into the pit and filled it to the brim with the foul looking, stinking excreta. And with a hoist of his left elbow and a twist of his right wrist, deposited the contents into the tank on the cart. Obviously an expert, he didn't make a splash, nor lose a drop of the indescribable mixture. With a wry smile, as if to say "put that in your pipe and smoke it", he handed the scoop to me.

They all stood well back when I took hold of the long pole. Which was just as well, for with my eyes closed and my teeth clenched, I dipped the bucket into the pit of disgusting, noxious filth, overfilled it and when I lifted it to empty the dripping contents into the tank, I spilled half of it onto the cart. The other half ran down the smooth handle of the pole into my trembling hands.

To cut a dirty story short, I threw the bucket down and said emptying schieszen-hausen cess pits was no job for an Englishman and I wasn't going to do it.

The Frau's face went a dead white and she came out with a

mouthful of German invective most of which I didn't understand. But I followed the gist of it. She would tell the Gefreiter in charge of the camp that I had refused to work. And then she had a sudden thought and changed her tune to try to blackmail me by appealing to my better nature. Saying if I didn't empty the pit, she would make Lilla do it.

I told her she could do what she liked but I repeated that emptying the schieszen-haus pit was not a job suitable for an Englishman. Especially me. (After all, in happier days, I was a specialist salesman selling the best Twyford's Silent Syphonic Closet Suites that money could buy.)

I won the argument and to my regret, little Lilla carried out the dirty work and filled the muck-spreader.

For my pains and insubordination I was told to help the hardfaced sixteen-year-old from the village, to kill and butcher a calf in the slaughterhouse. It turned out that the young lad was quite good at his job, and in fact played a trick on me with the animal. No doubt getting his own back for the drubbing down I had given him for his bullying of Lilla.

The killing of the calf brought back memories to me of Brennan's slaughterhouse in Cherry Lane, where, as a ten-year-old, I used to sneak in the back door to watch the slaughtermen kill the horses brought over from Ireland. At Brennans they used a humane-killer to kill the animals, carrying out the slaughter with the minimum of pain and distress. I expected Willie from the village to do the same.

But, instead, he looped a rope around the back legs of the animal, threading the other end through an overhead pulley and hoisted the struggling beast until it was hanging by its back legs, vertically, its head almost touching the floor.

On his instructions, I grabbed hold of the two front hooves of the terror-stricken animal. Whereupon he whipped out a long, gleaming, butchers knife from a holster on his belt, lifted up its head with one hand, its eyes almost popping out, and with a single, slashing stroke, cut its throat from ear to ear, directing a spout of brilliant red blood from the gaping slash into a bucket at his feet.

The young so-and-so laughed at me as, taken by surprise by his action, I grimly held on to the hooves of the animal thrashing wildly in its death throes, blood splashing over my boots and trousers. Then I realised he was taking the mickey out of me. With his long butchers' knife he was touching a nerve at the back of the throat of the now dead calf, causing it to violently convulse and throw me about as I hung on to its legs to control the violent spasms. I stopped his sadistic grin by releasing my grip and pushing the calf, heavily, against him, almost knocking him off his feet. He kicked over the bucket of blood just as the Frau walked into the slaughterhouse.

She wasn't at all pleased to see the floor awash with blood, and the newly white-washed walls of her slaughterhouse splattered with the animal's gore. And was not slow in saying so. Willie, frightened to death of her, made a scene. He started whingeing, the tears streaming down his cheeks and, through his sobs, blamed me for the fracas.

Frau Dreadnaught duly reported me to the Gefreighter for refusing to work, sabotaging the butchering of an animal and spoiling a bucket of blood about to be turned into a month's rations of German sausage for the villagers.

***

The next morning the Sergeant-in-charge lost his temper with me when I denied that I had refused to work, had hurt my wrist using the bucket on the pole and I wanted to see the doctor.

For the first time as a prisoner I was scared at the reaction of a German guard directed at me personally. To my horror, he pulled out his revolver, waved it at me, theatrically, and snarled that if the doctor said I was fit for work, he would shoot me. A bluff, of course – a fit of temper. I couldn't work if he shot me, could I? At that particular moment my bowels were telling me that I was in immediate need of the schieszenhaus and that I would be far better emptying it than having a bullet put between my eyes.

I had already seen the village doctor, on two occasions, with a young South African who had also recently arrived at the camp. He was quite determined not to work for the Germans and had been rubbing salt, or some other noxious substance into his eyes to try to toss the doctor. Both eyes were red, bloodshot and inflamed and shedding copious tears into his dirty handkerchief. At each visit the doctor had pronounced both of us fit to work. At this third visit he didn't even examine or question us. He just waved his hand to the door and said "Arbeiten".

When we returned to the billet, the Gefreiter had calmed down somewhat. Looking back, I suppose there was some excuse for his outburst and his attitude, for we had heard that he had lost a son in the fighting in France. He told both the South African – whose name I have forgotten – and me, that he was putting us on a charge for refusing to work. We were to attend a court-martial at his Battalion Headquarters.

The next day, accompanied by one of the elderly guards carrying the usual rifle with fixed bayonet, we set off to catch the local train. We took a wedge of black bread, our ration issue for the day and a couple of water biscuits with cheese spread, the remnants of our last food parcels. And a KLIM tin to brew tea.

We had a sort of day-out, really, changing trains at various stations, and having a short spell in an air-raid shelter at one station when the air-raid alarm sounded. We arrived at the Headquarters in the early afternoon to be told that the Commanding Officer was not available and we would have to return the next day.

So we made another trip the following day, this time travelling through typical Austrian thunderstorms, and heavy rain with hail as big as golf balls. We walked up the road from the station in driving rain, (the same road I had had a brief conversation with my neighbour from Liverpool two years before) and arrived at the German barracks like drowned rats.

Fully expecting a military court-martial in a courtroom full of Nazi Officers, Heiling Hitler and clicking their heels together, I was somewhat relieved to be marched into a private office. The Hauptman was sitting behind a large desk with his cap off and the top button of his tunic undone. I stood to attention before him like a schoolboy reporting to his Headmaster, after being caught throwing ink pellets at the classroom ceiling.

A tall man, iron grey hair thinning on top, his chest plastered with military ribbons, the Iron Cross dangling below them, this distinguished looking Officer looked old enough to be my father. He listened carefully as I explained in my best pidgin

German that I hadn't refused to work, but couldn't lift the bucket of schieszen because of the injury to my wrist and it was essential that I have treatment for it.

Like the woman doctor at Stadl he replied in perfect English. "You explain yourself well. Where did you learn to speak German?"

Two days later, by courtesy of the kindly old Hauptman, I was taken to a civilian hospital in Graz for treatment to the injury to my wrist sustained three years earlier in Murau.

Chapter 35

Return to Stalag

Unusually, I made the journey to Graz in a troop train full of German soldiers returning from leave to the fighting in Italy. I say unusually, for previously, I had always travelled in a separate compartment on my train journeys around Austria.

The guard with me had found seats at the end of a carriage containing fifty or sixty Germans in rather shabby, field-grey uniforms. Their kit, stacked in the racks overhead, overflowed into the narrow passage between the seats.

I had smartened myself up for the trip and felt very conspicuous in my khaki battledress and glengarry, as I walked down the carriage between the rows of grey uniforms, carefully placing my polished boots over kit-bags and haversacks strewn about the floor. Quiet and subdued, obviously not relishing their return to the front, the German infantrymen carried on with their talking and smoking and took little notice of me, or my escort. There was none of the camaraderie and laughter or the noise and squabbles of a coachload of British squaddies with their bottles of beer, games of solo and endless funny stories.

Two stations further down the line, I was joined by a tall, thin Australian. He was accompanied by two burly guards, handcuffed to one of them by the wrist. As he made his way between the seats of field-grey Germans my heart sank as I heard him loudly effing and blinding them, and the war, and the Italians, and the labour camp he'd been working in. He acted as though he wanted to start another personal war, taking on all the Germans in the coach.

After some considerable argument between his guards and the reclining infantrymen, three of them moved away down the carriage and he sat down beside me.

He greeted me with a friendly "Hiya, yer pommy bastard

where yer goin'. These Hun bastards are takin' me to Graz hospital, they think I'm round the bend because I made a Ned Kelly mask out of a bucket. But I had to get out of that working camp somehow, didn't I?"

Worried at first, that one the Germans would become impatient with his abuse and take it out on me as well as him, I was thankful when the train stopped at Graz Station, where I left the carriage-load of Germans to their fate in Italy.

I also parted company with the Australian when we reached Graz hospital. I never learned his name or what had happened to him in the hospital. I never found out whether he had become "barbed wire happy", his mind unbalanced, or whether he was making a formidable try for repatriation by 'tossing the doctor'.

***

Graz hospital, an old, red-brick building in the centre of the ancient city, reminded me of the Royal Infirmary in Liverpool.

I was put into a small ward, on my own. A room on the top floor containing three beds. There was no guard, but on the floor below the ward was full of German soldiers, casualties from the fighting in Italy. One of them, a Feld-Webel, his arm in a sling and a patch over one eye, watched over me with his one good eye and had the job of locking me in the room each night. When air raid warnings sounded, he shepherded me down to the crowded air raid shelter in the cellars of the hospital to join his walking-wounded comrades and most of the hospital staff.

In the air-raid shelter, at first, I was again very concious of my khaki battledress uniform, sticking out like a sore thumb amid the field-grey uniforms of the wounded Germans. But, generally, I was accepted without comment by these front line soldiers.

On the whole, I enjoyed my ten day stay in Graz hospital, and even began to hope at the end of the first week that the Red Tape would break, and leave me there. I thoroughly enjoyed my own solitary, silent company in the comfortable amenities of the little room. I didn't miss, one iota, the never-ceasing cacophony of noise and the stink of the smoky, overcrowded Schuster barrack. I was overwhelmed by the opportunity to take a proper

289

hot bath each day, in a proper white porcelain bath, with a proper white towel. The first time for years. And to sleep between clean white sheets again, like a forgotten dream.

I even came close to enjoying the potato soups ladled from a mobile aluminium container wheeled around the wards by an elderly, motherly nurse. This stout, matronly old dear took a liking to me, (or to the remains of the Cadburys chocolate I had in the bottom of my Red Cross parcel which I gave her for the three young grand-children she said she had at home). She pampered me with generous helpings of the awful soup. And with a smile of pleasure on her round, cheery face, accompanied by a sly wink, gave me the thickest slice of blut-wurst – spicy German sausage – she could find on her tray, to go with a slice of WHITE bread. The first time I had been fussed over since leaving home, and the first time I had tasted white bread in Austria.

My "holiday" in the solitude of the tiny ward, interrupted only by the ministrations of my new foster mother, the wail of the air-raid warning sirens, and the "gemma gemma, hurry, hurry", cries of the Sergeant as he jostled me down to the shelter, was broken by the arrival of a badly wounded British prisoner. A Scot, about my age. A small man, similiar to me in build and height. A one-time insurance clerk from Edinburgh.

I was truly shocked by his unfortunate, sorry appearance. His right leg, from his ankle to his groin, was encased in plaster-of-Paris. A gaping hole in the middle of the plaster on his thigh exposed bloody dressings on wounds both side of the leg. His left leg was plastered from the ankle to above the knee and both his arms were heavily bandaged.

Heavily sedated, it was two or three days before, haltingly, he was able to tell me how he had received these frightful and frightening wounds.

At that time air raids on Southern Austria were a daily occurrence and he had been drafted from a farm job to an airfield near Graz. There were about a hundred British prisoners, forced to work filling in bomb craters on the landing strip, under the direction of the Gestapo. They were guarded by SS men. Protests that this was war work and flouted the Geneva Convention fell on deaf ears. The conditions were atrocious and supervision by the SS men was strict. The work was heavy without any respite in bad weather. The food was lousy and the hours were long.

He had made numerous attempts to 'toss the doctor', without success. The last time earning him a beating with rifle butts by two SS guards, followed by three days bread and water punishment in a cell in the local police station.

So he decided to "do a runner".

Unfortunately, he chose the wrong time and the wrong place to make his escape and was spotted by one of the SS men. Apparently, ignoring the guard's cries to halt, he made a run for the cover of a nearby wood and the guard opened fire. A bullet went through his thigh leaving a gaping hole both sides. His left leg was broken when, lying in agony in a ditch, he received a vicious kick from the guard.

His story was interrupted by the sounding of the air-raid siren and, despite my protests, for I didn't want to leave him on his own, I was bundled down to the air-raid shelter in the basement with the German walking wounded from the floor below.

That afternoon, after the "all-clear" had sounded, I was told to get my things together as I was going back to Wolfsberg. I left Graz hospital before I could even learn the name of the young Scotsman, and I was never able to find out what happend to him.

But the thought of him lying, totally immobile, in the room on the top floor of Graz hospital, bombs dropping all around him, made me think again, rightly or wrongly, of the wisdom of trying to escape.

Copy of Graz hospital record.

I returned to Wolfsberg to meet up again with Dai Davies and Len Caulfield. They were in the throes of organising their escape and had already seen the Escape Committee, outlined their plan of action, and were waiting for a signal from the Kommandanteur that they had found a suitable working camp from where they could make their bid for freedom.

I found a dozen feeble excuses to tell them I had changed my mind about escaping. The time of the year was wrong. Winter was on us and the snows had started. The war was nearly over, anyway. By prisoner-of-war standards I had a comfortable place in the Stalag. I hadn't missed a weekly Red Cross parcel since I had arrived there. I was in one of the football teams and I had been asked to take a part in a new, very special show being staged in the theatre by the Padre.

But quite honestly, it was the sight of the awful wounds the young Scot had received in his abortive escape bid that had scared the life out of me, given me cold feet, and made me change my mind. But for the encounter with him, I am sure I would have gone along with my two friends.

There were no recriminations from either Dai or Len. They

carried on with their plan and left Wolfsberg shortly afterwards.

It was not until sixty years later I found out that Dai Davies had been successful in getting away.

A single paragraph in his brief letter tells of his experiences after his escape.

"I cannot remember how Len Caulfield and I got back to Wolfsberg. It was a good move because we both managed to get on a work party to a place called Gaas. Len I think wanted to make a break for either Italy or Switzerland and I wanted to get to Yugoslavia, so we went our different ways. Someone told me that Len got back to France and home. Roy Natusch (NZ), Joe Walker (a Geordie) and I made our break for Hungary, which we did, and managed to get a fair distance into Hungary. When we were caught, we were taken to a hell-hole of a place called Kormoran and confined to the dungeons. The Red Cross got us out of there eventually and we were sent to work on an estate in South Hungary in a place called Zigetvar. Picked up by the Germans again and taken to the Area jail in Siklos where we tried to escape again, but were recaptured. Eventually we were transferred to a concentration camp for Yugoslav partisans at Semun outside Belgrade where we were bombed by the USAF. From there I escaped with a Canadian Commando Roy McLean. Got picked up again by local Nazi supporters but made our get away again and eventually we joined the local partisans in Frusca Gora. There we stayed doing this and that and helping where we could behind the German lines until I was taken seriously ill with malaria and flown out to Bari in Italy and from there to the American hospital in Naples weighing about 7 stone."

In his letter, typically, Dai failed to mention that he had been awarded the Military Medal for his successful escape from a prisoner-of-war camp, and a Medal of Honour from Tito, the Yugoslav Dictator, for his exploits *"doing this and that behind the German lines"* with the Yugoslav partisans.

I had lost my job in the Schusters, although my bunk next to Dick Rimmer, after a little negotiation with the occupant, was still available. Ted McShea had been back for sometime after 'tossing the doctor' with his scabby heel, which was now on the mend. Ted and I were asked to appear in a new show about to be staged in the theatre and strings were pulled once more to find us work in the Kommandanteur. We were co-opted onto a special hospital detail. Collecting wood for the hospital stoves.

The detail of six men was allowed out of the camp on parole, every day, specifically to collect scrap ply-wood tea chests in which the Red Cross food parcels had been shipped to Wolfsberg. An Australian Sergeant, Ted Greenwood, was in charge of the party and responsible for getting us back to the barbed wire.

The empty plywood tea chests were piled from floor to ceiling in a warehouse at Wolfsberg railway station. It has to be said that, although fuel was in extremely short supply, even for their own use, the Germans never helped themselves to the Red Cross scrap wood. Neither would they let us have timber from the forests on the hills above Wolfsberg.

Officially, the scrap plywood was fuel for the cooking stoves of the hospital. But some of the props in the theatre bore the Red Cross sign on the back, and I had seen one or two realistic armchairs fashioned from the tea chests.

Each morning at about 9.30, the seven of us, dragging a four-wheeled V-shaped, open-sided farm cart would report to the German Kommandantur at the Camp gates. After a body search by SS Major Schafer and his henchmen, we were allowed out to collect the firewood.

It took an hour or more at our steady kreigsgefanganer stroll, to pull the cart to the station, including the unofficial stop we made at Boris's Bakery in the town.

Our unlawful, black marketeering with Boris started one morning after the air raid siren had sounded, and we had dragged the cart on a reconnoitre through the deserted streets of the town.

A typical baker, white shirt sleeves rolled up to his elbows and wearing a long white apron, he was standing at the door of his shop smoking and doffed his white trilby hat as we approached. We stopped the cart outside his shop and in response to someone's "brauchen sie zen cigaretten fur eine brot" "Do you want ten cigarettes for a loaf," without a word, he darted into the shop and handed over a loaf of his round, black bread for ten Craven A cork tipped cigarettes.

Boris the Baker wasn't allowed to forget that transaction. Almost every day, after the air-raid warning had sounded, we would take turns, two at a time, to dodge into his empty shop to lean on the counter like old customers. We usually came away with four or five loaves in exchange for cigarettes or Princes salmon or sardines.

The baker insisted on loose cigarettes. He was well aware of the dirty tricks played by certain of the treacherous kriegsgefangeneners. The wily ones of Wolfsberg, as well as making perfect reproductions of Official travel documents and railway warrants, could take the cigarettes out of a tin of fifty, cut off the cork-tip part of the cigarettes and re-pack the tips into the tin on top of paper. Without any damage or scratch to the tin or sign that the cigarettes had been disturbed.

The wood detail was not allowed to stay in the railway staion during air-raid warnings. Not that we wanted to. So the seven of us dispersed into the hills around the town until the "All Clear" sounded, usually some hours later. Ted and I always went to a farm where we had met up with an "auslander", a Yugoslav volunteer civilian worker. He was making himself scarce during the air raids, and at the same time dabbling in a little black marketeering on the side. So we were able to trade our cigarettes and tinned fish for delicacies like eggs and onions. On one auspicious occasion Ted swopped a pair of brand new winceyette pyjamas he had received in a comfort parcel from home, for a sizeable piece of beef.

Now, it was one thing to get hold of these luxuries on the black market, but it was quite another thing to get them successfully back in the lager. For we had to get the goods past the hawkeyed, English-speaking, bullying SS Major Schafer and his search party, at the gates of the Stalag. We tried all sorts of tricks to get the stuff in the camp. I had made special pockets inside the upper arms of my battledress jacket, large enough to conceal a packet of sugar or a tin of sardines or a bar of soap, to take out of the camp, and to bring back in, two or three onions or even a couple of eggs or tomatoes.

The idea was, that when I raised my arms for the customary body search, I lifted them up as straight and as high as I could trusting that the searcher's hands would stop at my armpits. Which they usually did. Except for one day when I finished up with four eggs trickling down the insides of my arms and poorer by forty cigarettes. This ploy was also used with the Army beret. But the guards soon got wise to this trick, patting the head with a fatherly grin, knowing full well that eggs were concealed in the beret and saying, "Good, good. You can go in now."

Trying to get five or six loaves of bread past the searchers presented a bigger problem, which was solved by the ingenuity and cheek of Ted Greenwood, the Aussie Sergeant.

The open farm cart was constructed around a heavy wooden six-by-six "tree" or beam running down the length of the base of the cart. So we nailed, or tied with string, the loaves of bread to the underside of the beam.

This ruse proved successful for the guards seemed to be reluctant to get down on their knees to look underneath the cart. But too many loaves were damaged or lost this way, the shaking of the cart dislodging or breaking them. And in wet weather they were apt to get a little soggy. So we hid them in the load on top of the cart. Or rather, Ted Greenwood did.

To carry a worthwhile load of plywood, we had to break down the two-feet-square tea chests into flat packs. Ted packed the bread inside the flat squares of plywood and then unloaded them himself under the watchful eyes of the German search party. He always outwitted them by lifting the packs, by the armful, with the bread well concealed inside the pack, and casually throwing them over the side of the cart. To be reloaded after the search and rescued when we dropped the wood off at the hospital.

The piece of beef however, was too big to play this trick with and I solved it by suggesting we take the cart the longer way back to the camp around the outside of the perimeter, passing the British compound on the far side.

When we came to the sentry box overlooking the compound,

I dropped three cigarettes on the ground at the foot of the ladder and shouted up to the bored sentry in his box to come down and pick them up before they got wet.

As the sentry clattered down the ladder to retrieve the cigarettes, Ted grabbed the parcel of meat and with a typical Australian Rules football throw, hurled it over the twelve foot high double wire fences to Dick Rimmer, waiting on the other side.

That night we had a gorgeous meal of Scouse. A stew made from the fresh, blood-red beef, thickened with Canadian biscuits, enlivened with a tin of Hartley's peas and slowly simmered on the Schuster cooking stove. Our dixies and plates were mopped clean with wedges of crusty black bread.

**

Most of my spare time in the early winter of 1944 was spent rehearsing the most spectacular musical show ever to be staged in Wolfsberg Theatre or for that matter in any Stalag Theatre.

Padre John Ledgerwood had obtained the full script of Ivor Novello's musical play, "Glamorous Night".

A popular West End musical before the war, "Glamorous Night" was an ambitious project to stage in a prisoner-of-war Stalag theatre with an all-male cast. Nevertheless, Padre John Ledgerwood produced the show entirely as it was written, except for the musical score. This was re-arranged by Ken Willmott to suit male voices and an orchestra of ten players. Everybody connected with the Theatre had been called on to help stage this popular musical. It was a huge success.

We were fortunate to have in the show Buddy Clive (Clive Dunne). He was the only professional in the cast of enthusiastic amateurs, some of whom like me, were press-ganged into taking part. Buddy played the leading lady, a vocal, non-comedy part, singing most of the popular numbers. I was in the line up of chorus "girls" enthusiastically applauded for a realistic interpretation of the "Skaters' Waltz", gliding over the bare wooden boards of the stage on imitation ice skates and, of course, dressed in short, ballerina costumes.

"Glamorous Night" ran for six, hectic, highly successful

performances.

But after the final curtain went down on the last performance and the cast had cleaned off their make-up, changed back into khaki and returned to their sleeping quarters, the wonderful Wolfsberg Theatre went up in smoke.

The fire started during the early hours of the morning in the "post office", a small bunk/room at the rear of the theatre, occupied by the "postman", an elderly Scot from the Black Watch. Jock had the cushy job of sorting and distributing incoming mail around the camp. Apparently, he had filched an electric fire from the Kommandanteur and tapped it in to the antiquated electric supply in his room. That night he left the fire switched on and woke up to find his room full of smoke and ablaze.

There was no emergency Fire Brigade in Stalag XV111A, nor even any simple fire precautions – verbal or otherwise, for that matter. In retrospect, it was a miracle that none of the old timber-built stables, veritable death traps for the overcrowded occupants, had caught fire earlier.

***

The two hundred men housed in the larger section of Barrack 1, evacuated the burning shed without casualties, to stand and stare as the whole of the barrack, all of their personal belongings, and our prize Stalag Theatre, was burned to the ground.

I believe it had been said in theatrical circles, that "Glamorous Night" was an unlucky play. I don't know whether there was any truth in that story, but it certainly was unlucky for Stalag XV111A.

John Ledgerwood does in fact relate a story of an earlier conflagration in the camp.

In 1942, the Germans had decided to build a special gaol, or bunker, in a small barbed wire compound of its own, within the main compound, to gaol prisoners sentenced to solitary confinement for escaping and other offences. The Germans used prisoners waiting to serve their sentence to

298

construct the hut. On the day it was completed and ready for occupation by the men who built it, the new wooden, purpose-built jail caught fire and was completely destroyed!!!

Chapter 36

Friendly Fire

From the spring of 1944, much to everyone's delight, American bombers made their first appearance in the skies over Wolfsberg.

Four-engined Flying Fortresses and Liberators, the largest aeroplanes of the time and forerunners of today's giant passenger aircraft, filling the skies in closely packed formations, almost wing-tip to wing-tip. Their Mustang fighter escorts specks in the sky above them.

The flight path of this daily armada, from air-fields in Italy in the South, to their targets in Germany in the North, took them directly over the Stalag. They flew every day, without fail, in ever increasing numbers as the months rolled on.

The first of the bombing raids brought everybody out of the huts to cheer the planes on their way, some to lie on their backs, crazily counting the numbers of aircraft flying overhead. We could virtually tell the time of the day when the first planes would appear. Ten-thirty in the morning. And about mid-day the first of the returning planes heading South to Italy, would fly over the last of the formations still flying North to their targets.

The bombing raids carried on continuously throughout the summer of 1944 and by early winter the American planes flying over Stalag XV111A numbered hundreds – if not thousands.

Nobody bothered to count them anymore. For like a flock of noisy, black starlings, bunched together in a tight ball, wheeling and circling over city lights in the dusk of a summer evening, there were far too many to count. On cloudless, sunny days the bombers completely filled the skies. North, South, East and West, as far as the eye could see, the vapour trails streaming from their engines merging to form a solid blanket of grey/white cloud completely blotting out the sun.

The vast aerial armadas gave off a continuous, deafening

rumble, the reverberations of the four-engined monsters causing the very ground to vibrate. The old wooden huts trembled alarmingly and the disturbed dust of years drifted down from the roof trusses to form a glittering curtain of dancing sunbeams in the mid-morning sun. Empty KLIM tins on the brick cooking stoves bounced and rattled like dancing marionettes until they jigged over the edge.

The 18th December, 1944, was just another brisk, sunny, winter's day in Wolfsberg and at mid-day the bombers were making their usual, daily, relentless, unstoppable flight north. After months of familiarity, we had become somewhat blase at the sight of the skies filled with the American aeroplanes, accepting the rumblings of the engines as part of a normal day. The awe-inspiring spectacle had ceased to be of any special interest. We would have been more concerned at their absence.

On that particular day, I had just finished my mid-day snack of a biscuit-and-bully sandwich and was strolling to the other end of barrack 3, carrying a mug of tea, to listen to the news being read out by John McDonald, the New Zealand Sergeant Major. Passing the open double doors in the centre of the barrack, by the ablution troughs, someone said to me "Look at those planes Doug, I've never seen them as low as that before."

I walked to the door to see a flight of six planes – I think they were Mustang fighter/bombers – flying in a tight, double vee formation over the fields alongside the camp. They were low enough, and near enough, for me to see clearly the friendly white stars on the wings and to hear the different sound of their engines above the din of the bombers overhead. We watched them until they passed from sight over the adjoining hospital barrack and I said to my companion, "They must be part of the fighter escort, I wonder what they're doing flying so low?"

After a few minutes we came to the conclusion that they must have been on a routine reconnaissance of the town and prison camp. As I was about to turn away they appeared again, this time flying slightly lower.

Thinking nothing more of the low-flying aircraft, I joined the crowd around the stove and, sipping my tea, listened to John reading the news bulletin, his voice raised to make himself heard over the noise of the bombers. I can't remember the details but he finished by announcing there would be another bulletin at tea-time.

On the way back to my place in the Schusters, I had almost reached the open doors in the centre of the barrack when the whole world seemed to erupt over my head. I was thrown heavily to the floor, a split second before I heard the first deafening detonations of a continuous, rolling wave of exploding bombs. Momentarily, I wondered why the barrack was collapsing, for roof-joists were dropping to the floor around me. Dazed and shaken, but without a scratch or a bruise, I picked myself up and opened my eyes to a fog of thick, black dust filling the barrack from floor to ceiling.

My first reaction when I realised the camp had been on the receiving end of a bombing raid was to run the four or five yards across the concrete floor of the ablutions, thinking that the Schusters barrack had been hit. I had just left most of my friends in there, ten minutes before, finishing their mid-day snack. Thankfully, the barrack had not been touched except for the shower of thick dust. I met Dick Rimmer coming out, shouting "The silly bastards have bombed us, they've hit the hospital."

We ran outside to find that the hospital barrack, ten yards away, had been reduced to a heaped pile of rubble and splintered timber. The only indication that the building had once been a hospital, was the pathetic sign, BRITTEN-LAZARETT, BRITISH HOSPITAL pinned on a short section of timber walling still standing.

The roof, with its two huge, red crosses painted on a white square background, indicating to "friendly", low flying aircraft that the building was a hospital, had vanished.

The British, Russian and French compounds received direct hits that day. Ironically, the German quarters at the entrance to the camp weren't touched. Losses among the prisoners were great and I have read different accounts of the numbers killed, varying from dozens, to hundreds. But from my recollection of the tragic and unnecessary event, the Russian compound took the brunt of the bombing.

The bombed British Hospital.

Another view of the bombed British Hospital.

Showing the devastation of the bombed British hospital.

There were over two hundred Russians, fifty French and fifteen British killed by the friendly fire of the United States Air Force. I never learned how many were wounded.

The British Officers' Mess was in the hospital and three of the five Officers in the camp were having lunch when the bombs dropped. The Mess Orderly for the day, was Danny Nolan MM, a 106th man, who was killed outright with Captain Woods, a Medical Officer and Captain Hobling, the Anglican Padre. Major Kinmont, the senior Medical Officer was badly injured but survived. Most of the patients in the hospital ward were killed with another of my good friends, orderly John McGeorge, a leading light in the musical productions of the Wolfsberg Theatre.

The tragic American bombing of Stalag XV111A Prisoner-of-War camp, Wolfsberg, was without doubt, a crass, stupid and careless mistake for which there was no excuse.

Wolfsberg was a small market and agricultural town and even in those days had been a tourist centre. It was not in an industrialised area, and there were no factories anywhere in Wolfsberg or near the camp. The town was situated in the middle of a flat, agricultural plain and the Stalag, two miles from the town, was surrounded on all sides by cultivated fields or grass meadows. Distinctive, high, watch towers were spaced at fifty yard intervals around the perimeter of the thickly wired double fence. Many of the roofs, like the roof of the British Hospital, were plainly marked with large red crosses painted against a white background. The day was clear, bright and sunny and they must have been distinctly visible to the six aeroplanes circling the camp. It is difficult to understand why the bombs were dropped.

To the best of my knowledge, there was no court of enquiry ever held over the "friendly fire" bombing of Stalag XV111A.

***

Life, in more ways than one, was never the same after the bombing. We were truly reminded that there was a war on. The general opinion was that if the Yanks had bombed us once, they would do it again.

The afternoon of the air raid the German Authorities decided to provide some sort of protection for the prisoners. They commandeered the field alongside the camp, and deep, wide zig-zag slit trenches were dug by hastily formed gangs of prisoners.

The next morning, when the warning sirens sounded, we were ushered out by the German guards, like sheep going to slaughter, and crowded into the muddy trenches. The guards were spaced at intervals along the top of the banked earth, their bayonets at the ready.

We spent four boring, wet, muddy hours in the slit trenches that afternoon. It snowed and rained as the legions of American bombers roared over our heads out of sight at 25,000 feet. Most of us resolved not to spend another day in the "air-raid" slit-trenches whether the Germans liked it or not.

There were, however, the nervous and the barbed-wire happy, who, for a few mornings, anyway, after the bombing, would queue at the gates of the camp waiting to go to the slit trenches after the sirens sounded.

***

It was about that time an event occurred which would have far reaching effects on the future lives of the Arthur Family and some of my siblings.

The Liverpool Scousers in Wolfsberg, most of them from the 106th RHA, were clannish. Like most Liverpudlians meeting in foreign climes. A favourite meeting place for the Liverpool lads was Dick Rimmer's bed-space, alongside mine, in the Schusters. Dick knew all the Scousers and they all knew Dick. Among them, was Brian Middleton, a medical orderly working in the Hospital. Brian and I became good friends, little realising that our friendship would last a lifetime and have far reaching effects on both our families.

It was sometime in the late summer of 1944 that Brian was selected to accompany a group of medically unfit prisoners being repatriated under an exchange system arranged by the International Red Cross. These were men with chronic or incurable medical disorders or were limbless or blind, being sent back home via Switzerland in exchange for similiar German prisoners in the U.K.

Brian of course was excited at the prospect of leaving Wolfsberg and believed he would be back home in Liverpool in a matter of weeks, if not days. Shortly before he was due to leave, he approached me and Dick Rimmer, and one or two more of his Liverpool friends, and said he would go to our homes and personally assure our families of our wellbeing. He suggested we give him a photograph or a letter or a keepsake of some sort to hand over to a mother or a wife or a sweetheart, as proof that he had actually been with us.

I gave him the silver pocket watch I had liberated from an Italian Officer at Beda Fomm in 1941, which I had carried around with me, through thick and thin, ever since. It was to be a souvenir of my wanderings which I had kept as a coming home present for my father.

In fact, the war nearing its end, Brian did not make it home with the party of repatriates but finished the war out in another Stalag.

Chapter 37

Now is the Hour

One rainy, cold afternoon in April, 1945, Arthur Albrow, the Cockney street-busker, was leading the whole of Barrack 3 in a chorus of the popular New Zealand anthem, "*Now is the Hour, for us to say Goodbye*". Prophetically, as it turned out.

Although a very sick man – Arthur's way of explaining his illness was to say he was the only man in captivity with two arse holes – Arty Albrow's one man show, after the loss of the theatre and the bombing of the camp, had kept the British compound entertained. He would stand on his feet for a couple of hours at a time, playing his banjo, singing song after song and cracking joke after joke.

The impromptu concert that day, however, was suddenly interrupted by the arrival of The Chief Man of Confidence. Jumping up on the brick stove he announced without any preamble, the news that we had been expecting for some weeks. Stalag XV111A was to be evacuated.

We were to form up on the parade ground in groups of a hundred. Immediately. Every man-jack in the camp, fit, unfit, bludgers, hospital bed-cases, men with assumed names and "wanted" men hiding in the Dreaded Bog, were to leave. The elderly guards were to accompany us.

We were to march to an unknown destination.

So into a scrap of blanket, hurriedly converted into an improvised hold-all, went the most valuable of my worldly possessions. My share of the remnants of our last Red Cross food parcels pooled with Ted McShea.

A packet of Instant Yorkshire Pudding Mixture, half a tin of Klim milk powder, a tin of sardines in tomato sauce, an opened tin of Hartley's raspberry jam, half a dozen hard, round water biscuits, a two ounce carton of cheese spread, three hoarded packets of the life-saving Brook Bond tea and six small, wizened, sprouting potatoes. Little did I know that I was to survive the rest of the war on these sparse rations, for we were to receive no more food from the Germans.

There was barely room in the bag for the two pairs of spare socks, a shirt and the woollen balaclava which I was to find a boon, later. I filled the pockets of my battledress tunic with photographs, letters from home, and what was left of my Army paybook. Odds and ends like a knife fork and spoon and my last tin of Halibut Liver Oil capsules slotted into the pockets of my trousers. I tied an aluminium army dixie and a battered white enamelled mug to a loop on my belt.

Discarded without a second thought were the souvenirs I had collected in my wanderings around Austria. A pair of wooden sabots, a mandoline, three Austrian tasselled, long-stemmed meerschaum pipes and a patent cigarette making machine. The well thumbed copy of Cuthbertson's "The Art of Bridge" (I never was able to master his five clubs convention, anyway) and a spare pair of old boots which I had "acquired" when working in the Schusters, were thrown on the growing heaps of what had lately been necessities for existing in a prisoner-of-war camp. Later I was to regret not taking the old boots with me.

We left piles of the carefully acquired possessions of a thousand men on the floors of the wooden huts. I was to learn, many years later, that a warehouse at Wolfsberg railway station was crammed from floor to roof, with letters and parcels which had failed to reach the thousands of prisoners in the Stalag and attached arbeitslagers.

At four o'clock next morning, in pouring rain, I left Stalag XV111A, Wolfsberg, for the last time.

Nobody knew our destination. Apparently, not even the guards. They told us that we were to make our way to the West, ahead of the Russians approaching from the East. The distant sounds of Bolshevic artillery and bombing had been music in our ears for days.

It was months after the war ended I learned the true reason for the exodus from Wolfsberg. One of the last maniacal proclamations issued by Hitler, before he committed suicide in the bunker in Berlin, was that all prisoners-of-war were to be herded like sheep into a redoubt in the Berchesgarten area. There, in his mountain fortress, he planned to make his "last stand" and to liquidate all prisoners-of-war, in the process.

***

In the utter confusion of those last three or four weeks of the war I remember little of the dreadful, forced march across Austria.

There was chaos on the main roads. As we trudged along, we mingled with convoys of German troops more confused than we, going this way and that, aimlessly. Some of them making their reluctant way eastwards, impeded by scores of civilians fleeing westwards from the Russians and thousands of prisoners-of-war being herded into the Redoubt.

Crack German infantry units, or SS detachments, in disciplined ranks, ignored us completely as they marched past smartly, singing their German marching songs, and "heiling Hitler" to fellow regiments, as they passed them marching in the opposite direction. Artillery regiments lumbered along, their guns and limbers caked with mud, intermingled with farm carts stacked high with sundry rolls of carpet and antique sideboards and black iron bedsteads, the personal possessions of the fleeing populace. Parties of panic stricken "auslanders", the foreign civilian workers the Germans had conscripted five year previously, added to the chaos, fearful of both the advancing Russians amd their German hosts.

Our guards – now guides, in effect – took us away from the main roads, avoiding the headlong, mad dashes for cover when flights of marauding American fighters, spitting frightening, lethal doses of death at friend and foe alike zoomed over the packed roads. We scrambled across country via the quieter mountain paths and country roads. As the column became more strung out and supervision became more lax, it was quite easy to make a break for "freedom". Indeed, a few did so. But the senior Brtiish N.C.Os in the group had, to all intents and purposes taken over as far as discipline was concerned and issued common sense orders that we should all stay together.

One morning in the second week of the confused and

disorderly march, my heart lifted and my stomach rumbled in anticipation, when we came to two International Red Cross lorries. Parked at the side of the road the white canvas covers of the 3-ton trucks were conspicuous with red crosses painted on the sides and roofs. At great risks to themselves, they had driven from Switzerland handing out food parcels to the starving groups of evacuating prisoners. The cupboard was bare, however, when I reached them, for the trucks were empty. They had also run out of petrol and were stranded at the roadside with nothing to do but wait for the Americans.

The spring weather had turned bitterly cold and at the end of a day's march through heavy rain or sleet and snow, dog-tired, starving hungry and sometimes soaked to the skin, we would stagger to a halt to kip down in any shelter we could find under dripping trees and hedges at the roadside. If we were lucky we dossed down in the luxury of a straw-filled, rat-infested barn or the cold comfort of a deserted village school.

I remember sheltering one night, with Ted McShea, under an overhanging cliff at the side of a mountain road. It was teeming with rain but we had managed to gather some dryish wood and after taking it in turns to puff and blow at glowing embers of the remains of Ted's Army Pay Book, had got a fire going. There was more smoke than flame but we were able to warm the damp, congealed contents of a packet of instant Yorkshire Pudding mixture, the last of our precious store of Red Cross food. Rainwater from the overhang dribbled down the back of my neck as, like a Red Indian sending smoke signals, I bent over trying to coax more life into the fire and response from the "instant" pudding mixture.

We kept ourselves alive by stealing what food we could find stored in barns and farmhouses vacated hurriedly by some of the farmers in their panic to avoid the Russians. We helped ourselves to potatoes and turnips and beet from straw-filled vegetable clamps under twelve inches of frozen soil and straw in frost-bound farmyards. If luck was on our side and we were the first of the fleeing refugees, sometimes we found eggs in a deserted hen coop. At one farm, the autumn brew of apple cider made a marvellous, if somewhat noisy, nightcap for the 106th lads in my group.

We commandeered hay-wagons and farm-carts, parked in the frozen mud and mire of farmyards, to carry casualties with blistered feet and knees swollen with the unaccustomed walking. And it wasn't unusual to see a khaki-clad Britisher pushing a babies' bassinette containing a mate with badly blistered feet, his legs dangling over the side of the pram like Stan Laurel in a Laurel & Hardy film.

Even one or two of the elderly guards finding the going too much, won places on the over-loaded farm-carts with the "walking wounded" to be pulled along by the prisoners.

**

After a two week trek over more than two hundred miles of mountainous roads, we arrived at a camp on the outskirts of Markt Pongau, a country town near Saltzberg. I was unwashed, smelly, and sported the beginnings of a luxuriant black beard that aged me by ten years. Although the griping hunger pains had stopped I reeled with dizzyness if I stood up too quickly. I had kept walking throughout the march, but was limping badly with a huge blister on the heel of my right foot, and a hole in the ball of my left foot caused by a nail I had stood on in a dark barn some few nights previously. My starving, skinny frame was host once again to the body lice I had brought with me from Greece four years before.

Stalag XV11A was a replica of the Wolfsberg camp but smaller. At one time it had been a gruesome concentration camp holding Jewish civilians en route to the death camps. It was turned into a prisoner-of-war Stalag, in 1941, for Allied prisoners taken in Greece and Crete.

Now packed with prisoners from all over Austria and Germany, there was no room in the overcrowded huts when we arrived. We slept anywhere we could find an empty space in the mud on the parade ground or the areas between the huts.

There was absolutely no organisation. There was no fuel for fires. There was no food. We barely survived on scraps of raw potato and turnip. Long queues formed at the water taps and the overflowing, stinking cess-pit latrines.

Despite being advised and ordered by the senior N.C.Os. to

stay in the camp, a few decided to take matters in their own hands and go and find the advancing Americans.

It was easy to walk out of the camp. The guards, still obeying their orders, but now making only a token pretence of manning the sentry boxes on the perimeter of the wire, made little protest if someone walked out.

Dick Rimmer and Mick Bolger, two of the group of 106th men in my party who had all stuck together on the march across the mountains, decided to have a go.

Not exactly to look for the advancing American army but to find a Benedictine Monastery where Mick had been employed in a working camp six months previously. He said it wasn't very far and that he knew the village people and was sure there was plenty of food to be had. But more importantly, he knew where a cache of gold and silver ornaments and valuable jewellery and an unknown quantity of "American Silver Dollars" and English five-pound notes had been buried in a corner of the monastery garden. Dick was the only volunteer of our party to go with Mick on his hair-brained scheme.

So off they went, probably the first looters to search for the buried gold of the Nazis at the end of the war.

They came back to Markt Pongau in the middle of the next afternoon with their tails between their legs, Dick Rimmer soaked to the skin and beginning to show the effects of a heavy cold.

Apparently, they had been making their way down the main road to Saltzberg alongside a river. The road was teeming with German troops and vehicles of all kinds. A three-tonner, loaded with German sappers looking for the Americans to give themselves up, caught Dick Rimmer's shoulder as it drove past. Dick, knocked off his feet, went rolling head over heels down the bank and tumbled into the river. His homemade haversack did a double somersault over his head on to his chest to vanish under the swiftly flowing water.

Mick Bolger's shouts of alarm and waving of arms brought the truck to a swift halt. The German Engineers in the back jumped out and ran down the bank of the river just in time to fish Dick out of the water as he came up for the second time. After drying off as best as he could they made their way back to

Markt Pongau. For years afterwards, Dick Rimmer talked about the fortune he missed when the German truck knocked him into a river.

Next morning, the 10th May, 1945, we woke to find the sentry boxes surrounding the camp and the German quarters by the gate, were empty. Our German guards had done a bunk.

The war was over.

***

An Australian Regimental Sergeant Major assumed control of the camp and, that morning, we gathered around him when he stood on a farm-cart in the centre of the parade ground.

He told us that we were under strict orders not to leave the camp as the Americans would be bound to reach us shortly. He advised us not to go wandering about as there was complete chaos on the roads.

But that afternoon, desperate for food, I walked out of the camp with Jack Ward and Ted McShea to see if we could find anything to eat in Markt Pongau. Passing a small hospital or nursing home, we saw three young girls in blue dressing gowns at an open window on the first floor. We stopped to ask if we could buy bread or potatoes from them in exchange for Lagergelt, the worthless camp money Ted McShea and I still had in out pockets. They said they had had nothing to eat for days and wanted to know if the American soldiers would reach them before the Russians.

Markt Pongau was deserted of civilians, but an open air swimming pool in a park Lido was crowded with naked prisoners attempting to rid themselves of the muck of months. We decided to give it a miss when we saw the colour of the dirty water.

Shops were closed and boarded up but our wanderings took us to the railway station, and to a locked storeroom or warehouse at the end of the platform. We broke down the door with a shovel and pickaxe from the Station Master's office and to our delight, found the shed half full of sacks of an unsavoury looking, dark flour.

We staggered back to the barbed wire under the weight of a

313

50 kilo sack of flour, the first of a chain of twenty sacks to make their way from the station to the camp. That afternoon, in an old bucket, Sergeant Jack Ward added water to the grey, gritty flour to make a sort of a gruel, and said he was going to paper the Sergeants' Mess with it. But I made pancakes with the unsavoury looking mixture, griddling them on a slab of roofing slate over an open fire. We burned the wooden doors of the latrines, the only timber left in the camp.

***

Happily, it turned out to be my last makeshift meal as a prisoner-of-war. The following morning a cry went up around the filthy compound. A cry which I had been waiting for four years.

"The Yanks are here, the Yanks are here, they're outside the camp."

Excitedly, I ran to the gates, half expecting to see John Wayne at the head of a squadron of battle-scarred tanks with smoking guns, or a battalion of infantry with sub-machine guns and fixed bayonets. Instead there was a single, battered, dirty-looking vehicle manned by two khaki-clad figures. The only indication to me that they were American were the Stars and Stripes painted on each front mudguard of the truck, barely visible under grime and mud, and a torn, bedraggled Stars and Stripes flag, fluttering in the breeze on the top of a ten foot high wireless aerial by the driver's seat.

I was to learn that the vehicle was a jeep. The work horse of the American Army.

An Officer was standing on the front passenger seat, trying to make himself heard above the shouting and cheering of the excited ex-prisoners massed around the vehicle. Every time he managed to quieten the crowd the cheers would ring out again immediately he made an announcement.

"OK you guys. The Jerry guards have vamoosed."

(Cheers and boos and cat-calls, loud raspberries and obscene curses telling the Germans where they could go.)

"The Yanks are looking after you now. From now on you're in the American Army. For the time-being anyhow."

(More cheers and hand-clapping and a chorus of "I'm a

314

Yankee Doodle Dandy")

"And you guys'll get no potato soup from us.

(Howls of sarcastic derision and scorn)

"K rations will be issued to you right away. The Americans fought the war on K rations. You'll never eat anything else again once you've sampled them."

(Even louder cheers and whistles and shouts of "let's be 'avin' them, then, let's be 'avin' them")

And the biggest cheer of all was when he said that we would all be flying home, just as soon as the necessary arrangements could be made.

To add to the noise and hullabaloo, the American in the back of the truck was picking up cardboard boxes and throwing them, willy nilly, to the prisoners – or should I say ex-prisoners – surrounding the jeep. A resounding cheer from the starving men echoed around the hills of Markt Pongau, as each parcel thrown from the truck was caught by a gleeful prisoner. Cartons of "Chesterfield" cigarettes and flat boxes of "K rations", the emergency rations issued to American troops in the field.

The Yankee doughboys were scathing about their "K rations", but we found them luxurious compared with the bully beef and biscuits we had existed on in our Army. There appeared to be an endless supply of "K rations" and cigarettes.

In fact our American rescuers seemed to be equipped with everything. The next day, in a huge, articulated, mobile ablutions truck, I had a hot shower followed by a liberal application of delousing powder, down my trousers and up my shirt, with a garden syringe.

I was spellbound when a mobile canteen, the size of a Pickfords removal van, put in an appearance. It was a sort of travelling NAAFI. When the side of the truck was dropped, to form a counter, I could see it was fully stocked, like a corner shop, with soft drinks and candy (as they called their sweets), Hersey bars, chewing gum and cigarettes. (When I was on the front line at Fort Cappuzzo, Libya, Christmas Day 1940, our NAFFI truck was the Troop Sergeant Major's three-tonner with one bottle of beer per man!!)

This NAAFI on wheels was staffed by three glamourous, heavily made up, Hollywood beauty queens, smartly turned out in light brown uniforms and spotless white shirts and khaki ties. I fully expected them to break out into a song and dance routine, "This is The Army Mr Arthur", before opening shop. These friendly girls all had immaculate, blonde hair, looking as if it had been permanently waved that morning. And their elegantly manicured, red-laquered pointed finger nails matched the cupid bows of their brilliant red lips. They smilingly doled out, without question, as many cigarettes, sweets and chocolate as we wanted. It was not surprising that the ex-kriegies, goggle-eyed at their first sight of these fascinating females, kept joining the queue for more of the goodies.

Our American liberators did everything possible to keep us occupied and entertained during what turned out to be three or four impatient weeks before I left Markt Pongau.

There was a mobile cinema in the extensive administration camp they had established near Markt Pongau and for the first time in years I "went to the pictures". Sitting on the grass in front of a giant white screen I saw a Frank Sinatra World War II film, emulating the Errol Flynn World War I film, the last film I had seen in Larissa four years before.

Baseball dominated American sporting life then, as it does today, and they had set up a baseball diamond in their camp. They issued a challenge match to the British, if enough men could be found who knew anything about the game to make up a team.

Now, I had played "English Baseball", (the forerunner of the American game,) as a boy at school and in youth teams prior to the war, and went on to play a little of the American version, until the war interfered with my sporting activities. (I was – and still am – the proud owner of a genuine, if somewhat battered, Spaldings American baseball bat which I bought for the princely sum of six shillings and six pence, in 1936, at Spaldings Sports Shop in Lord Street, Liverpool. More than half my week's wages at the time).

However, once again, I digress.

Thinking I knew a little bit about the game, and ever ready to hold my hand up to try something new, I said I would have a go. We just about made up a team from the hundreds of reluctant ex-kriegies and one of them, anyway, was a young American.

316

Michael Davies from Pittsburgh, who had reluctantly joined us in Stalag XV111A in December, 1944.

Imagine my disappointment when I found that the game was "Softball", a training or junior version of the proper game. The normal, hard, leather-skinned baseball was replaced by a large, white, kind of stuffed tennis ball the size of a coconut. The bat was bottle-shaped, like the Indian club thrown about by jugglers, and was half the size of my American bat standing in the wardrobe at home. Their fielders wore a large leather glove on the left hand to catch the soft ball and emphatically refused to believe me when I said that we never used gloves in the game we played, although our leather ball was the same as the American ball.

I would be very pleased to say that I beat the Americans at their own game, but I found I was unable to hit the ball of compressed cotton wool more than twenty yards. Anyway, I was still feeling the effects of my two weeks hungry hike across the hills of Austria. When I did succeed in clouting the ball, I had no energy to run fast enough to first base.

But it was well worth the effort. For after the game the team sat down in the Sergeants Mess to a dinner of tinned "roast" turkey and lashings of vegetables and gravy, followed by tinned fruit and cream and gallons of sweet coffee. Our poor showing at American Baseball, too, was softened when, challenged to a game of soccer, our new American friends couldn't get a team together.

Chapter 38

The Flight of the Phoenix

It was shortly after the baseball game that we received the glad news we were all waiting for. We were being flown home. Or we were to make the first moves to fly home.

We formed ourselves into numbered groups of twenty, with an N.C.O. as a spokesman for the group. Because flights were limited each day the group numbers were put into a hat, and a draw was made to decide the order of departure. The sick and the walking wounded, the bludgers and those with blistered feet, had already left.

My usual good luck deserted me when the draw was made, for my group was almost the last to be drawn out of the hat. But, at long last, after days of impatient hanging about, and saying my goodbyes to old friends and familiar faces departing in earlier groups, it was my turn to leave the shambles and stink of Stalag XV11A, Markt Pongau.

We were transported to Saltzberg air-field in the back of trucks driven by cheerful, good natured black drivers plying us with cigarettes and chewing gum. They were black Americans, conscripted into war service and serving in segregated, black transport battalions.

Arriving at Saltzberg air-field in heavy rain, we were told that the weather had turned sour and we would not be flying out that day. It was not until we had landed safely in England, we learned that the hold up was because two Lancaster bombers ferrying returning prisoners from Germany had crashed, with the loss of all those on board.

We bivouacked in tiny, three-man tents on the wet grass at the edge of the air-field and were told not to leave the area. As soon as the weather cleared we would be flying out. By prisoner-of-war standards we were fed like fighting cocks, on "K" rations and black, sweet coffee and the glamour girls in their NAFFI wagon visited us everyday, so there was no shortage of cigarettes and goodies. To pass the time we played solo whist in the cramped tents. When the rain eased up a bit, we took walks around the perimeter of the field, eyes and ears at the ready for any signs of landing aircraft.

It was on a path within yards of our makeshift camp at the edge of Salzburg air-field that I came across a carefully laid out cemetery for pets. The animal graves, in neat, orderly rows along weed-free gravel paths were mostly for dogs. Framed photographs of alsations and long-eared dachshunds were fixed above ornate inscriptions of pet names and dates on marble and wooden headstones. There were a few "in loving memory" of black cats and pet rabbits and there was even a picture of a parrot or parakeet. I had never before heard of such a burial ground, never mind seen one.

Many of the animals had been buried in recent months, even weeks, and I was at a complete loss to understand the reason for such grief for animals, when all over Europe, human beings had been slaughtered in their millions. Most of them cremated in gas chambers or buried by the thousand in deep lime pits.

Even if the local populace had been unaware of the slaughter of the Jews, as I too was unaware at that time, they must have been aware of the thousands of starving Russian and other auslander workers in their midst. It is ironical to think that Russian prisoners would gladly have disposed of the dead animals by eating them. Indeed, there were a number of occasions in my four year stretch as a prisoner-of-war that I, too, would have enjoyed the tasty, roast leg of an alsation or German Shepherd.

*****

Three days later it was still drizzling and I was crammed in the little bivouac three-man tent, with George Martin, Ted McShea and Billy Brougham, trying to play solo whist. My head was pressed against the canvas roof of the tent, cold rainwater was running down the back of my neck. I'd forgotton that my feet were protruding through the wall of the canvas until my wet socks reminded me.

I had just declared abondance over George Martin's solo call, when Sergeant Charlie McIlroy, our group leader, poked his head through the damp fly-sheet and said, "It's on, lads, it's on. We're going home today and we're leaving right away."

We had seen planes land on the grass strip that morning but as the clouds were heavily overcast, we didn't expect to move that day.

Charlie McIlroy was, in fact, a reluctant leader of our group. He had already approached the American Major overseeing the repatriation, to say he didn't want to go home by aeroplane but would prefer to go by boat. The Officer would have no truck with this, of course, and ticked Charlie off for not "setting an example to the men".

Sergeant McIlroy was not the only person in the group who had a "fear of flying". And I must say that when I saw at close hand the scruffy, battered aeroplane that was to carry me home, I had doubts myself about making my first flight in an aeroplane.

The twin-engined plane was a US Douglas DC-3 Dakota, the universal workhorse of the Allied forces during the war. Thousands of Dakotas were used as troop or cargo carriers and in airborne operations towed gliders and dropped paratroops. The Dakota is still being flown in many parts of the world today.

The one I was about to board looked as if it had taken part in all of those manoeuvres, very recently, for it was, undoubtably, a little the worse for wear, not to say battle-scarred. The fuselage and wings were patched with 12" riveted squares of dull, unpainted aluminium, repairing the shrapnel or bullet holes of previous missions. The wings were heavily marked with broad, black oily streaks fanning out from the exhausts of the two engines. My sensitive nose picked up the reek of petrol and stale engine oil before I climbed the ladder into the plane. My concern was somewhat eased, however, as the Captain and his crew of two, ignoring the stink, passed in and out of the flight cabin with glowing cigarettes in their mouths.

So the sight of the casual, cavalier puffing of the cigarettes by the crew and the thought that I would be in England in a couple of hours or so, overcame any misgivings I had about my first ever flight in the battered old crate.

Climbing up a short ladder hooked on to the sill of the door, I found myself in a dimly lit, long, bare, aluminium-lined compartment or tube. At first sight it reminded me of the lower deck – the "inside", as the conductor called it – of an ancient No 13 double-decker tram in Liverpool, on the Dale Street run from the Pier Head to Norris Green. Popularly known as the "bone-shaker" to all Scousers.

As in the bone-shaker, a simple, polished plywood bench-seat ran down each side of the tube, beneath a row of small, tobacco-stained windows. There were no seat-belts or safety harnesses. (There were'nt any seat belts on the bone-shaker, either, if it comes to that). Drooping from the rounded ceiling, was a cable, like the bell strap on the No. 13, which you pulled, twice, to let the driver know you wanted to get off at the next stop. But the cable on the Dakota was where the courageous paratroopers had clipped their parachute harness before jumping out into the unknown.

As we sat, apprehensive and subdued, facing each other on the uncomfortable plywood seat, nervously puffing away at American Chesterfield cigarettes, the tall lean figure of the captain, a double of James Stewart in "The Flight of the Phoenix", put his head round the door of the flight cabin at the front of the compartment.

"OK guys," he said, casually, "we're gonna take off now. Cigarettes out and no more smoking until I say the word."

All conversation ceased and the Chesterfields were dowsed (I had already put my cigarette out when I smelt the petrol fumes) and, two minutes later, the engines burst into a rumbling roar ten times louder than the noise of a modern 747 Jumbo Jet. The aeroplane, like the bone-shaker of old, began to tremble and judder alarmingly as if reluctant to make the effort to leave the safety of the wet grass. Five minutes later, to my relief, although the noise was still deafening, the vibrations eased to a steady throb, throb, throb, as the aircraft rolled and bounced along the grass strip of the airfield.

I turned to look out of the tiny port-hole window as the old flying-horse picked up speed and was alarmed to see the broad, oil-stained wing swaying up and down as if hinged to the body of the aircraft. And then I realised we were in the air, banking sharply over the neat paths of the pet cemetery and the deserted camp of green, camouflaged bivouacs where I had been playing solo whist an hour ago.

Still slowly climbing, we flew over the half-demolished Rathaus of the town of Markt Pongau, and then circled the sentry boxes and barbed wire of Stalag XV11A Prisoner-of-War camp with its rows of wooden huts and litter-strewn compounds. We cheered as the pilot, on our behalf, made a victory roll in ironic farewell. I caught a brief glimpse of blue-grey uniforms being herded into the enclosure by khaki-clad figures with rifles at the ready. And then the plane was enveloped in a thick layer of billowing, dark grey clouds before serenely sailing into a fantastic panorama of snow-white hills of shining cotton-wool, dazzling in the brilliant sunshine of a clear blue sky.

But my appreciation of the magical, sun-strewn landscape above the clouds, was short lived. For at that moment, I was appalled to see dense black smoke and a six foot long finger of wavering red flame gushing out of the exhaust pipe of the engine. The reek of petrol still in my nose, my heart turned over at the sight and I came to know the true meaning of the phrase, "my bowels turned to water".

I had just dug my elbow into the ribs of George Martin sitting alongside me, to draw his attention to the firework display, when James Stewart came out of the flight-cabin. His peaked cap was set at a rakish angle on the back of his head, after the fashion of most Hollywood greats, and an enormous fat cigar was clenched in his teeth. Unable to make himself heard over the din and clamour of the two engines, he indicated with a flourish of his cigar, that we could smoke if we wanted to.

My first thought was, somehow, to put him wise to the fact that his aeroplane was on fire, but when I glanced out of the little window again, I saw that the exhaust was now only discharging wisps of thin grey smoke. There was no sign of a fire and the aeroplane was flying at a steady, stable course over the rolling, white clouds just below. James obviously knew something that I didn't. All the same I didn't have a cigarette on that first heart-stopping flight.

The rest of the journey was incident-free and I almost

began to enjoy the experience, thinking that my first dramatic flight would be a fine tale to tell my grandchildren in the years to come.

I gradually relaxed my grip on the rounded edge of the plywood seat beneath me and waited impatiently for the white cliffs of Dover to loom over the horizon.

Chapter 39

Welcome Home Doug

I didn't see the cliffs, though, white or any other shade. Not that day anyway.

After we had been in the air an hour or so, the Flight Lieutenant came out of his cabin and indicated with a dipping motion of his hand, that we were going down and that cigarettes were to be stubbed out. As the Dakota slid into dark grey, menacing clouds again, my hands renewed their vice-like grip on the edge of the seat and I swallowed compulsively in an effort to rid myself of the crackling and pain in my ears. The plane swept around in a half circle, apparently balancing on one wing, then straightened out beneath the blanket of grey clouds.

To my relief, the old Dakota made a perfect landing, albeit with a bit of a bounce and bump, on an apparently completely deserted airfield in the middle of nowhere. Taxiing over the wet grass we finally came to a halt near a derelict concrete hangar. When the engines were switched off we all broke into loud and prolonged applause like children at a Saturday afternoon matinee at the Clubmoor cinema applauding the arrival of Tom Mix's dust coated stagecoach at the abandoned gold mine.

In the unearthly silence, after the noise of the engines had died, the Flight Lieutenant told us we were near the city of Reims, in Northern France, and that we were going to stay the night to "get cleaned up" before going on to England in the morning. As he spoke trucks made their way across the field to stop by the plane.

Within half-an-hour we arrived at an extensive, hutted, military camp, the Stars and Stripes fluttering on flag-poles each side of the main entrance. Two smartly turned out American G.Is with rifles were on guard at the gates.

After disembarking at a long, shed-like, pre-fabricated

building we were shepherded into a reception area at one end and informed by a cigar-smoking, gum-chewing American Officer that we were going to be registered, interrogated, showered, de-loused, medically inspected and kitted out once more, as soldiers of the King.

The building was, in effect, a factory. The first stage in the refining and refurbishing of a lately released prisoner-of-war, into a human being again. The conveyor belt in the factory was operated with remarkable efficiency by the Americans and I had never before seen anything like the American camp at Reims, neither in the British Army nor in the four years I had spent as a guest of the German Reich. And to be honest I've never seen anything like it, since.

In a kind of reception room at the end of the building, I was handed a cardboard box and told to put my name and army number on a white label stuck on the lid. In the box I put in the few personal belongings I was carrying with me. My Army Paybook, some letters from home, (the letters were, eventually, to be the basis for my book DESERT WATCH), a few photographs taken in the arbeitslagers, souvenir programmes of the Wolfsberg Theatre shows, and the Cherry Blossom Boot Polish tin with the silver pocket watch I had pinched from an Italian officer four and a half years before. I was told I would get the box back after my shower.

After stripping naked as the day I was born, I was handed a large, rough, white towel and directed through a door at the end of the reception area into a communal shower room. Even as we started to file in, two American orderlies were shovelling our discarded uniforms into the open door of a furnace. Every article of clothing we'd been wearing went in the fire. New, old and in tatters, clean or filthy. Worn-out boots, battle dress uniforms, tatty pullovers, great-coats, glengarries, leather belts, old haversacks and webbing.

I was more than happy to part from mine for they were stinking, and I had spotted signs of the blood-sucking lice of the compound in Crete and the concentration camp of Salonika, in the seams of my trousers.

Wallowing in the glorious hot water for ten minutes, I soaped, shampooed and showered under the watchful eye of a white-coated medical orderly. Watchful, because surprisingly, some men seemed reluctant to take a bath, as if ashamed of their snow-white skin stretched over their emaciated frame.

In an anti-room at the end of the luxury ablutions, I waited in a line to be "medically examined" by an American Army doctor in a white coat, a red rubber-tubed stethoscope hanging from his neck. He looked me up and down like Dr Jew Baiter back in the timber camp in Paarl and asked me if I was feeling OK buddy. Then a masked, white-coated orderly, with a realistic impression of gangsters James Cagney or Edward G. Robinson, pointed a Flit-gun at me and sprayed me from head to toe with clouds of pungent, snow-white delousing powder.

Looking and feeling like Marley's ghost, I passed into what seemed like a stock room in the basement of Lewis's, or the Fifty-Shilling-Tailors. I was handed a huge, green American Army kitbag with my name and Army number, in two inch black characters, stencilled on the outside. Not the thin, white, paltry canvas bag of the British Army, with its draw-string at the top, but a thick double-handled American Army duffle-bag with a metal clasp and padlock, long enough to carry a full set of golf clubs. Inside was the cardboard box with my few worldly possessions, which I had left at the door before going into the shower.

A long counter, divided into sections, and staffed by gum-chewing, cigarette-smoking American G.Is, ran down one side the length of the warehouse. Behind the counter, in each section, were shelves stacked with clothing and uniforms.

As I walked alongside the counter, holding open my new kit-bag, the G.I. in each section threw articles of clothing and kit from the shelves behind him into the bag.

Two vests, two underpants, two shirts, two pairs of grey woollen socks, two khaki handkerchiefs, one battledress blouse, one pair of battledress trousers, one pair of white braces, one pair of gaiters, one pair of boots, one glengarry, one webbing belt, one long-sleeved khaki pullover. A knife, fork and spoon, an enamel plate, an enamel mug, a comb, a hairbrush, two boot brushes, a tablet of soap, a slab of chocolate, a box of matches and a tin of fifty Players Medium cigarettes.

There were no questions asked except, "what size are yer,

326

buddy?"

Staggering out of the Fifty-Shilling-Tailors, under the weight of my now half-full kit-bag, the broad strap cutting into my shoulder like an overloaded golf bag on the eighteenth fairway on a cold winter's Sunday morning, I passed into a dressing room at the end.

After I was dressed, grateful for the familiar feel of the rough khaki cloth with its "new" smell, and feeling more like a human being again, I was briefly interrogated by a British Officer. A captain in the Intelligence Corps who seemed to be in a hurry to get back to his evening meal. He asked me for names of any Germans who had "ill-treated" me during my four years as a p.o.w. but seemed uninterested in the fact that I had been half-starved most of the time. He laughed when I told him about Frau Dreadnaught and the scheisen hause. The pistol stuck in my ribs by the Feld-Webel seemed to be unimportant as I couldn't remember his name.

He handed me a signed and dated billet-doux to say that I had been duly interrogated.

That night, after reneging half-way through my third plateful of roast chicken with all the trimmings, I slept like a log between white sheets on a steel framed G.I. cot. I believe it was called a truckle bed.

***

Breakfast next morning was early. And substantial. In fact, I could eat as much as I wanted. Long-dreamed-of rashers of bacon, fried eggs, sausage, beans, fried bread, tomatoes, All swamped in hot bacon fat, to be soaked up by crisp, white bread rolls. And, new to my eyes, a strange looking, but delicious mixture which the man in the white cook's stovepipe hat told me was "hash browns". Longings and daydreams and fantasies and wishful thinking of the starving prisoner-of-war at last come true.

Certified that

No....390650......   Rank....DvR..............

Name (BLOCK LETTERS)....DOUGLAS....ARTHUR............

UNIT....106ᵗʰ....R.H.A....................................

~~been fully~~ / briefly interrogated by an Intelligence Officer

of I.S.9. (W.E.A.) on ....26ᵗʰ....May,....... 1945.

has completed M 19/GEN/

~~and~~ / should not be re-interrogated.

....
I.S.9. (W.E.A.) Rear E.Q.

IMPORTANT

THIS CERTIFICATE MUST BE RETAINED AND SHOWN WHEN ......

ON ARRIVAL IN U.K.

Interrogation Certificate.

Identity Card.

Breakfast was early, they said, "Because we had a plane to catch."

The plane waiting for us on the deserted air-field was a Royal Air Force Lancaster four-engined bomber. Another battered veteran of the skies, it looked as if it had been in far more engagements than the Dakota.

A caricature of a boomerang in flight was painted in red over the door beneath neat images of a row of bombs. I was to learn that each bomb denoted a successful bombing mission.

The cheerful, friendly R.A.F. crew of the massive bomber, each with three stripes on his arms, looked as if they had just left school. Sergeant Charlie McIlroy's ernest request for a parachute, made to one of the young Sergeants as he counted us into the aircraft, was met with a laugh.

"What do you want a parachute for, Sarge?" said the chubby-faced Sergeant sixth-former, who by the wisps of blonde down on his upper lip looked as if he hadn't started to shave yet. (For the first time in my life he made me feel quite old.) "The crew don't have a 'chute. We wouldn't know what to do with one. Anyway, you'll be back home in England, safe and sound, in an hour or so."

They packed us in, carefully, like sardines in a can of Princes, on the ribbed aluminium floor along the length of the aeroplane, my huge, green duffle-bag taking up almost as much

329

room as I did. We received definite instructions to sit down, keep still and on no account to move about. I sat with my knees drawn up, at the feet of the wireless operator, who, when the engines roared into life, grinned and gave me the thumbs up sign.

I remember little of my flight in the Lancaster.

Unlike the Dakota, some of the tiny bullet and shrapnel holes, the battle scars of previous encounters, had not been repaired and a freezing, brass-monkey draught howled along the floor. The noise was deafening and I struggled to overcome the claustrophobia of the aluminium box. Towards the end of the flight, I became bothered when the plane suddenly tilted at an alarming angle, and four thick metal rods running along the length of the aircraft in brackets on the wall by my shoulder, began to jerk, noisily, backwards and forwards, as if the pilot was having difficulty getting into the right gear. That's what I imagined, anyway.

But the Lancaster lumbered on and landed, in glorious sunshine, at a Bomber Command airfield "somewhere in Kent" as smoothly as a modern coach drawing to a halt in a parking lot at Blackpool.

The day was the 1st of June, 1945.

Exactly four years from the 1st June, 1941 when I was abandoned on the island of Crete to become a prisoner-of-war.

I have forgotten the name of the airfield, one of dozens built all over the United Kingdom during the war. But it doesn't matter, now, anyway, for it has long reverted to the agricultural land from whence it came.

Ushered by attractive, smartly turned out WRAFS from the Women's Royal Air Force, I walked across the tarmac, new kit-bag slung across my shoulders, to a cluster of marquees and corrugated iron Nisson huts. In front of the rolled-back sides of one of the tents, Union Jacks flying bravely from the ridge in a stiff breeze, a Royal Air Force band broke out into a rendering of "Land of Hope and Glory" as we walked towards them. For some reason I thought it was directed at me and my eyes filled with tears.

This time there *was* a welcoming reception committee and there were understanding, sympathetic ladies from the Womens' Institute, and there was an endless supply of sausage rolls and meat pies and cream cakes.

In my four years absence, the British Army seemed to have acquired a leaf out of the American conveyor-belt system, for I was home in Liverpool, and knocking on the front door of 26, Vanbrugh Crescent, within twenty-four hours. I spent the afternoon in a huge military camp somewhere in London, to be once more medically inspected and instructed to attend a civilian hospital when I got Home. After being kitted out, yet again, with a new and better fitting uniform I attended a Pay Parade to receive a handful of the old, familiar two-shilling pieces and half-crowns and Post Office drafts enabling me to cash more money if I wanted it. My pay, less the weekly allotment I had made to my Father, had accumulated during the four years I had been a prisoner-of-war and I found I was, at last, a rich man as well as a free man.

The following morning I collected a sheaf of what I was told were "Food Coupons", a pass for four weeks leave, and a third-class railway warrant for a journey from Euston Station to Lime Street Station, Liverpool.

Although it was my first visit to the great Capital, crammed in the back of an overcrowded Morris 3-tonner, I saw nothing of London. After a bumpy ride I was dropped off at Euston Station with George Martin, Dick Rimmer, Ted McShea, Billy Brougham and Sergeant Charlie McIlroy. Six of the six hundred and fifty 106th Lancashire Yeomanry who had left Lime Street Station early in September, 1939 (Charlie pleased as punch that he had flown back to England instead of walking across Europe as he wanted to back in Salzberg).

We sat, contentedly, on our American duffle bags, for more than eight hours, in the corridor of the overcrowded, overheated train, as it puffed and huffed and back-tracked and jolted and jerked its way up the London and North Western line. A luxurious ride compared to the Forty Men Eight Horses trip in the 1914 cattle truck of four long years ago.

At Lime Street Station I left my stalwart friends and comrades, my companions of five years of hardship in the scorching heat of the desert and the freezing cold and hunger of a prisoner-of-war stalag and caught the No. 13 bone-shaker home.

Vanbrugh Crescent appeared to be very much the same as it

was when I left five years before, except the houses looked smaller and for the most part were unkempt and in need of a coat of paint. The wooden fences in front of the tiny front gardens were in need of repair and the overgrown privet hedges wanted clipping.

I wasn't too much worried about that, however, especially when I came to No. 26 to see painted across the roadway outside, in two foot high letters,

"WELCOME HOME DOUG."

POSTSCRIPT

For three years after I got home I sowed the somewhat belated wild oats of an old, young man.

Most of the seeds fell on stony, non-productive ground. With my usual good fortune, however, one or two were blown by the winds of chance and came to rest in a veritable English Garden. I met my lovely wife, Maureen.

After she broke off an engagement of marriage to a six foot two Royal Marine from Sheffield and returned his expensive engagement ring, we were married on the 28th May, 1949.

In January, 1951 I received the most treasured letter of my life.

C. Ward,
Broadgreen Hosp.
18th January, 1951

Hello Darling,

I've been wanting to write to you all week, but haven't had a minute and I didn't want to rush your letter. I wanted to be able to settle for an hour and write all that came into my head.

You know, Dear, I don't half love you. I didn't think I could possibly love you more than I did, but now I'm just full up with love for you. When you came Wednesday night I just wanted to hug you and keep on hugging you. I've missed you terribly, love, and am glad I'll soon be home. Don't worry, though, love. I'm not making myself miserable wishing for home. I'll be in here till Monday at least. In the meantime we are having a good many laughs. My goodness

333

some of the women don't mind what they say.

Today I had my stitches out – blessed relief. This afternoon I had my first bath – it was marvellous.

Isn't it wonderful, love, being Mummy and Daddy. You know I feel as though I have everything in life. They can all say what they like about winning their pools. I've got all I want. You wouldn't get me swapping my two men for anything. I love you both very much. I know we are all going to be very happy. Incidently David has gained three ounces since he was weighed Tuesday, and the Doctor today said he was fine. I'm glad he's settling down to his feeds. He did worry me. The only thing that stopped me getting really worried was the fact that it might have affected my milk and I knew he would come all right eventually. Mother instinct guided me in my crisis, I think. He used to look so helpless, I just felt like gathering him up and crying. However, I'm really glad I was sensible over it as it is paying dividends now. Sister has been really good with me. That in itself proves that she has approved of my behaviour. She really persevered with David. Used to force him on my breast, to see him now feeding away you wouldn't think he was the same baby. Mind you love ours was a usual complaint and nothing to worry over. Every mother in the ward has feeding problems and believe me they are problems. One girl, too silly to realise the damage she could do, didn't express (get rid of the milk) after each feed, now her baby is on a bottle. She has milk but her breasts are sore. She will have to get that milk away.

Doug do you think we could possibly afford a shawl for Baby. All the mothers going out have had shawls. I'd feel awful if I didn't have one. Instead of buying me a present we could have a shawl. Maybe Mother or Dee would go for one on Saturday. Then I could have it for coming out instead of the blue blanket. Will still need the white blanket though. If Dee has got those brassieres Doug would you bring them in Saturday. By the way love don't bring any food or fruit in as I've plenty, and I don't really need a lot of extra stuff now as I will be out soon.

An hour later.

Well Dear I had to leave off to feed our son. It would do you good to see him sucking away. Am afraid love I haven't time for any more.

I love you, always will. Good night & God Bless,

All My Love, Your Maureen. XXX
XXXX From David to Daddy.

And we lived happily ever after.